Ethics and Human Well-being

Introducing Philosophy

Introducing Philosophy is a series of textbooks designed to introduce the basic topics of philosophy for any student approaching the subject for the first time. Each volume presents a central subject of philosophy by considering the key issues and outlooks associated with the area. With the emphasis firmly on the arguments for and against a philosophical position, the reader is encouraged to think philosophically about the subject.

1   An Introduction to the Philosophy of Religion   *B. R. Tilghman*
2   Ethics and Human Well-being   *E. J. Bond*
3   An Introduction to Business Ethics   *Jennifer Jackson*
4   An Introduction to Epistemology   *Charles Landesman*

Forthcoming
5   An Introduction to Ancient Philosophy   *R. James Hankinson*
6   An Introduction to Aesthetics   *Dabney Townsend*

Ethics and Human Well-being

An Introduction to Moral Philosophy

E. J. BOND

BLACKWELL
Publishers

First published 1996

2 4 6 8 10 9 7 5 3 1

Blackwell Publishers Inc.
238 Main Street
Cambridge, Massachusetts 02142
USA

Blackwell Publishers Ltd
108 Cowley Road
Oxford OX4 1JF
UK

Library of Congress Cataloging-in-Publication Data

Bond, E. J. (Edward Jarvis), 1930–
    Ethics and human well-being: an introduction to moral philosophy / E. J. Bond.
      p.   cm.
    Includes bibliographical references.
    ISBN 0-631-19549-1 (hbk.: alk. paper). – ISBN 0-631-19551-3
(pbk.: alk. paper)
    1. Ethics. I. Title.
BJ1012.B57 1996
170 – dc20

96-4573
CIP

British Library Cataloguing in Publication Data

A CIP catalogue record for this book is available from the British Library.

Typeset in 10 on 12 pt Bembo by Best-set Typesetter Ltd., Hong Kong
Printed in Great Britain by Hartnolls Ltd, Bodmin, Cornwall

This book is printed on acid-free paper

To my inamorata
Sheila Carnall
teacher extraordinary
and students' friend
with love and gratitude
this book is dedicated

Contents

Preface

This book is based on more than 25 years of thought, interchange of ideas, and the successful teaching of ethics or moral philosophy, often to first-year students. It differs from standard introductions to the subject in a number of significant ways. First of all, it does not condescend, but assumes that the reader is intelligent, literate, has a serious interest in the subject, and is willing to work hard at it. Secondly, I speak in my own voice from the start, offering my own deeply serious views on a subject which I believe to be of fundamental importance, although always writing with the understanding that this is the reader's first acquaintance with philosophy.

The book is not, therefore, a survey of moral theories, but takes a clear position from the beginning, aiming at a definite conclusion. Nevertheless, in the course of developing a quite specific moral theory, every existing moral theory of importance comes under survey. An attempt is made to lead the student – often by appealing to what she herself must certainly believe – into an understanding of the view that is presented. The book is essentially an *unfolding*. (The debt to Aristotle in the view presented will be obvious, and no apology is made for it.) It is hoped that the book will be useful not only as an introductory textbook, but as an introduction to the subject for any intelligent reader who has an interest in it.

The various forms of moral skepticism, or of views leading to moral skepticism, must be dealt with in detail and at length at the very beginning. Otherwise, as I know well from experience, there will be no audience, for 90 percent of my readership, unless they are religious believers, will certainly be skeptical of the possibility of a universally valid morality that is not purely egoistic. I begin with an examination of psychological egoism because the arguments against it are very solid and centrally philosophical – psychological egoism is based on an easily discernible confusion of thought – and I know from long experience that this is the best way of gaining the students' interest and attention.

My experience has taught me that it is wise to instruct the student first to read an entire chapter (or, in the case of longer chapters like chapters 2 and 4, a significant portion of it) to catch the overall drift, then to read it again, slowly and carefully, making notes of questions and criticisms to be raised. It is also extremely important to read the text itself. The chapter summaries are nothing but reminders or aids to memory, and will be useful only *after* the text has been read. The charts for the more complex chapters and for the whole of part I will be of help in a similar way.

Acknowledgments

I wish first of all to acknowledge my indebtedness to the Centre for Philosophy and Public Affairs of the University of St Andrews, Scotland, and its Director, Dr John J. Haldane, where I had the honor to be Royal Bank of Scotland Visiting Fellow for two terms in the winter and spring of 1993, and where, thanks to the facilities so generously provided, this book was begun. I must also express my gratitude to Queen's University at Kingston for granting me sabbatical leave in the academic year 1992–3.

I would also like to thank Floyd Switzer of Frontenac Secondary School in Kingston Township (Ontario) for inviting me several times to lecture and take part in discussions with his senior students in philosophy, where some of the ideas in this book were presented. These were happy and profitable occasions.

My greatest thanks, however, go to my *bonne amie*, Sheila E. Carnall, teacher of English at Bayridge Secondary School, also in Kingston Township, who designed the charts, and whose editorial help in trying to make this difficult subject intelligible to philosophical beginners is quite beyond praise.

"That a thing may be honest without being profitable; and again, may be profitable without being honest [is] the most pernicious error, and most destructive of all goodness, that ever could have crept into the minds of men."

Cicero (*De Officiis*, II, 3)

Introduction: What is Moral Philosophy?

To the question "What is moral philosophy?" not all moral philosophers will give the same answer. That is because this is a question *within* philosophy, and philosophy is a subject in which different and opposing views are normal and to be expected. You will quickly discover these differences for yourself if you go on to study the subject further, either in a university or college course or by doing some more reading on your own. You will discover them, too, when you listen to what different philosophers have to say in answer to your questions, or when you listen to them talking, either to an audience or just among themselves. Still, there are some important issues that just about every philosopher will agree do belong to the subject matter of philosophical ethics. (The term "ethics," when used to refer to a branch of philosophy, simply *means* moral philosophy.)

Whether you realize it or not, some of you will already have views on some of these issues. For instance, some of you quite certainly believe that moral judgments (judgments about moral right and wrong, moral good and evil, morally good and bad character) are value judgments and therefore purely subjective, or purely a matter of personal opinion, unlike facts, which are objectively true or false. Some of you will think that morality is relative, not to personal opinion or attitude or feeling, but to culture, to the kind of conduct or character that is approved or disapproved within a given society. According to both these views, there are and can be no standards of morality that apply to all human beings no matter who they are or in what place and time they happen to be. These are philosophical views, and they will be discussed in part I under the heading "Moral Skepticism."

If we decide in favor of one of these forms of subjectivism or relativism, that is where moral philosophy ends. If moral questions are purely matters of what a particular individual happens to believe or feel, or of what a particular society or culture happens to approve or disapprove of, there is simply no more for moral philosophy to do. Psychology, sociology, and anthropology take over at this point. But if these views are rejected as unsound and not worthy of belief, as they will be here, then we are left with the whole question of what *really is* morally good and evil, right and wrong, and what *really are* good and bad qualities of character and what it is that makes them so. If we have succeeded in defeating the various forms of moral skepticism, moral understanding becomes at least a possibility, and it is worth our while to try to answer these questions, which are philosophical questions. If moral skepticism has been defeated, such questions are part of the legitimate subject matter of ethics or moral philosophy.

What makes these *philosophical* questions is that they are problems for *thought* rather than for scientific investigation. We cannot come to a deeper understanding of what is good or evil, wrong or allowable, admirable or contemptible, by any investigation of actual beliefs and practices, whether our own or other people's. This could only give us knowledge of what particular individuals happen to believe and act upon, something which belongs to psychology, or it could give us knowledge of customary morality at a given place and time, which is the business of anthropology or sociology. It is only by thought and reflection that we can even try to answer questions about what *actually is* morally good or bad and why, and that places them squarely in the domain of philosophy.

Ethics, or moral philosophy, is usually divided into two parts: *meta-ethics*, or the study of the nature of moral judgments and how moral language functions, and *substantive ethics*, which deals with what actually is good or bad, right or wrong, admirable or contemptible. Substantive ethics, in turn, is divided into (a) *theoretical ethics* (a general account of the nature of good and bad conduct and character); and (b) what is called either *applied ethics*, or, somewhat confusingly, *practical ethics*. Applied or practical ethics deals with particular moral issues, especially difficult ones, such as war, abortion, and capital punishment, and with such social issues as racism and sexism. Or it may deal with moral questions as they arise within a particular area which gives us business ethics, professional ethics, medical ethics, and so forth.

The division of substantive ethics into theoretical and practical ethics is confusing because it suggests that theoretical ethics is a mere intellectual exercise that might help us to think clearly but has no real practical importance or significance. The implication is that we only get down to the nitty-gritty when we start doing *practical* ethics. But substantive theoretical ethics, because it deals, at the most general level, with the nature of good and evil, with what makes acts right or wrong, with what makes qualities of character admirable or contemptible, and the difference all of this makes for the best life we can have for ourselves, *could not be* more practical. What we believe about these things cannot help but affect the way we choose to live, and if questions about these things are real questions that need to be answered, it is important to try to get the answers right.

More than that, we cannot even begin to do applied or so-called practical ethics, unless we have some idea of the answers to these general questions. If we try to handle particular moral issues on a piecemeal basis, without any appeal to general moral considerations, either we will be making certain assumptions at the general level that we haven't bothered to examine, or we will be blind and at sea. This is not to say that we should not make use of examples when doing substantive theoretical ethics – we do have to keep ourselves anchored in real life – but understanding at the general level (theoretical understanding) is an absolute necessity.

Of course, if you accept the skeptical arguments of the subjectivists or the relativists, meta-ethics is the whole of the subject, and even to believe that there is or could be such a thing as substantive ethics is to be under some sort of delusion. But even if we reject the arguments of these skeptics, we still have some meta-ethics to do, for we have to try to show what it is or could be for a moral judgment to be objectively true or false or, if that is too strong, to be worthy or unworthy of belief. Only then can we begin to do substantive theoretical ethics proper. This issue is dealt with in part II, "A Rational Basis for Ethics," where we also begin to deal, in the most general way, with substantive moral questions. The details, however, are the subject matter of part III, "What Morality Is," and part IV, "Tying Things Together," where we also try to reach a summary and conclusion.

Unlike some other subjects that you may have studied, there are no authorities in philosophy, and nothing said in this book is, or could be, offered as authoritative. You have no choice but to consider the views put forward here, to question them where they appear dubious, and to judge for yourself whether or not they are acceptable. In other words, you can only consider what is presented here and *think it through for yourself.* There is no other way of doing philosophy. But you need first of all to understand what is being said. Then you need to consider it carefully. Where you disagree, you should understand and be able to explain *why* you disagree. Philosophy is not a matter of assertion *v.* assertion, or opinion *v.* opinion; it is an attempt to come to a deeper understanding of important issues, an understanding that can only be arrived at by thought and reflection. Much thought and reflection have gone into what is presented here, and of course you are being invited to believe it, but all you can do is try to understand, to relate it to your own experience, to reflect, and then to exercise your own judgment.

Part I
Moral Skepticism

1

Psychological Egoism

At some time in your life you will have heard somebody say that all acts are basically selfish, that whatever anyone does she does for herself, or for her own gratification, and that it would be stupid to believe anything else. According to people like this, the idea that anyone ever does anything for others, or for the sake of some ideal or principle not directly related to her or his own private satisfaction, is nothing but pretense, hypocrisy, or delusion. There is nothing trivial about this view of things, nor is it just an intellectual game, for if what these people believed were true, then acting out of care, concern, or sympathy for others would be literally impossible. Nor could there be concern, apart from one's own benefit (e.g. keeping up appearances), for justice or the public good, or even for being decent or honest, unless to give oneself a pat on the back for one's goodness, or in order to feel superior to others.

Of course, this would apply to everybody. It's not just that you don't give a damn for anyone else; no one else gives a damn for you either, or for anything else besides himself. If anyone does anything for me, that's only because he wants something in return, or because it somehow satisfies some selfish desire. If all this were true there could be no love, or even friendship, except as an exchange of favors, a kind of mutual back-scratching. Everybody is basically out for himself or herself and let there be no pretending about it. And since we have to share a world, everyone is in competition with everyone else for the goodies of pleasure, status, power, and material wealth. That is the name of the game. Even the so-called "good" people, those who pretend to themselves or to others that they have any concerns besides their own profit, are really only concerned with reputation or advantage or appearances, or how good it makes them feel. Everyone is fundamentally selfish. That is how human nature is.

Such a belief, if it is taken seriously, is bound to affect one's attitude toward oneself and other people and to color one's whole outlook on life – to color it cynical in fact. If it is true, cynicism about human pretensions to acting for anything but self-satisfaction is fully justified. If it is false, it is a terrible mistake. If it is true, the only reason we have for being decent to one another is self-protection, and what passes as love or friendship is nothing but self-interest. If it is false, we have no reason for doubting that we can, and sometimes really do, care about things other than ourselves including, most importantly, other people. What different worlds these are, and what a difference it must make to our lives, both as individuals and as a society, which one of these worlds is the real one, and whether we've got it right or wrong.

Psychological Egoism Stated

The view we have been considering here is called by philosophers *psychological egoism*, "psychological" because it states a belief about human motivation, and "egoism" because it claims that all human motives are *self-regarding*. This term "self-regarding" may be the first technical term or "term of art" that you will have encountered in doing philosophy. Many philosophers prefer it to "selfish" because, unlike that word, the word "self-regarding" is *morally neutral*. If we say that an act or a person is selfish, we usually mean to imply that there is something wrong about the act or something bad about the person, but if we say that an act is *self-regarding*, all we mean is that the person is doing it for himself or herself, and there is nothing inherently wrong or bad about that.

Many of the things we do – eating, sleeping, brushing our teeth, going shopping or for a walk, going to a football game or a concert, long-range projects such as career planning, and many other things – we do for ourselves, but we would not normally call these things *selfish*. An act is not normally called selfish unless it is unfair to others or is mean and grasping when kindness and generosity are called for. Many acts are *innocently* self-regarding; only some self-regarding acts are selfish in the sense that they are mean or grasping or unfair, and therefore morally bad. Nevertheless – and this is important – while not all self-regarding acts are selfish in the sense that condemns them morally, we can and do call acts that are not self-regarding *unselfish*, and this is a form of moral praise.[1] Because only some self-regarding acts are selfish in the moral sense, we need the morally neutral term "self-regarding," but we do not need the clumsy term "non-self-regarding" because acts that are not self-regarding are quite properly called unselfish, even if they do not involve any self-denial or self-sacrifice.[2]

The doctrine of psychological egoism, stated in a morally neutral way – not meaning to praise or blame – is that *all human acts are done from self-regarding motives*. Nothing else, the psychological egoist insists, can seriously be believed. Though the psychological egoist need not claim that all acts are selfish in the *moral* sense, he will insist that there is no such thing as an unselfish act because there is no such thing as an act that is not self-regarding. But even if we state psychological egoism as "All acts are self-regarding" rather than "All acts are fundamentally selfish" we are still expressing a cynical or dark view of human nature. If goodness involves concern for something beyond oneself, say, genuine sympathy for others, then we are saying that goodness is impossible. We are saying that because no one can *help* but act exclusively for his or her own benefit, no one can really be good. According to this view, we are all trying to get the best we can for ourselves, and saying or believing anything else is either pretense and hypocrisy or foolish innocence.

It is important to see how very strong the position of psychological egoism actually is. *All* human acts, it states, actual acts or merely possible or imagined acts, are done from self-regarding motives; hence no act could be anything but self-regarding. *One single instance* of an act that was not self-regarding, whether actual or merely possible or imaginable, would be enough to prove the theory false. We can all agree that many acts are self-regarding and that some of these are selfish in the moral sense of being mean or grasping or unfair (and therefore wrong or bad), but the psychological egoist claims that every single act *must* be self-regarding, that nothing else is possible.

Of course, if this were true, while many acts would remain innocently self-regarding, we would all be selfish people by our very nature. Why? Because we would not be capable of real concern for others or for anything besides our own satisfaction, although we could not be blamed for our selfishness since there would be nothing we could do about it. That is why psychological egoism, though its claim is simply that all acts are self-regarding, really does seem to justify a cynical view of human nature. It is not that we are by nature evil. We cannot help being the completely self-regarding creatures that we are. But goodness, if it means acting in ways that are not self-regarding, say out of genuine concern for others, is simply beyond our powers. We all know that there are many people in the world who never do anything except for themselves, and we can say that these people are thoroughly selfish, true kindness and generosity being quite unknown to them. But the psychological egoist says that *everyone* is like this because *all* acts are self-regarding.

Understanding Psychological Egoism: Some Mistakes to Avoid

We must be careful here not to confuse a psychological egoist, who is someone who holds a certain view of human motivation, with a person whose every act is self-regarding and who is therefore selfish. Nor should we make the mistake of supposing that because there are many such selfish people in the world, psychological egoism is true. Psychological egoism is only true if *nobody* ever does *anything* that is not self-regarding. Nor, for that matter, are selfish people necessarily psychological egoists, for they may in fact believe that people sometimes do act from motives that are not self-regarding. They may regard such people as fools, or they may admire them while despising themselves for their own selfishness. Another mistake we must not make is to suppose that a person who opposes the doctrine of psychological egoism believes that *no* acts are self-regarding, or that there is anybody who is completely selfless. The opponent of psychological egoism only believes that *some* acts are not self-regarding, that we have no reason for believing that *every* act is self-regarding, that we *sometimes* really do care about something other than ourselves.

Finally, we must not make the mistake of supposing that psychological egoism is a theory of what sort of person we *ought* to be, or of how we *ought* to conduct our lives. That is to confuse psychological egoism, the theory that we *can only* act self-regardingly, with ethical egoism, the theory that we *should always* act for our own greatest advantage. Because it deals with the question of how we *should* conduct ourselves, ethical egoism is an ethical or a moral theory. Psychological egoism, on the other hand, because it deals only with *motivation*, is not an ethical but a psychological theory, according to which the only thing that *can* move us to action is self-interest. According to one form of *ethical* egoism, our one guide to dealing with anyone and anything should be our own profit, and anyone who thinks or acts otherwise is a fool. Nice guys finish last.[3] This obviously implies that we could act in ways that were not self-regarding if we chose, but that this would be a foolish choice. But a common form of ethical egoism that goes hand in hand with psychological egoism is this: since we are all out for ourselves and it can't be any other way, the thing to do is to be as clever as you can at controlling things to your own advantage. Since we are all adversaries anyway (there are no nice guys), the thing to do is to get, or try to get, whatever it is you want, using whatever means are available. And why should the greatest rewards not go to those who are best able to bring if off? On either view, we are admirable to the extent that we are clever, forceful, and able to work things so that we come out on top. Domination is the name of the game.

Interestingly, if psychological egoism is true, no account of what we should do or be makes any sense except some form of ethical egoism. Virtue (the quality of character that is admirable) can only consist in being clever at pursuing your own advantage. People who conduct their lives in this way thus have an *interest* in psychological egoism being true, for if every act is necessarily self-interested, how could anyone be to blame for pursuing his own advantage to the best of his ability?

Psychological Egoism: a Seemingly Irrefutable Position

Some of you, reading this, will recognize psychological egoism as something you yourself believe, while others, strongly opposed to it, will remember the frustration of having got absolutely nowhere with somebody who was arguing for this view. That is because the defender of psychological egoism can take *any example whatever*, actual or invented, that is offered as an other-regarding or ideal-regarding act and find a plausible ulterior motive for it that is self-regarding. (The ulterior motive of an act is its true but hidden motive.) Here are some of the things offered by defenders of psychological egoism as the *real* motives for acts that are supposed not to be self-regarding. If I do someone a favor, that is because I expect something in return. If I appear to do something or stop myself from doing it for the sake of an ideal, such as protecting the environment for the sake of future generations, or in order not to be hurtful or dishonest or unjust, that is simply because, with my upbringing or my social conditioning (indoctrination), it would make me feel bad. If I seem to care about anyone at all, other than myself, that is only because of the threat of personal loss, or because I expect good treatment in return for the good treatment I give. If I display courtesy or kindness, that is only to make myself well thought of by others, and so on and so forth, endlessly.

In desperation, the opponent of psychological egoism will turn to acts of extreme heroism and bravery, either at the risk of losing one's life or in the certain knowledge that one will die: jumping into dangerous waters to save a child from drowning (social conditioning, says the psychological egoist, or not wanting to seem a coward, or wanting to be a hero), rushing into a burning house to save the occupants (same thing, says the psychological egoist), and finally and inevitably, the soldier who throws himself on a grenade, knowing he will die, in order to save his comrades. (If he didn't do it he would suffer so much from shame that he couldn't live with himself, says the psychological egoist.) The psychological egoist seems to be in a position where he cannot be defeated. It doesn't matter what is offered as an example of an act that is not self-regarding; it can always be rejected by producing a plausible-sounding ulterior motive that *is* self-regarding.

If pushed to the wall, the psychological egoist will usually say that if there is no obvious conscious ulterior motive, then there is an unconscious one. The act simply cannot be understood, the psychological egoist will say, unless its true motive is self-regarding. This absolute refusal to give up the position, however hard pressed, shows that the psychological egoist sees his position as certain beyond the possibility of doubt, without any need for observation or investigation or, as philosophers say, true and certain *a priori* (a term meaning independently of, or prior to, observation or investigation).[4]

The psychological egoist sees an act that is not self-regarding as something *beyond the possibility of understanding.* Such a notion is, to the psychological egoist, literally incomprehensible. Notice that even though the doctrine *is* used to justify cynicism about human nature, the psychological egoist does not suppose that people lack the power to act with regard to anything other than their own interest *because they are weak.* It is rather that, to the psychological egoist, the idea of an act that is not self-regarding simply *does not make sense.*

The psychological egoist may not realize that this is what she thinks; she may think she is drawing attention to a universal human weakness or failing. But her underlying belief, which is that we cannot even make sense of the notion of an act that is not self-regarding, is revealed by her refusal to accept any example, actual or imagined, as counting against her theory. In philosophers' jargon, her theory, because (knowingly or unknowingly) it is held to be true *a priori*, has *no empirical content.* (This is a technical way of saying that it has no basis at all in observation, investigation, or experiment.) It is just clear and certain, period. It cannot be doubted. There is no need to look and see. What we observe or might observe in the world does not make the slightest difference.

Psychological egoism is not, therefore, a theory about human nature *as it is actually found in the world,* for such a theory would have at least to allow for the *possibility* of evidence that would count against it. A theory about human nature of this kind would have to be *based on* what we actually find in the world. A theory of human motivation as it actually is *but that it was possible for it not to have been,* cannot be assumed in advance to be true, and so we cannot know automatically that any and every motive will conform to it. Certainly, it can easily be seen that many acts are self-regarding, some of them when they pretend not to be, but this fact does not make it a law of nature that every act is self-regarding. We are not forced to reject in advance *anything* offered as an example of an unselfish act. We are not forced to accommodate anything and everything to the theory of psychological egoism.

Psychological Egoism: Why Does it Seem so Certain?

Now when a person clings to a belief so strongly that he does not think anything *could* count against it, when he thinks that nothing could possibly show it to be false, this is a sure sign that, lurking underneath, there is something that one could understandably think to be true and certain without investigation. One takes it to be true *a priori* because denying it does not seem to make sense. Psychological egoism certainly looks like an example of this. What the psychological egoist says is that all human acts are self-regarding and that, in fact, you would have to be a fool not to see this right away. You don't even have to bother to investigate. We must ask: is there something here that we can know on the basis of understanding alone, without investigation? Let's think carefully about this. Well, it really does seem absurd to deny that every human act is done to satisfy *some desire of the person whose act it is*, or, as philosophers say, some desire of the agent. For every conscious, voluntary, and intentional act – and we are not interested in any other kind – is done to achieve something that is actively desired by the person who does it, either for its own sake or as a means to some further desired end. *Otherwise we could not understand it as his or he act.* As her act it must have her motive which means that it must be done to satisfy her desire.

Two Principles Confused (Psychological Egoism Disarmed)

We seem to have uncovered, in the previous paragraph, a principle that we might very well be unwilling to give up under any circumstances, for giving it up would require us to believe that someone could do something without any motivation for doing it. The question now is: does this principle amount to a statement of psychological egoism? Look carefully, for the correct answer is "no." Remember, what the psychological egoist says is that all acts are *self-regarding*. But this principle that we have just uncovered says nothing of the kind. It only says that agents always act to satisfy *their own* desires and that nothing else can be made sense of. It doesn't tell us anything at all about what the *object* of those desires might be, about what they are desires *for*. It doesn't rule out the possibility, for instance, that *I* have a desire for *your* well-being. The desire is still *mine* but it is not self-regarding. And so we have two principles, as follows:

1   Every act of every person is done to satisfy some desire of his or her own
2   Every act of every person is done to satisfy some self-regarding desire

These principles, although they are quite different, look very similar, so similar, in fact, that they can easily be confused, and it seems that this is what the psychological egoist has done. We have just seen that the first principle is arguably true *a priori*, for the reason that we cannot imagine what it could even *mean* to say that someone knowingly did something without having any desire to do it. She may not have wanted to do it because she liked doing it, or because she had a strong urge to do it, but at least she wanted to do it to bring about some further thing that she thought worth the effort, or to prevent something she wanted to avoid. So, in some way or other, she *wanted* to do it, and this desire was *her own*. Nothing else seems to make any sense.

But this principle, unlike the second, does not say that the desire must be self-regarding. In fact, it leaves the question of what is desired completely open.

The psychological egoist has made the mistake – all unconsciously, of course – of attaching to the second principle (psychological egoism) the certainty that quite rightly belongs to the first. The two principles have been confused. *Own* desire is not the same as and does not imply *self-regarding* desire, and only the belief that it is or does could make psychological egoism seem certainly and indubitably true.

Psychological egoism has not been *disproven* by this argument, but the psychological egoist can no longer claim to occupy an impregnable fortress. If one is to go on defending the view, one must do so on the basis of evidence. Now, as has already been said, many supposedly unselfish acts really do have an ulterior motive that is self-regarding. In fact, any motive offered by the psychological egoist as the true underlying motive (ulterior motive) of an act supposed to be unselfish (not self-regarding) could be the real motive *sometimes*. But there must at least be reasons for suspicion based, say, on what we know about a person's character. Or we may know that the person obviously has something to gain by doing the thing in question (possibly a tax advantage). But there are many ordinary acts of kindness, compassion, and good will, where we have no reason at all to suspect that there is an ulterior motive, and the psychological egoist's claim that there must be one no longer has any force. Certainly, there are plenty of grounds for cynicism about many people's seemingly unselfish motives, but we run into examples every day where there is no reason to doubt, unless we appeal to the now discredited *a priori* version of psychological egoism, that the unselfish motive – simple kindness or concern, for instance – is genuine and real. There is no need to look for heroics; thinking of something other than oneself is a very ordinary thing. And, remember, the psychological egoist has been deprived of his (her) power. There is no longer any *must* about the matter.

Psychological Egoism: the Last Defence

But perhaps it is too early to proclaim victory. The hard-line psychological egoist is not finished yet. If we always act to satisfy our own desires, she says, doesn't this mean that we act *for the sake of* their satisfaction, and since this is *our own* satisfaction, doesn't that make all acts self-regarding? To this she may add that it is only the thought of the satisfaction that produces the desire, that without this thought there would be no desire. And so we really do always act to satisfy *ourselves*; no acts are *really* unselfish.

Before we can finish this off we must deal with an ambiguity in the notion of satisfaction. We say (1) that *a desire* is satisfied if, in fact, we get what we want. This does not necessarily mean (2) that *we* are satisfied, for we might not find any value in the thing we wanted when we get it. And even if we are satisfied, that does not necessarily mean (3) that we have a *feeling* of satisfaction, if by that we mean a rush, a buzz, or a high.

Now, to answer this final objection. In sense (1) of satisfaction, a desire *just is* something that wishes to be satisfied, so simply to *have* the desire is to have the thought of its satisfaction. This is *a priori* and harmless – part of understanding what it is to have a desire. Like the first of our two principles, it leaves the question of what is desired completely open. No egoism is implied. Still, we do suppose (2) that getting what we want (the satisfaction of our desire) will satisfy *us*. Does this mean that it is really *for the sake of* this satisfaction that we act? Finally (3), suppose that when I get what I want I have a strong *feeling* of satisfaction. Does this mean that it had to be *for the sake of* this feeling that I acted, that I only did it for the kicks?

Let's consider an example. Suppose you have a headache, and I give you a pain-reliever because, out of sympathy or compassion, I do not want you to be in pain (I want you not to be in pain). If your headache does go away, not only is my desire satisfied, but my distress on your behalf is relieved and I am really pleased. In other words *I* am satisfied. I may even have a strong *feeling* of satisfaction. Does this mean that I did not really care about you – that I was only thinking of my own satisfaction? The answer here is "no," for my satisfaction is precisely *in* your no longer suffering pain, and if I hadn't wanted you not to suffer, I would have received no satisfaction at all. *My satisfaction is dependent on my caring about you.* Nor did I act for the sake of the *feeling* of satisfaction, to get a particular kick, as a person does when, out of malice, hatred, envy, or spite, he tries to make another person suffer. (We can say that such a person takes pleasure in the other person's suffering, but he wants the other person to suffer *for the sake of* the pleasure that this gives him. The act is therefore self-regarding. Unlike the giver of the pain-reliever, he does not act for the other person's sake.) Certainly, I took pleasure in the relief of your pain, but I did not try to relieve your pain *for the sake of* the pleasure it gave me. The disappearance of your headache may have made me very happy, but that does not mean that I tried to cure it for the sake of my own happiness or to prevent my own misery, that I really did not care about you at all. In fact, if I had not cared about you I would have felt nothing. Not only does my feeling satisfied *not* mean that I acted for the sake of that feeling and not really for your sake at all, but my feeling of satisfaction *depends on* my having cared about you.

This does not mean, of course, that I *might* not have given you the pain-reliever to make you like me better, or just to demonstrate my powers, or to place you under an obligation or a debt to me. Any one of these things *could* be the true story sometimes, but nothing like this *has* to be true. We have no reason to doubt that I acted in this case simply in order to relieve your suffering (for the sake of relieving your suffering), and the fact that my success satisfied me or even gave me a feeling of satisfaction in no way changes this. It does *not* show that I was really only thinking of myself. Finally, it should now be plain, without further argument, that while I would not be motivated to do something without the thought of some satisfaction in it, that does not necessarily mean that it is *for the sake of* that satisfaction that I act. And when I am satisfied, it may be only because my desire for the relief of *your* pain or burden, for the sake of which I acted, has been satisfied. Because I am sympathetic and concerned, what satisfies *me* could easily be that something good has happened to *you*. It may very well have been for *your* sake and not my own that I acted.

Psychological Egoism: a Form of Moral Skepticism

There is a kind of moral theory, originated by the English philosopher Thomas Hobbes (1588–1679), which is a relatively benign form of ethical egoism.[5] According to theories of this kind, morality is a matter of people agreeing among themselves to treat one another decently. This they will do for their own benefit, if they are smart, because trying to go it alone is too risky. Breaking the agreement would be discouraged by the threat of isolation and the loss of the benefits of cooperation. According to Hobbes, the parties to the agreement should willingly submit to a ruler or governing authority who or which would ensure by force or the threat of force (punishments for violators) that the most important rules, those ensuring peace and good order, were obeyed. Since it only benefits people to obey the rules if others are doing so too, they need to know that violations are discouraged in this way, for only then can they be sure that sticking to the rules won't be to their disadvantage. Theories of this kind are compatible with psychological egoism and often assume it to be true. And while, unlike other forms of ethical egoism, they do tell us that we should be decent to one another, this is for purely self-interested reasons. Moral goodness is still unrelated to anything beyond my own interest as distinct from, and in competition with, the interests of others. Such things as kindness, generosity, or concern for the common good beyond my own profit have no part in it.

To be a skeptic about something is to have doubts about its reality or even its possibility. If being morally good means not just thinking of ourselves all the time, then psychological egoism is a very serious form of moral skepticism. But we have now defused or taken the sting out of psychological egoism in its most dangerous, menacing, and persuasive-sounding form. This is the form that reveals itself upon inspection to be based upon a confusion of two identical-looking but actually quite different principles. The first is a harmless one that can plausibly be claimed to be true *a priori*; the second is a threatening one (psychological egoism) that most certainly cannot. We are not required to discard, in advance, any theory of morality according to which being morally good involves sometimes thinking of something other than ourselves.

The Defeat of Psychological Egoism and the Possibility of Altruism

One final but very important point. You will notice that I have been careful to avoid the use of the word "altruism," even though egoism and altruism are often opposed. If an act is not egoistic, it is said, it must be altruistic, by which is meant selfless. But if a person always acts, necessarily, to satisfy some desire of his or her own, to do or bring about something he or she wants, and if she is pleased to do it or to bring it about and frustrated if she does not, how can we speak of altruism? She is not being selfless; she is doing what matters the most to her, even if it is for the good of another person or group or the community as a whole. In an important sense, there is no real sacrifice or self-denial involved – something usually claimed for altruistic acts. For how can we say that a person is denying himself when he is doing what matters the most to him? He may be giving up something he could otherwise have for himself, but this is his choice; this is what he prefers to do and he would not have it any other way. In an important sense, there is no such thing as altruism, if altruism means self-sacrifice, self-denial, or selflessness. A person is not denying herself in doing things that are not self-regarding; she is doing what means the most to her. She is doing precisely – and nothing else is possible – what she wants to do, and if her expectations are fulfilled, she is satisfied. Although unselfish acts are not egoistic, they are not altruistic either. We may call this the grain of truth in psychological egoism.

SUMMARY

1   Psychological egoism is the doctrine that every act of every human being is motivated by *self-regarding* considerations, and that it could not be any other way.

2   This would mean, if it were true, that no one could ever act for the sake of anything besides herself or himself – not for other people nor for any ideal such as justice or the betterment of the world.

3   If psychological egoism were true, I *could not* care about anything

besides myself, and this would be true of everyone else as well. Therefore, any notion of moral goodness as involving concern for others, or for the community as a whole, or for any ideal, would be a vain and foolish notion.

4   Psychological egoism is not a moral theory but a theory of human motivation. Still, if it were true, it would justify cynicism about supposedly unselfish motives. Since most of us do see moral goodness as involving concern for something other than ourselves, it is a form of *moral skepticism*.

5   There is one kind of moral theory, however, that psychological egoism will allow, and that is *ethical egoism*. If psychological egoism is true, then everyone is really in competition with everyone else to get as much as he or she can for himself or herself. Ethical egoism can take the crude form that the admirable thing is to be *smart* at outdoing others in this competitive struggle.

6   Ethical egoism can also take the more refined form, first advocated by Hobbes, that since not everybody can make it big, and you can never know whether you will be a winner or a loser, it is better to enter into an agreement with everybody else to restrict your conduct so that people do not have to live in perpetual fear of one another. (This is a form of what is called *contractarianism*.) (Note that what is being said is that it is *in your interest* to enter into such agreement. There is no appeal to motives that are not self-regarding.)

7   Psychological egoism is an extremely nasty view of human nature – nobody really cares about anybody or anything else besides himself – and whether we believe it or not greatly affects our outlook on life. We should therefore examine it carefully.

8   People who believe that psychological egoism is true typically do not let *any example whatever* count against their position. For any act whose motive seems not to be self-regarding, they are always able to produce a plausible-sounding *ulterior* motive that *is* self-regarding, and which they say *must* be the real motive. They regard their position as undefeatable – nothing can or could count against it.

9   Now when a person sees his or her view as undefeatable in this way, that is a sure sign that she has latched on to something that is true *a priori*, or, in other words, something of which one can be absolutely certain without appealing to any actual evidence.

10   The *a priori* truth that the psychological egoists have latched on to is this: *Every act of every person is done to satisfy some desire of his or her own.* This seems to be genuinely true *a priori*, because we cannot *make any sense* of the idea that someone might consciously, voluntarily, and intentionally do something without having any desire to do it. Desire is

necessary to motivate, and, of course, if it is going to motivate *me*, it must be *my* desire. (I may not want to do the thing for its own sake; I may want to do it because it achieves something else that I want.)

11   Psychological egoism states, however, that *every act of every person is done to satisfy some self-regarding desire*, and this is *not the same* as the principle stated in (10) above. Because a desire is *mine*, it need not be *self-regarding*. In fact, its object could be your good, or the good of society, or anything you please. "Own desire" does not mean the same as "self-regarding desire," and the believer in psychological egoism has confused the two.

12   *The certainty that quite properly belongs to the first principle in (10) above has been mistakenly transferred to the second (11).* In other words, the *owner* of the desire has been confused with its *object*. Coming to see that this is so takes the ground out from under the feet of anyone who would claim that psychological egoism is true beyond the possibility of doubt.

13   One difficulty remains. The believer in psychological egoism might say that if everything is done to satisfy some desire of one's own, does that not mean that it is done *for the sake of* that satisfaction? Is it not, therefore, basically egoistic in the final analysis? But suppose that I do something to relieve your pain because I really care about you. Naturally, I am satisfied if I succeed; that, after all, was what I wanted. But not only does this *not* prove that I really didn't care about you at all, but if I *hadn't* really cared about you, I would have experienced no such satisfaction. Of course, I am satisfied when I achieve what I want to achieve, but that does not mean that I only acted *for the sake of* that satisfaction. Here my concern was with *your pain* and its relief. *That* was what mattered to me.

14   Of course, I can only act for the sake of what matters to me, even if that is another's good, or justice, or the good of society, or whatever you like. In *that* sense there is no such thing as altruism or selflessness. This is the grain of truth in psychological egoism.

Some Mistakes to Avoid

1   Do not confuse *psychological* egoism, which denies that unselfish acts are *possible*, with *ethical* egoism, which says that one *should* always act in one's own self-interest. (One can be an ethical egoist – saying that people who act for anything but their own self-interest are simply fools – without being a psychological egoist.)

2   Do not confuse a psychological egoist (someone who believes that

psychological egoism is true) with someone who is completely selfish. A completely selfish person need not believe that psychological egoism is true.

3   Do not confuse psychological egoism with the view that some or many or even most people are selfish. (This could be true while psychological egoism was false.) Psychological egoism claims that *every* human act is *necessarily* self-regarding.

4   Do not confuse psychological egoism with the view that some or many or even most of a person's acts are self-regarding. (This could be true while psychological egoism was false.) Psychological egoism claims that *every single one* of a person's acts is self-regarding and that it could not be any other way.

5   Do not suppose that if psychological egoism is false, then all or most of our acts must be unselfish. If there ever was, or ever could be, even *one* unselfish act, then psychological egoism is false.

QUESTIONS FOR THOUGHT

1   The world is full of selfish people. Does this mean that psychological egoism is true?

2   Do you agree that a person can only act to satisfy some desire of his/her own? Why does this seem undeniably true? Does this mean that psychological egoism is true?

3   If psychological egoism were true, would this mean that *no* morality was possible? Why is psychological egoism a form of moral skepticism?

4   Is altruism possible? Explain why or why not.

2

Cultural Relativism

Psychological egoism is a view that, if it were true, would make it impossible for there to be a moral goodness that involved thinking of anything besides oneself. The only kind of goodness or virtue that psychological egoism allows for is being *smart* in getting the most we can for ourselves, regardless of the consequences for other people (unless these consequences happen to affect us). This is because psychological egoism declares that, *of necessity*, all human acts are self-regarding. We have defused psychological egoism by pointing out that the only thing *necessarily* true is that every act of every person is done to satisfy some desire *of his or her own*, which places no limit on what may be desired. The *object* of desire could be anything, including the good of others. My own desire may be self-regarding but it need not be. *Own* does not mean or imply *self-regarding*. There is no necessity in psychological egoism, and without necessity it seems to have nothing going for it at all. And that, if it is true, means that we have succeeded in removing what looked at first like a very powerful threat to the very idea of goodness or morality as involving concern for justice, the community, other people, or anything other than oneself.

But some may think that it was a mistake even to consider that goodness or virtue might consist in being clever at maximizing your own profit (which we said was the only thing that virtue could be if psychological egoism were true), let alone to think seriously about a morality that (unlike ethical egoism) did involve concern for something other than ourselves. For in both cases we were trying to say something about moral goodness *in general*, whatever the time or place, and perhaps, as many people think, goodness, virtue, and morality are purely *local* matters. To say that because morality is a local matter we cannot even think about a moral goodness that would apply to all human beings at all times and in all places is the thesis of *cultural relativism*. Morality, it is said, is simply a matter of conduct or character that is approved of or disapproved of, and that is something that varies from culture to culture, that is different at different times and in different places. Thus, there is no *universal* morality, no morality that applies to all human beings regardless of the historically and geographically located culture in which they happen to be living.

No doubt you are all familiar with the view that morality is simply a matter of accepted standards of conduct which, of course, vary from time to time and from place to place. If we wanted to be nasty, we could call this the "film censorship board" theory of morality; it is all a matter of "what the community will tolerate." If sexual abuse of children is tolerated by the community, then sexual abuse of children is perfectly all right. By similar reasoning, if clitoridectomy (so-called "female circumcision") is the done thing, then clitoridectomy is what is to be done and there can be no objection to it. There can be no objection to it from within the culture because it *is* the accepted social practice. There can be no objection from outside the culture for this amounts to trying to impose *our* standards on a culture which happens to be different from our own. This view is often given out in the name of *liberalism*: we should respect our own morality, but we should be allowing and tolerant of the morality of other cultures, which is as valid from their perspective as our own morality is from *our* perspective.

Simple Cultural Relativism

There is a simple form of cultural relativism which derives from the ethnologists of the earlier part of the twentieth century, William Graham Sumner, Ruth Benedict, Edward Westermarck, and Margaret Mead.[1] Their argument is as simple as this:

> *Premise*: Accepted norms of conduct vary from culture to culture
> *Conclusion*: Therefore, morality varies from culture to culture

From simply observing the difference in the kinds of behavior that are approved of or disapproved of in different cultures, they derived the conclusion that morality was entirely relative to culture. Questions of good and bad, right and wrong, could be settled only by reference to cultural or community standards or they could not be settled at all. There was nothing else *objective* to appeal to. Furthermore, this was announced as if it were a new discovery, although cultural relativism was a commonplace among the educated in Plato's time, and was famously taught by the sophist Protagoras.[2]

Unfortunately, however, the argument as it stands is no good. We cannot derive the conclusion from the premise. What makes the argument *seem* sound is that it contains a suppressed or unstated premise, namely that morality *consists in* following accepted norms of conduct. Now when, in an argument, a premise is left out (unstated, suppressed), as not being necessary for the argument to be convincing, that is nearly always because the unstated premise is thought to be so obvious that there is no *need* to state it.[3] This is certainly what has happened here. The full argument, including the suppressed or unstated premise, is the following:

> *Premise 1*: Accepted norms of conduct vary from culture to culture
> [*Premise 2 (unstated)*: Morality (being moral or good) consists in following accepted norms of conduct]
> *Conclusion*: Morality varies from culture to culture

The argument is obviously valid. "Valid" is a technical term in logic which means, when applied to an argument, that the conclusion follows logically from the premises. What *this* means is that you cannot affirm or assert the premises and then go on to deny the conclusion without contradicting yourself, and *that* means that if the premises are true the conclusion *must* be true. For to affirm or assert something is to say that it is *true*, and so, when the conclusion *follows logically* from the premises, we must, if we take the premises to be true, accept the truth of the conclusion as well. Why? Because if we don't, we will have contradicted ourselves. What this means for us, here and now, is that if premise 1 and premise 2 are true, then *necessarily* the conclusion is true, and the case for cultural relativism in ethics has been proven.

Now let's examine this argument for cultural relativism step by step. First of all, no one in her right mind would challenge the truth of premise 1. Accepted norms of conduct certainly do vary from culture to culture and, for that matter, from subculture to subculture within a complex culture such as our own. But, because the argument is valid, if we go on to accept premise 2 we are *forced* to accept the conclusion. The only way to escape is to challenge premise 2, in the hope that we can show it to be false, and that is exactly what I now propose to do. There are two different ways of looking at this second premise: we can interpret it as *definitional*, as saying that "being moral" ("morality") simply *means* "following accepted norms of conduct," or we can read it as a *substantive moral claim* saying, in effect, that if you want to be morally good you must conform to the norms of conduct of the culture you inhabit, and if you fail to conform to these norms then you are morally bad.

These two interpretations of the second premise are quite different. Let us consider the first possibility, namely that it is true by definition. If "morality" or "being moral" or "being good" simply *meant* "conforming to accepted practices" or "doing the done thing" (following accepted norms of conduct), then no one could challenge any of the norms of her or his culture or subculture *without contradicting herself or himself*. For on this reading of premise 2, it is established *by definition* that something is good if it conforms to the accepted norms, and bad if it does not. I would therefore be contradicting myself if I said: "I know this is an accepted norm of conduct, but I believe it to be wrong." But it is perfectly obvious that such remarks are not self-contradictory. And whatever we think of the would-be moral reformer, there is nothing wrong with his or her understanding of the meanings of words! Somebody getting ready to heave a stone at the adulteress might have thought that Jesus (Rabbi Yeshua)[4] was a bit weird when he said (assuming the Bible story to be true): "He that is without sin among you, let him first cast a stone at her."[5] After all it was (according to the story) a norm of conduct and an accepted social practice and (again according to the story) the rabbi obviously knew that – but no one would have thought he was contradicting himself, even though he was saying, in effect, that the practice was wrong and should be done away with. It cannot be true by definition that to be morally good is to do the done thing and never to do anything that is not done.

Now let's consider the second way of interpreting premise 2, that is as a *substantive* moral claim, namely that the way to be moral or good is to conform to accepted social practices. Notice it is no longer being claimed that this is true *by definition*; rather, it is taken as telling us how we must behave if we are to be moral or good. The moral reformer is no longer contradicting herself or himself; now he or she is simply mistaken if she claims that there is something morally wrong with some accepted social practice, or that there is a practice that *should be introduced* because it would be morally good, or morally better than some present practice. However, this is nothing but pure moral conservatism, and no argument for it has been offered. In fact, we have been given no reason at all to believe it. Apparently, we are supposed to accept it as being obviously true or, as philosophers say, self-evident! The rabbi wasn't contradicting himself; he simply didn't see that to be morally good is to do the done thing and to avoid doing what is not done. But moral conservatism (extreme conformism) is plainly *not* self-evidently true. The accepted practice or, to use the ethnologists' word, the *mores* of a culture *can* be criticized from within, and on *moral* grounds. It is obviously not self-contradictory to say, from within a culture in which slavery is an accepted institution or practice: "Slavery should be abolished because it is morally wrong; human beings should not be bought and sold or be merely used for their owners' purposes; human dignity forbids such exploitation." It is equally plain that it is not self-evidently false simply because it is made from within a slave culture. We must, therefore, be able to appeal to something other than accepted practices in making our moral judgments.

But the argument is even worse than this. For if premise 2 is taken not to be true by definition, but as telling us *what we all must do if we want to be morally good* (namely, follow the accepted social practices of the culture in which we happen to be located), then it has to be a moral principle that is *not* relative to culture. It is clearly transcultural, i.e. it cuts across all cultures, applying in all times and places, and is not relative to any particular one. What it says, in effect, is "Always do the done thing, whatever that may be, in the place you happen to be" or "When in Rome, do as the Romans do," and this can only be a universal or "absolute" principle of morality, applying to all persons at all places and times. But what was the argument trying to disprove? Precisely the possibility of there *being* any such universal principles! Thus the argument undermines itself by taking as a premise something that contradicts the conclusion! We cannot use a universal moral principle as part of an argument for cultural relativism in ethics since, if cultural relativism is true, there *are* no universal moral principles!

Of course, none of this proves that cultural relativism (the conclusion of the argument) is false. It only shows that this particular argument for it is no good, and so if we are going to try to show that cultural relativism is true, we will have to produce a better argument than this. And if there *is* no better argument, or if no better case can be made, then we have *no* reason for accepting it. There *are* more sophisticated arguments for cultural relativism, which is still a very popular doctrine, and we shall look at some of them now. We won't have such an easy job with these more complex views and understanding both the positions themselves and my attempts to undermine them will cost you a major effort.

Sophisticated Cultural Relativism: (1) Bernard Williams

We will begin with Bernard Williams. According to him,[6] there are moral truths, but these are *perspectival* truths, or truths only from *within* the particular culture to which they belong. Williams calls them "non-objectivist truths," part of a way of living that belongs to a particular culture, and valid only from within that "evaluative perspective." They are "non-reflective," that is they are not in any way argued for or thought out. They use what Williams calls the "thick concepts" of the culture to which they belong, such as, to use his own examples, "liar" and "brutal," which are drawn from our own culture.[7] Thus, "You are a liar" and "His treatment of his wife is brutal" are used to state *moral* truths (not morally neutral facts) from within our own evaluative perspective. For us, terms like "liar" and "brutal" carry within themselves their moral meaning. However, these concepts cannot be used by anyone who does not share our perspective. Someone outside our culture can recognize that we use them to state moral truths, but these need not be moral truths from within his or her evaluative perspective. We might also recognize "She is a chaste and humble patriot" and "She is a diligent and obedient wife" as capable of stating moral truths *from within our own cultural past*, but no longer capable of stating moral truths for us now. (And he's right in one respect, isn't he? They just won't do any more.)

Similarly, says Williams, "non-objectivist" moral truths cease to be truths for someone within the culture as soon as he or she reflects upon them or calls them in question, asking such questions as whether something is really wrong or really right or really good or really evil, or whether something really ought or ought not to be done. One may ask these questions, which involve thought and reflection, using such "thin" concepts as "good," "right," "ought," "wrong," but there are no answers to be found. We have made the mistake, according to Williams, of looking for *objective* moral knowledge of universal moral truths, knowledge that is independent of any particular evaluative perspective. Thus morality has lost the "non-objectivist truths" with their 'thick' concepts, which were the cultural anchor that gave it reality and substance. In Williams's words, "reflection destroys knowledge."[8] As he sees it, when one steps outside one's "evaluative perspective" and tries to answer moral questions, as it were *transcendentally*, or from above, one finds oneself completely at sea and no answers are forthcoming. (We shall see in what follows – I hope – that one need not adopt or try to adopt a transcendental standpoint in order to put forward and defend something as a universal moral truth, by which I mean one applicable to everybody, regardless of time and place.)

But think for a moment. Do the people within a culture recognize what they take to be their moral truths as non-objective truths or as truths simply *for them*? Clearly they do not. They take them to be truths, pure and simple. In fact, if they did not, these "truths" would carry no weight with them; there would be no moral conviction. In fact, one cannot even *say* "These are truths here and now but not necessarily there or then, truths for us but not necessarily truths for them," for we cannot make any sense of such a statement. Try "That huge boy beating up other children in the schoolyard is a bully and a brute. But of course that is only *our* truth. From another evaluative perspective there might be no such truth." Clearly this won't do, for the person first says that someone is a bully and a brute and then effectively takes it back by saying that this might not be a truth from another evaluative perspective. Indeed, in saying that it might not be a truth from some other evaluative perspective he is adopting, or trying to adopt, the very transcendental standpoint (the standpoint outside all evaluative perspectives) that Williams says destroys knowledge!

If we say, with Williams, that the only moral knowledge is non-objectivist knowledge, we have already destroyed that knowledge, for we can no longer say simply "That boy is a bully" and, angry and distressed, tell the principal or headteacher about it. As soon as we declare it to be non-objective or perspectival, it ceases to *be* knowledge or conviction for us, and will no longer move us to action. Thus, if we accept Williams's position, we effectively wipe out all our moral convictions, for in accepting it we have already stepped outside our evaluative perspective! In fact, we have ceased to be moral beings. It turns out that even in order to *state* Williams's position, we *must* stand outside all evaluative perspectives, adopting a transcendental standpoint that looks on all of them from above, but this means, on his own account, that all our moral knowledge is thereby destroyed! The poor fools within the perspective may go on taking their moral statements to be simply true and go on acting on their convictions, but we philosophers, who know better, can no longer do so! Again, on Williams's own account, we are completely at sea! Thus his position undermines itself. According to him, as soon as we adopt the transcendental standpoint, real, living, effective morality disappears, but it is only from the transcendental standpoint that we can even speak of non-objectivist moral truths! Thus, in the very act of thinking and speaking of non-objectivist moral truths we destroy them. We can only conclude that there is no such thing as non-objectivist moral truth.[9]

Let me say now, although this really belongs to a future discussion,[10] that if that beefy boy really is beating up smaller children in the schoolyard, then he is a bully, and let me suggest that that is a moral truth. If so, Williams is right in saying that we often do not need to use reflective "thin" concepts like "good," "bad," "ought," "right," and "wrong" in making moral judgments. Surely bullying *is* bad; it is an evil *in itself*, or *of its very nature*, and a habitual bully is, in that respect, a bad person, or a person of bad character. (If we know what bullying *is*, we already know that it is bad.) What do you think? Again, if I discover that you are in the habit of telling lies for personal advantage, without any thought for the person lied to, and you do so easily, without a shred of conscience, then you *are* a liar, and "You are a liar," said to you, is a moral truth. Telling lies without some moral justification is morally wrong, and a habitual liar is a bad person or a person of bad character in that respect. Again, what do you think, and why? (Place yourself in the position of the person who trusts the liar, and is lied to.) Williams does seem to be right about one thing: the word "liar," like the word "bully," in its familiar use, does all the moral work by itself. We do not, in the context of daily life, need to *make out a case* for bullying and lying being wrong or bad, whether in making our own judgments or in discussing the matter with others.

Williams is also right when he says, by implication, that "She is a chaste and humble patriot" is not a moral truth for us, although it may have been accepted as a moral truth by our great-grandparents. Some woman of our own time may very well be a chaste and humble patriot, or a diligent and obedient wife, but to say these things about her is not, for us (unless we are out of step with the times), to praise her character. Our moral views have changed and – dare I say it? – they have changed for the better (see figure 2.1).

Transcendental standpoint

*The perspective of the person who
evaluates or questions or reflects upon a
moral issue by consciously examining the
issue from an objective perspective*

*Uses "thin" concepts such as
"good" or "ought" in the process
of reflecting upon a moral issue.
Take the question "Is it really
true that I ought not to tell lies?"
In order to answer this question
some moral authority or standard
must be referred to. No answer
can be found because there is no
universal moral standard to
appeal to.*

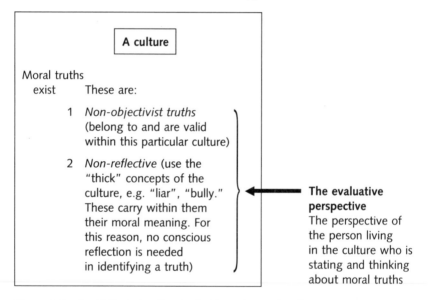

Figure 2.1   Sophisticated cultural relativism: Bernard Williams

Sophisticated Cultural Relativism: (2) Alasdair MacIntyre

The position of Alasdair MacIntyre[11] is in some ways very similar to that of
Bernard Williams. As with Williams, morality is embedded in culture and one
cannot arrive at any moral conclusions, particular or general, by attempting
to take a position outside all living moralities. Unlike Williams, however,
MacIntyre claims that moral judgments *can* be defended rationally. Still they

can only be defended, or justified, *from within a particular living tradition*. There can be no *external* justification for moral judgments and hence no universal morality. Agreement can be reached on moral questions only among those within the *same* tradition, and one cannot arbitrate among traditions from some position outside them all.

MacIntyre also sees morality as something that develops over time within a culture. We, as individuals, and as a society, must quest (search) for the good, for the best life, by living it, and we can only begin from the point in time where we happen to be historically located, from a position within some living tradition that we ourselves accept. No matter how hard we might think about it, we cannot work out the good in advance. There is no fixed or eternal good discoverable by thinking, no good outside history and tradition, no good independent of an endless quest for it from within the time and place in which we happen to find ourselves.

MacIntyre believes that there is so much disagreement on moral questions in our own culture because of the clash of different traditions now mixed together in an incredible mish-mash − traditions which come from different times and places in our history − with no possible way to arbitrate between them. The answer to a particular moral question may be one thing according to one tradition and another according to another, and there is no way in which the two can be brought together. Thus moral argument has degenerated into a shouting match. How can this state of affairs be overcome? MacIntyre says all one can do is declare one's allegiance to a particular tradition, inviting others to understand and come to agree by some sort of imaginative sympathy. If one succeeds this could be part of a movement of cultural change. There can be no *argument* for one tradition over another.

It is important to notice the differences, as well as the similarities, between Williams and MacIntyre. For Williams, there are "non-objectivist moral truths," truths from the evaluative perspective of a particular culture, using its "thick" concepts, but these are "non-reflective," which means they are not and do not need to be defended or argued for. If, for instance, some person *really is* a bully or a liar, then that is that. MacIntyre, by contrast, claims that moral judgments can be supported or argued for by an appeal to agreed-upon rational criteria, but that these criteria are rational only from within a particular tradition, and by the standards of rationality of that tradition. There can be no appeal to a common or universal reason shared by all. Thus moral questions cannot be settled and there is no moral truth except *from within a particular living tradition*. For neither author are there any *universal* moral truths applicable to all persons at all times and in all places.

We were able to defeat Williams's position by showing that the position itself was only understandable from the very transcendental perspective (the perspective outside all evaluative perspectives) that he declared to be destructive of moral knowledge. The minute we declare moral truths to be "non-objective," we have rendered all of them inoperative, and that includes our own. Thus his position defeated itself! But how are we going to deal with MacIntyre?

MacIntyre claims that what counts as practical rationality (rationality about *what to do*) – and this is understood to include morality or being moral- depends upon the tradition from which one is speaking. Thus, from the perspective of one tradition, MacIntyre says, to be practically rational is to act wisely in one's own interest, from another it means an impartiality that does not favor one's own interests, and from yet another it means acting so as to bring about the final and true good for humanity in general.[12] Thus there is no such thing as practical rationality plain and simple. It all depends on which tradition you are (for the moment) speaking from.

In answer to this claim of MacIntyre's, it is surely obvious that people may disagree about what *is* practically rational without disagreeing about what practical rationality *is*, and there is no reason why this should not apply here. Can we not say that to be practically rational is to act for the best reasons, or for the sake of whatever it is that is most worth pursuing or accomplishing? The differences can be seen not as coming from completely different ideas of what practical rationality *is*, but from disagreement over what *is* practically rational, that is over what thing or things, generally speaking, *actually are* most worth having, getting, or doing, hence things that we have the best reasons for going after. We can reinterpret what MacIntyre says as follows. Tradition 1 says the supreme value for a person is prudence, or one's own best long-range interest, and therefore this is what all action should aim at; tradition 2 says it is the good of everyone equally, with favor to no one; tradition 3 says it is the final or true good for humanity in general. These are claims about *just what is practically rational* rather than about *what practical rationality is*, and the question of just what is most worth pursuing (what is practically rational) can be debated by any two or more parties. We can discuss, consider, and reflect upon just which tradition is best, or whether we can't, in some way, combine all of them. People may even be persuaded by thought and reflection (as perhaps some of you will be) that some one thing or some combination of things is what is most desirable, most worth our while to aim at or pursue. One is not forced to adhere to one or another of these "traditions" and on no rational basis whatever!

Let us now consider MacIntyre's claim that there are many important moral issues upon which no agreement can be reached in our culture because the arguments on one side or the other use premises based on different and incompatible traditions. Remember that, according to MacIntyre, there is no morality *independent of* one tradition or another and hence no *universal* morality. MacIntyre gives three examples of areas of unresolvable dispute to try to prove his point: war, abortion, and the question of whether health care and education should be state or private matters.[13] According to MacIntyre, these disputes are unresolvable because, in each case, the parties to the dispute base their arguments on premises that derive from different and incompatible traditions. In the first dispute (war), these premises, supposedly deriving from two different traditions, are respect for justice and innocence on one side, and the need for survival and success on the other. In the second dispute (abortion), they are respect for rights on one side, and the obligation to give others the same treatment that one would require for oneself ("universalizability") on the other. In the third dispute (health care and education), they are respect for equality on the one side and respect for liberty on the other. We may roughly summarize the disputes as follows.

On war, the first party says that the only just wars, in present circumstances, if there are any just wars at all, are wars of liberation against oppression, where the good to be gained outweighs the evil, major wars leading inevitably to the loss of many innocent lives. The second party says that if you are going to survive you must prepare for war (in other words arm heavily) and let everyone know that you are ready and willing to go to war if necessary; potential enemies must be intimidated into not doing anything nasty. (This is called "deterrence.") Otherwise, a war *in which you lose* cannot be avoided. The slogan is, "If you wish peace, prepare for war."

On abortion, the first party asserts that everyone has certain rights over his or her own person including her own body, of which the embryo is a part. Therefore, a girl or a woman should be able to make a free decision on whether or not to have an abortion. The second party points out that I could not, retroactively, permit my mother to abort the embryo that became me, for had she done that I would not now exist as a person in the world. But there is nothing special about me. I cannot therefore (unless the embryo is badly damaged or defective) allow any pregnant girl or woman to proceed to have an abortion, abortion being, in effect, equivalent to murder.

On education and medical care, the first party asserts that everyone should have equal opportunity, and this is not possible without universal access to medical care and education, regardless of financial means. The second party says that everyone, including medical practitioners, educators, and those who require their services, has the right to freedom of choice. Therefore, medical practice and education should be strictly private, and the state should not interfere in these matters.

As MacIntyre would have us see it, the first party in the war dispute follows a tradition that includes justice and innocence among its highest values, while the second party belongs to a tradition that gives the same exalted status to success and survival. But why must one choose between justice and innocence, on the one hand, and success and survival on the other? Are not all of these values values for us? Must they belong to incompatible traditions? If we value success and survival, must we exclude (or ignore or demote) justice and innocence? And if we value justice and innocence, does this require us to exclude (or ignore or demote) considerations of success and survival? Or is it supposed to be simply a question of which of these sets of values ranks higher or of which one takes precedence over the other? If this is all that is being said, why can't we debate the matter rationally? Is the question really nondebatable because the differing views on which set of values takes precedence belong to different traditions? And why must we give a *general* answer to the question of precedence? Why should we not favor one or the other according to the circumstances in a particular case?

First of all, we must survive. This is a precondition of everything. If, indeed, the only way to survive is to arm to the teeth and intimidate everybody into leaving us alone, then that is what we must do. But what about negotiation conducted with sincerity and good will by both parties in their mutual interest? Isn't that a better way to peace? Isn't arming to the teeth, with the potential enemy doing the same, more likely to lead to war than to prevent it? I will not try to answer this question here, for it is not a philosophical, but a psychological and sociological question. But whatever answer we give, it will certainly be relevant to the debate. If negotiation in good faith by both parties, and the establishment of trust is, in fact, the only way of ensuring peace and security, that is clearly the way we should take. And we may then cease to slight justice and innocence. War is an evil, clearly to be avoided, unless it is forced upon us in order to prevent or eliminate an obviously greater evil, for it is bound, however limited it may be, to take many innocent lives. Is that not a consideration that should appeal to all of us? Must the people who say we must arm to the teeth in order to avoid destruction simply be speaking *from a different tradition*? Couldn't they just be mistaken?

In order to explain our apparently not being able to resolve this dispute, we do not need, as MacIntyre claims we do, to invoke different and incompatible moral traditions. The main issue, which would resolve the dispute if it could be settled, is the question of just exactly what is the best or the only way to peace and security. No one needs to choose between success and security, on the one hand, and justice and innocence on the other. After all, justice and innocence would only need to be set aside if one actually had to seriously risk a major war, and if one is really arming to the teeth for the sole purpose of ensuring peace, then one is attempting to eliminate or minimize this risk! One could, of course, simply not care about the loss of innocent life, but to what moral tradition could that belong? I suppose one could say that there is a "tradition" of military conquest and victory over one's enemies, for the sake of glory, territory, and destruction or exploitation of the conquered, a "tradition" closely associated with the supposed virtue of patriotism. There are plenty of historical examples of this, up to and including Adolf Hitler. There is also the "pre-emptive war," in which you try to destroy the enemy before the enemy can destroy you. This is success and survival with a vengeance. But is MacIntyre telling us that those who say "If you wish peace, prepare for war," are speaking from within *this* tradition? If, in fact, this were so, they would be displaying the grossest hypocrisy, for they are claiming that they are only interested in peace. If we are to take them seriously, we can only assume that peace is what they really want.

To turn now to his second example, it is easier to demolish MacIntyre's claim that the unresolvable dispute over abortion, as he sets it out, results from the two parties appealing to different and incompatible traditions. To begin with, MacIntyre give us the most extreme positions on both sides of the dispute: on the "pro-choice" side that the embryo is a part of the female's body; on the "pro-life" side that abortion, even early abortion, is indistinguishable from infanticide, and is therefore equivalent to murder.

To begin with, let us ask, in general terms, whether we have here two different and incompatible moral traditions. The two principles appealed to are (1) that a person has a moral right over what she (he) does with her (his) own body, and (2) that we are not to commit murder. Assuming that suicide is not murder, where is the incompatibility here? Why cannot both of these things be true, or why can't we accept both? Do rights belong to one tradition, while the principle that we are not to do to others what we would not have done to ourselves belongs to another? Well, a person has the right to do what he (she) likes with his (her) own body (tattoos included), which means that others must stand aside and let him (her) exercise that right if he (she) can't be persuaded otherwise. Why? Because a person must not treat others as she (he) would not be treated herself (himself). What is the matter with this reply? And I am not to commit murder? Why? Because everybody, or every innocent person, has the right to life. What is the matter with this reply? And doesn't it sound familiar? Don't the opponents of abortion speak constantly of the "right to life"?[14] So both sides in the dispute appeal to rights. And could not both appeal to so-called "universalizability," or of allowing only what any person would allow universally, including the times when he or she is on the receiving end? Would you allow anyone else to decide what you should do with your own body, without your agreement and consent? Do people not, except under unusual circumstances (perhaps war, perhaps self-defence, perhaps having committed some vile crime), have the right to life, the right not to be killed? So where is the incompatibility, and what are the different traditions alleged by MacIntyre to be in unresolvable conflict here?

But the dispute goes on. Why is it unresolvable? Well, so long as one party says the embryo is a person and killing it amounts to murder, it obviously can't be resolved! Why? First of all, because the two claims are incompatible simply as statements claiming factual truths about the world, *not including the moral dimension*. If the embryo is literally part of the pregnant female's body, then it is not a separate organism, and if it is a separate organism, then it is not part of the pregnant female's body. *That* is not an *ethical* dispute. What is the fact of the matter? Well, the embryo is clearly *attached* to the pregnant female's body and is dependent on it for life, but it is, undoubtedly, an individual of the species *Homo sapiens* in a very early stage of its development. After all, if evolution had taken a somewhat different course, we might have been egg-layers, like platypuses, or marsupials, like kangaroos. It just so *happens* that with our species, as with most mammals, the organism in the first stage of its development remains within the mother's body. What this means is that the extreme "pro-choice" people are basing their argument on a claim – the claim that the embryo is a part of the pregnant female's body – that is factually false and is easily shown to be false by a simple appeal to biology.

And what about the other side? Is the embryo of, say, 8–12 weeks a person? The answer seems to be pretty clearly "no," although it is true that if left alone and the pregnancy comes to term, it will, after birth (given that it is normal), *become* a person. Furthermore, it is plain that if the *conceptus* (from single-celled zygote on) in my mother's fallopian tubes and then her uterus, had not developed to the point where viable independent life was possible, *I* would not exist, and I could not, unless my life were unbearably miserable, will the abortion of that pregnancy. But I could not will that abortion even if it were spontaneous (what is called a "miscarriage"), and equally I could not will that the human organism that is now me had not been conceived in the first place! In none of these cases would I now exist.

So is abortion murder or its equivalent? Because the embryo or fetus is not a person, the answer seems to be "no." But nevertheless abortion is not *morally neutral*, for it is after all the knowing destruction of a human life with real potential, and that is different both from its unintended destruction and from the failure to bring that life into being. Thus it is a regrettable act and is not equivalent to cutting your hair or paring your fingernails! Abortion, in some cases – to take an obvious example, when the pregnancy results from the rape of a 13-year-old – seems to be the lesser of two evils. The position of the pregnant girl or woman who is, after all, a person in the world, as the embryo is not, cannot simply be ignored. Perhaps she herself *should* have the last word. After all, it is she who would have to bear the child, and why should a decision be forced on her? So, if we retreat from the extreme positions, we seem to see at least the possibility of a solution, although undoubtedly full agreement (consensus) on this particular issue will never be reached. In any case, the continuing and seemingly endless dispute does not, as MacIntyre insists, result from an appeal to different and incompatible moral traditions!

MacIntyre seems to have the most going for him in the third dispute, the dispute concerning health care and education. It might at first seem plausible that liberty and equality really are incompatible, that there is no meeting ground between the two, that we can choose either one or the other but not both, because they belong to two different traditions. But consider, are they not both values for us? And can't we give both of them due weight? Cannot a compromise of some sort be reached? Of course, there cannot be a *restricted* equality of opportunity because if it is restricted it ceases to be equality. But what about liberty? Can it be given full and unrestricted reign? Certainly not, for some (the stronger or more powerful) would be encouraged to take advantage of others (the weaker or less powerful) in ways that we could not help but recognize as unjust. There must be *some* restrictions on liberty if we are to have a society at all, for when there is none, everyone is at risk. (We must not forget that the tide can always turn.) So liberty is something that must be restricted, no matter what.

Well then, why should liberty not be restricted in the interest of equality of opportunity, given that that is regarded as desirable and just? Given a free and private money economy, there are bound to be wide differences in income. Some will not be able to afford private medicine and education. And why should the poor be deprived of the schooling and access to medical care that are necessary for equality of opportunity? Should people only be entitled to what their money can buy? Why can't we say: let us have as much liberty as possible, compatibly with other values that cannot be sacrificed? Isn't this at least a reasonable position to take?

Absolute equality is not a viable ideal. Neither is absolute freedom. Are the two incompatible "traditions" supposed to require one or the other of these but not both? Can we not say that sanity requires freedom, yes, but not at the expense of equality of opportunity? If the communist ideal requires absolute equality at the cost of the freedom necessary for living a good life, then there is something wrong with it. If the capitalist, free-market ideal requires that the devil take the hindmost, that many be forced to live under intolerable conditions from which there is no hope of escape, then there is equally something wrong with it. Surely, given that we live in a money economy, some compromise is necessary? Whether you agree with this or not, isn't what is being said here at least intelligible and worthy of consideration? Where is the incompatibility if, accepting both liberty and equality of opportunity as moral values, a compromise may possibly be reached?

According to MacIntyre, all three disputes are unresolvable, the positions irreconcilably opposed, with no hope of settlement or compromise. This, he says, is because they are based on premises that belong to different and incompatible traditions, traditions hopelessly existing side by side in the same culture – ours. On this view there can be no real debate, no appeal to reason on such issues, reason or rationality being something different within each different tradition. Moral "argument" on such questions can therefore be nothing but a shouting match. But we have seen, in all three disputes, that this is false. The issues can be rationally debated and the *possibility* of solution exists, even if complete and general agreement (consensus) cannot be reached.

In the first dispute, everything depends on the answer to the non-moral question of whether arming to the teeth and threatening potential enemies with destruction *really is* the only way of ensuring peace and security (which in some historical circumstances, Hitler's Germany for instance, may indeed be true). If it is, then the second party's position must be accepted, and if it is not, that position is totally undermined. However, one suspects that these people are often more interested in the glory of military might and the possibility of winning a war than they are in ensuring peace – *that* may only be a smokescreen for the naïve. (There may be a tradition of military conquest, glory, and the subjection of conquered peoples to the victor's rule. But *that* tradition is not relevant to *this* dispute, or not if we take the dispute at its face value.)

In the second and third disputes, some compromise between the two extremes must be sought. In the abortion case, both extreme and supposedly unalterable positions contain falsehoods: on the one side, the biological false-hood that the embryo is part of the pregnant girl's or woman's body; on the other, the false assimilation of abortion, however early, to murder. Reason obviously requires a solution somewhere in between, and I have indicated some of the lines the – fully rational – debate might take. In the education and health care dispute, we have two things, equality and liberty, both of which we may recognize as values, but on both of which we may agree that some restrictions are necessary and desirable. There is no way to compromise equality of *opportunity*, so we must either abandon it or place certain restrictions on liberty (for instance, by introducing taxation for education and health care). One may not *agree* with this position, but one cannot deny that it is an understandable position to take. There is no need to carry placards labelled "Freedom" or "Equality" – depending on your tradition – and then simply shout at one another, even if this is sometimes done! Of course, there would be nothing else to do if this were, as MacIntyre claims, nothing but a conflict of different and incompatible traditions.

I hope that these criticisms have made it clear that, contrary to MacIntyre, we *can* reason about these issues, even if we can never reach complete agreement. Therefore, such moral disputes cannot be seen simply in terms of an irreconcilable opposition between incompatible moral traditions. Further, practical reason or rationality, plain and simple (not confined to any particular tradition), can be applied in the attempt to reach a solution to every one of these issues and there is at least the possibility that agreement (even if not full consensus) could be reached. Thus we have been *given reason* for supposing that practical reason and rationality are *not*, as MacIntyre claims, relative to a particular tradition or phase in our cultural history.

MacIntyre is also in trouble on another point. His claim that unresolvable moral disputes are the result of a clash of traditions seems to imply that within a *single* tradition all moral problems would be resolvable. There would be no moral dilemmas. But moral dilemmas are an inescapable fact of life. Suppose, for instance, that we hold the view that there are valid moral principles which forbid or require certain actions, because we cannot accept the consequences of their being done or omitted by others when we would be affected ("universalizability"). Let us indeed suppose that this is our tradition. How can we avoid conflicts of two principles both of which we accept, say the principle that we should not needlessly cause hurt to others and the principle that we should show respect to fully rational and innocent people by telling them the truth if they trust us and that is what they wish and expect? Do we tell the cancer patient that he or she is dying? Or do we either lie or mislead by withholding the information for the sake of preventing pain? Or suppose we are unable to obey a single principle, say keeping one's promises (doing what one has solemnly agreed to do, having been trusted to do it), when two promises to two different people have been made but, because of unforeseen circumstances, only one can be kept? Tradition is not going to help here.

MacIntyre appears to have assumed that some form of cultural relativism *must* be true and then tried to tailor his examples to fit this assumption. But, as we have seen, this doesn't work. We are forced to conclude from all that has been said here that the moral judgments we make are not valid, sound, true, acceptable, justifiable, or capable of being agreed upon, from within and only from within a particular historical tradition, and that MacIntyre is wrong.

Sophisticated Cultural Relativism: (3) Sabina Lovibond

There is one more argument for a form of cultural relativism, again more sophisticated than the ethnologists' argument (see above), that we need to consider – that of Sabina Lovibond. According to her,[15] there are moral truths, but like all truths these require consensus (general agreement) or the possibility of consensus. In so far as moral truths are objective, they are the "truths" embedded in the existing institutions of a culture, including "the family, the nation-state, schools, universities, professional bodies," and in such "quasi-institutions" as relations of power and differences in status. "Moral rationality," she says, "rests upon a shared practice which is embodied in institutions."[16]

So, as Lovibond presents it, there are moral truths which, like all truths, are objective. But, like other truths, they are dependent for their truth and objectivity on consensus ("intersubjective agreement") or its possibility. Moral truths, therefore, are those embodied in the institutions and practices of their place and time, and it is the existence of those institutions and practices that makes them objective, providing an "intellectual authority" for moral judgments. This morality, which is grounded in existing institutions and social structures, is called by Lovibond, "intersubjective morality," "consensual morality," or "*sittlich* morality."[17]

Now what this sounds like is an extreme form of moral conservatism (conformism). There is nothing you can do but obey the "intellectual authority" of existing institutions and social relations, for these provide the only moral objectivity or truth there is. However, Lovibond is aware that she is in danger of advocating pure conformism, and she goes on to state that criticism of "the values upheld by the consensus" does make sense.[18] She even states that it makes sense for *one person* to believe and say, "I am right and they are wrong." But such a statement, she says, only makes sense if we see it as looking forward to a *future* consensus, when everyone agrees with what I now believe![19] The judgment is made, as it were, in an imaginary future world. And the same would presumably be true of any criticism, say by a minority group, of the existing (*sittlich*) morality. Their views must be seen as "prefiguring" a future consensus, for it is only consensus that can give them real objectivity.

But if, from within a slave culture (a culture where slavery is one of the institutions of the customary morality), I, as an abolitionist, proclaim: "Slavery should be abolished because it is incompatible with human dignity!" am I anticipating a future consensus? Or am I stating what I believe to be a moral truth here and now, no matter what other people believe? Do I see my belief – that slavery is a moral evil that should not be tolerated – as objectively true only in some future society where everyone agrees? And do I suppose that until then it is only true for me and for those who agree with me?[20] The answer to this question is clearly "no," for, as an abolitionist, I see the institution of slavery as *a present moral evil* in the full, rich sense. That is why, filled with moral conviction, I am working with others toward giving the slaves the freedom to which as persons I believe they have every right. Furthermore, I am attempting to persuade others of the truth of this – to persuade them of its clear and present truth. If I did not so see it, it could have no force for me, nor would I have any means of persuading others. Yet, as Lovibond would have it, the slave-owners are objectively right, for it is their institution that is in place, and simply because it is in place, and for no other reason, this institution is part of the "intellectual authority" that determines present truth and objectivity in moral questions.

Conclusion

For Lovibond, as for all cultural relativists, the only external thing I have to appeal to for an answer to moral questions is the existing moral consensus (or norms of conduct, or evaluative perspective, or living historical tradition). Otherwise I draw a blank. But on what basis, then, can I suppose that I am right and that others are wrong? Anticipating a future consensus just isn't good enough; I must have *something* on which to base my belief. But, apart from present institutions and social practices, there is nothing there. Did my belief just fly in through the window?

The simple cultural relativist, the one who accepts the ethnologists' argument or some form of it (see above), holds that there are no moral *truths*, only beliefs and practices. On this naïve view, the person unaware of anything beyond her own culture *thinks* there are consensual (agreed upon) truths because she thinks, speaks, and acts from within that culture, not knowing of any other practices or traditions. However, those who are aware of cultural differences think either (1) that their tradition is right and all others are wrong (heathens, infidels, barbarians) or, if they see things objectively and dispassionately, (2) that *no* culture or tradition is right, that there is no moral truth, and that morality is *nothing but* a matter of custom and tradition.

The consequence, however, of their holding the belief that morality is simply a matter of custom or convention, is that they cease to have *any* moral convictions, that is unless they adopt the "When in Rome" or "Do the done thing wherever you are" principle. But that would mean that they had committed themselves to a universal, transcultural and non-relative morality which, according to their own relativist view, they cannot do! And, anyway, they'd have a hard time doing it if they tried. Suppose eating a few of your slaughtered enemies was the tradition. Would you be happy, as a visitor, to join in? Would you feel morally comfortable? Would you feel you had done the right thing? Can a person switch moralities at will? I agree with Bernard Williams that this is not possible,[21] although I know some people have tried.

The simple cultural relativist has no real alternative, then, but to take a transcendental view, above all cultures, and abandon her moral convictions. In spite of the fact that this too is difficult if not impossible, it is the lesson to be learned from this form of cultural relativism – if you assume it to be true – and many have accepted the consequences. This is why so many people nowadays are lacking in any moral beliefs, and why they declare themselves to be *amoral* (to have no morality). Of course, if moral views are entirely culture-dependent and, because of this, have no basis in any truth, what other position is there to take?[22]

Unlike the simple or naïve cultural relativist – the one who accepts some version of the ethnologists' argument – the more sophisticated relativists, like Williams, MacIntyre, and Lovibond, do not deny that there are moral truths. However, these truths are always relativized. On Williams's view, there *are* bullies and liars, and there *is* such a thing as murder, all of these terms carrying moral weight as terms *within our evaluative perspective*. But these terms, which yield only *non-objectivist* truths which are not open to thought or reflection, may not be translatable into terms belonging to another culture, for that other culture will have a different evaluative perspective. According to MacIntyre, moral objectivity, moral truth, and sound practical reasoning (practical rationality) exist, *but only from within, and relative to, a living historical tradition*, a tradition which cannot itself be justified or argued for. According to Lovibond, there are *objective moral truths*, but these (like all truths on her view) are dependent upon consensus or intersubjective agreement and, as *moral* truths, are embedded in the existing institutions and social relations of a culture which, of course, vary over place and time.

But all of these views run into very serious trouble. We have seen, after examining Williams's argument (see above) that non-objectivist truth is an impossibility. The very concept undermines itself, for as soon as we begin to think of moral truths as non-objective, they cease to carry any moral weight. The people who use the "thick" concepts not only do not but *cannot* regard the moral truths expressed in them as non-objective. In MacIntyre's case, we have seen that moral reasoning is possible, even in the very examples that he chooses as revealing a conflict of irreconcilably different traditions. This shows that we *must*, in our moral reasoning, do more than simply appeal to the "tradition" from within which we speak. Lovibond at least recognizes that we *can* disagree with the consensual or customary (*sittlich*) view, but she excludes any possible basis for this disagreement. We are, she claims, appealing to a *future* consensus, but we can have no reason for claiming that this future consensus would yield a better morality than our present one. We cannot even begin to justify the claim "I am right and you are wrong." There are other arguments – none of them as good or as sophisticated as these – for cultural relativism in ethics, but there is no need to waste our time on them.

Some Final Reflections

Why, then, is cultural relativism in ethics so prevalent a view, and why do so many people feel that some form of it *has* to be true? Well, the only alternative position for many seems to be that there are moral truths *written in the sky*, truths that are independent of human life as it is actually lived, of human interests and concerns as they exist in any actual, living culture. Of course, this does seem like foolishness, but as we shall see, I hope, in what follows (parts II–IV), belief in a common morality for all human beings does not require any such foolish and implausible belief.

Another important source of the belief is the confusion between morality proper, on the one hand, and aspects of custom or tradition that have nothing to do with morality, on the other. Questions of dress, deportment, food, manners and propriety, for instance, are purely matters of custom. Unconventional hair styles and outlandish dress are usually disapproved of in any culture (except on special occasions), but this does not make them moral issues; they are at worst improprieties. Being proper is a matter of great importance to some people but that does not make it a moral matter. Indeed, if morality were simply a question of propriety, we would have no very good reason (except to create a good impression) for paying much attention to it. By contrast, questions of loyalty, trust, honesty, kindness, cruelty, malice, betrayal, causing needless hurt or harm, injustice, oppression, intimidation, exploitation, and things of this kind, clearly belong to morality properly understood.

The ethnologists certainly confused these matters as, I suspect, MacIntyre and Lovibond occasionally do as well, or at least they are not careful to distinguish them. Custom and deportment may vary immensely from culture to culture − and cultural variety is undoubtedly a good thing − without genuine moral questions (honesty, trust, etc.) varying in the least. Custom is, of course, a major part of tradition, and we genuinely do not have any right to impose our customs and traditions on others. Does Western-style schooling really help poor Africans, for instance? And in the interests of what do we require women to cover their breasts, or people to wear shoes, where going bare-breasted or bare-footed is the custom or tradition? This has sometimes been done *in the name of* morality, but these are not moral issues.

And, of course, we should, as visitors, respect the customs and traditions of other cultures. In Japan, for instance, street shoes are never worn inside the house. It would therefore be boorish and offensive to disobey this custom when we are in Japan. This is where the "Do the done thing" or "When in Rome" principle has its place. We do not need to join in the head-hunting expedition if we believe it to be immoral or wrong, but we should not cause needless offence by simply ignoring the customs of the culture in which we find ourselves. Notice that this is based on a *universal* principle, namely "Do not cause needless offence." It is transcultural, just as is any form of the "When in Rome" principle. But as coming under "Do not cause needless offence," it is a principle that is reasonable and acceptable.

While a single morality is compatible with an infinite variety of non-moral customs and traditions, if, as anthropologists, we were to discover that there were transcultural moral beliefs and attitudes, this would not prove that these beliefs and attitudes were universally right, any more than discovering different moral beliefs in different cultures would prove that none of them was universally right or that nothing was universally right. For in both cases we would only be appealing to the fact that they were accepted. It would still be possible to judge even universally accepted moral beliefs to be wrong or mistaken, and on moral grounds. If *suttee* (the burning of a widow on her husband's funeral pyre) or clitoridectomy were practiced the world over, that would not make them morally right or acceptable. The most that the discovery that some, or even all, cultures find a certain practice acceptable (or required) shows is that this is the belief or the practice of that particular culture, or of all cultures if that happens to be true. It cannot show that something is good, or right, or wrong, only that the people of that time or place *believe* it to be so, and we may challenge the belief or the practice on recognizably moral grounds. We may even challenge the moral beliefs and practices of our own time and place, and *not* by appealing to the values of other cultures. Thus the institution of slavery was challenged by appealing to the notion of *human dignity* as a universal and non-relative value.

We may revise the ethnologists' argument to read:

Premise 1: Accepted norms of conduct, including moral norms, vary from culture to culture

Conclusion: Therefore moral beliefs and practices vary from culture to culture

If we had to supply a second premise, it would be:

[*Premise 2 (unstated)*: Moral norms involve moral beliefs and practices]

This is not only a valid, but also a *sound* argument, since the premises are both true and the conclusion follows, but it is *all* the ethnologists can get from their discovery of variety in norms of conduct. Nor can the sophisticated cultural relativists get any farther. Of course, to believe something is to suppose it to be true and, if it is a *practical* matter, to be disposed to act upon it. But believing something (supposing it to be true) does not make it true indeed. (We can, after all, mistakenly believe that today is Tuesday when in fact it is Monday!)

Finally, the more sophisticated relativists insist that we can only speak from our own place and time and from our own personal and intellectual history. We cannot stand outside ourselves, and adopt a transcendental standpoint (which, ironically enough, the simple cultural relativist seems forced to do, the "When in Rome" principle being unacceptable because it is universal or "absolutist"). And, of course, the more sophisticated cultural relativists are right, for to stand outside ourselves as we have become through our own personal and intellectual histories, embedded as they are in time and place, is inconceivable. But that does not mean that we cannot make truth claims and attempt to justify them by reasoning. Furthermore, we have seen that at least some of the more sophisticated relativists are trapped by their own position on this matter. (The simple cultural relativists have no alternative but to accept it.) Thus Bernard Williams, for instance, must adopt (or try to adopt) a transcendental standpoint in order to state his position on non-objective moral truths, and both MacIntyre and Lovibond might be accused of a similar mistake. But we do not have to adopt (or attempt to adopt) a transcendental standpoint in order to offer a view of universal moral good and evil. Of course, it will come from our place and time and from our intellectual and personal histories, and it cannot be judged except from some non-transcendental standpoint or other, but that does not mean that the claims we may make about the nature of morality, claims such as those that will be put forward in parts II–IV of this book, and the arguments in support of them, are not worthy of consideration or even of belief, especially if they seem convincing or if they have the ring of truth.

SUMMARY

1   Cultural relativism is the view that there is no *universal* morality applying to all humanity, but that morality is strictly a *local* matter that varies from time to time and from place to place.

2   Since most of us who make moral judgments believe them to be applicable to everybody, cultural relativism is a form of moral skepticism.

3   The simplest argument for cultural relativism is that produced by certain ethnologists (investigators of culture) in the early years of the twentieth century, although cultural relativism argued for on this same basis was common in ancient Greece. We may call this *simple cultural relativism*.

4   The argument is as simple as this:
    Premise: Accepted norms of conduct vary from culture to culture
    Conclusion: Therefore, morality varies from culture to culture

5   However, this argument is valid only if we supply a missing premise:
    Premise (unstated): Morality consists in following accepted norms of conduct
    Obviously, if we include this premise, the argument does go through. (The conclusion follows logically from the premises).

6   The original premise ("Accepted norms of conduct vary from culture to culture") is obviously true. This means that if we accept the unstated premise ("Morality consists in following accepted norms of conduct"), we are forced to accept the conclusion. All we can do then is to go after this unstated premise.

7   If one of the premises of an argument is left unstated, that is usually because it is thought to be so obviously true that it doesn't need to be stated, and that is clearly the case here. But is this unstated premise obviously true?

8   There are two ways in which this unstated premise can be interpreted: (1) it can be treated as true by definition – being moral or good simply *means* following accepted norms of conduct; or (2) it can be regarded as a substantive moral principle telling us what to do if we want to be morally good, namely follow the accepted norms of conduct.

9   If we take the unstated premise as *definitional*, then a person could not challenge any accepted norm on moral grounds without contradicting himself, and this is obviously false. If we take it to be *substantive*, then no one could challenge an accepted norm without being *immoral*. But it is obviously not immoral to challenge an accepted norm. Why should we accept *pure moral conservatism* without being given any reason for doing so?

10   Worse, if the unstated premise is taken to be a substantive moral principle telling us what we are to do if we want to be morally good, it amounts, in effect, to the principle "When in Rome, do as the Romans do." Unfortunately for the argument, though, this can only be read as a *universal* or "absolute" principle, applying in all cultures at all times and places. But obviously you cannot use such a universal or "absolutist" principle as a premise in an argument trying to establish that no such principles exist!

11   Therefore, the ethnologists' argument for simple cultural relativism fails.

12   There are, however, more sophisticated arguments for cultural relativism. Three of the most impressive are those produced by Bernard Williams, Alasdair MacIntyre, and Sabina Lovibond.

13   Whereas simple cultural relativism implies that there are no moral truths, but only customs and practices, Williams, MacIntyre, and Lovibond all claim that there *are* moral truths, but *only from within the perspective or point of view of a culture or tradition*.

14   Williams claims that "world-guided" terms ("thick" concepts) like "bully" and "liar" are used to make moral judgments which may be true from within what he calls an *evaluative* perspective ("non-objectivist" truths). These judgments are *nonreflective*. When we try to reflect, using "thin" concepts like "ought," "wrong," and "good," no answers are forthcoming. That is because we have stepped outside our evaluative perspective and, in doing so, have destroyed moral knowledge. Unfortunately for Williams's argument, we must step outside our evaluative perspective – hence (on his account) destroy moral knowledge – in order to formulate the concept of a "non-objectivist" truth. In order to *accept* Williams's position, we must throw away all our moral convictions. Therefore Williams's position refutes itself.

15   MacIntyre, too, claims that there are moral truths that can be rationally defended, but only from within a *particular historical tradition*, many of which exist competitively in our own culture. People arguing from within different traditions, he says, can never reach agreement on moral questions. That is why, according to MacIntyre, there is so much moral disagreement in our culture. However, none of the disputes he uses as examples establishes his point, for we were able to see how agreement

might be reached on all of them, appealing to considerations that are *not* based on any particular tradition. Therefore his claim fails.

16 Lovibond claims that there are moral truths but that these are established by *consensus* (general agreement within a culture), and that the authority for these truths lies with existing social institutions. Since this smacks of extreme moral conservatism, Lovibond says that we can disagree with the consensus, saying "I am right and you are wrong." However, this only makes sense, she says, if it can be seen as appealing to a *future* consensus where everyone agrees with me. Lovibond leaves no room for any *rational ground* to appeal to in order to defend my maverick moral view. But this is clearly false. Such claims can be and are regularly defended by an appeal to recognizably moral considerations that are independent of any consensus, present or future. Lovibond's position will not hold water.

17 If it fails so badly, why is cultural relativism so prevalent a view? Why do so many people believe that some form of it *has* to be true? The first reason is that it is natural to believe that if it is *not* true, there must be some airy-fairy realm of moral values to appeal to in making our moral judgments. But we will see in what follows that we can accept that there is a universally valid morality without believing any such silly thing. The second reason is that questions of *morality* (being morally good) are jumbled together with questions of custom, practice, and tradition, many of which have nothing to do with morality at all.

18 There is, however, a grain of truth in cultural relativism. This grain of truth is that we should respect the customs and traditions of the culture we find ourselves in, provided that they do not offend against our sincere *moral* convictions. But this falls under the principle "It is morally wrong to cause needless offence," which can only be seen as a universal, transcultural moral principle.

QUESTIONS FOR THOUGHT

1 Accepted norms of conduct vary greatly from culture to culture over time and place. Does this mean that morality is a purely local matter? Explain.

2 What does Bernard Williams mean by a "non-objectivist" moral truth? Do you have any difficulties with this notion?

3 Must moral arguments be a mere shouting match based on different fundamental assumptions stemming from different traditions, as MacIntyre claims? Explain why or why not.

4 Is there anything to appeal to beyond consensus (general agreement) in making a moral claim? Explain.

Chart summary for chapter 2 Cultural relativism: a comparison

	Simple cultural relativists	Williams	MacIntyre	Lovibond
Overall similarities				
1 Universal morality	No universal morality exists. There are no objective moral truths, only beliefs and practices (norms of conduct) defined within a culture	No universal morality exists. In adopting a "transcendental standpoint" there is no possibility of discovering a moral truth. In fact, all moral knowledge is thereby destroyed	No universal morality exists. No appeal can be made to a common or universal morality shared by all. There is no justification for moral judgments external to a particular living, historical tradition which exists within a complex culture	No universal morality exists. All moral truths are embedded in the institutions and practices operating within the culture
2 Morality is relative to culture	Yes. Morality is entirely relative to culture. Morality consists only in following accepted norms of conduct	Yes. Morality can only be defined by the culture	Yes. Morality can only be defined by an existing living tradition operating within a culture	Yes. Morality can only be defined by the existing institutions and practices within the culture
Similarities and differences				
3 Moral judgments (a) Are there objective moral truths?	There are no objective moral truths. Moral decisions are made based on the beliefs and practices (norms of conduct) in the culture. Morality is nothing but a matter of custom and tradition	There are only "non-objectivist moral truths." These are valid only within the particular culture	There are no objective moral truths. Moral truths exist only within the framework of each living, historical tradition within a culture. Morality is tradition-based	There are objective moral truths as determined by consensus or general agreement within the culture
(b) What "group" defines moral truths in the culture?	The beliefs and practices (norms of conduct) in a culture define any moral truths	The culture defines its own moral truths. These moral truths are "non-objectivist," which means that they are true only from within the "evaluative perspective" of a person living within the particular culture	Each living, historical tradition within a culture defines its own moral truths. In our complex culture many different traditions exist	The institutions and practices embedded in a culture define the moral truths. These institutions vary over place and time (some examples from our culture include the family, the state, schools, professional bodies, relations of power, and differences in states)

(c) What is the basis for all moral judgments (the moral authority)?	The conventions and customs (accepted norms conduct) of the particular culture	The "evaluative perspective" (common to all people living in a particular culture). "Non-reflective" moral truths ("non-objectivist moral truths") are drawn from the "evaluative perspective"	Practical reason, defined within each living, historical tradition within a culture	The existing institutions and practices in a culture which provide "the intellectual authority" to define the "norms of conduct" for each society. This authority is called "intersubjective" morality, "consensual morality," or *sittlich* (customary) morality
(d) What (if any) role do reflection and reason play in making moral judgments? (These would involve conscious analysis of a moral problem)	Essentially non-reflective. The beliefs of a culture cannot be challenged from within. *If* a person reflects upon (or questions) the belief that following the accepted moral practices in her society is valid, she is in danger of abandoning her moral convictions. She would realize, in the process of questioning, that there are no moral truths (outside these) to refer to. People who go through this analytic process and abandon their moral convictions are called *amoral*	Non-reflective. Moral truths do *not* need to be defended or justified. This is because people use the "thick" concepts of their culture in stating moral truths. Using these does not involve conscious thinking, evaluating, or reflecting (i.e. a "thick" concept like "bully" carries within itself its own moral power). Consensus within the culture is assured	Reflective. Moral judgments can be argued for or defended by an appeal to agreed-upon rational criteria within a particular living historical tradition – but *not* within a complex culture as a whole	Non-reflective. If a person should disagree with the standard moral line on a particular issue, he is merely stating an opposing view and it *cannot* be defended by rational argument. A person can challenge "the values upheld by consensus" in the culture. These judgments are made as if living in an imaginary future world – where consensus would exist on the new view
(e) What is the scope of moral judgments?	Moral judgments are only accepted within a particular culture	Moral judgments are only true or valid within a particular culture	Moral judgments are only true or valid within a particular historical tradition in a culture. There may be many conflicting traditions with opposing views within one complex culture such as our own	Moral judgments are only true or valid within a particular culture with its entrenched institutions
(f) Do moral truths require consensus, or the possibility of consensus, within a culture?	Moral agreement or consensus is expected to exist within a culture. If a person questions the existing system, she will have no moral authority to appeal to and, as a result, may abandon all her moral convictions	Moral agreement or consensus is expected to exist within a culture. It is embedded in the "thick" concepts of the culture (e.g. "bully")	No moral agreement can be reached within a complex culture, such as ours. There are too many conflicting traditions. No one tradition is arguably superior to another in itself	Moral truths *require* a consensus within a culture – or the possibility of a consensus. The authority embedded in institutions and practices ensures this general agreement within a culture

3

Subjective Relativism

According to cultural relativism, there can be no right or wrong, good or evil, that is independent of the culture in which a person happens to be located, or the living tradition from which he or she speaks. If you accept what I have been calling the ethnologists' argument, or simple cultural relativism, then there are no moral truths, only customs, beliefs, and practices. If you accept one of the more complex views, like those of Williams, MacIntyre, and Lovibond, then there are truths, of a kind, but these are truths only from within the culture one inhabits or the tradition within which one thinks and speaks. Either there is no objectivity (Williams) or that objectivity is firmly tied to the living tradition to which one holds, which, although it has its own rationality, cannot itself be rationally defended (MacIntyre), or it is dependent upon consensual agreement based on existing institutions and social arrangements (Lovibond).

According to these more sophisticated views, there is a moral reality all right, but it belongs exclusively to an existing culture or tradition, varies as that culture or tradition varies, and is real only for the inhabitants of that culture or tradition. This limited moral reality is entirely dependent on its consensual acceptance, and no grounds can be given for this acceptance. Also, because there is no appeal to anything beyond the culture or tradition to which one belongs and which one accepts, there can be no external justification, appealing to universal reason, or reason plain and simple, for any particular moral belief. Moral reasons exist, but only in the context of some specific culture or tradition, and cultures or traditions simply are; they are there; they are in place. They cannot themselves be defended, nor can a particular moral judgment be justified by an appeal to anything other than the shared beliefs of the culture to which one belongs or the tradition to which one adheres. A simple way of putting it is that, according to these more sophisticated views, moral truth and moral reality exist, but they are internal to culture or tradition.

I tried to show, in chapter 2, that in making our moral judgments we not only do appeal to something beyond the shared beliefs of our culture or tradition, but we must do so, in which case cultural relativism, in both its simple and more sophisticated, versions fails. We have also seen the grains of truth that lurk in the cultural relativist view and help to make it seem plausible. These are, first of all, that custom and tradition do vary from culture to culture, and that there is nothing wrong with this, provided that we are careful to distinguish between what are simply questions of custom and tradition, having no moral implications, and truly moral questions – questions about what is morally good or evil, morally right or wrong. Secondly, we have seen that there is some truth to the "When in Rome" or "Do the done thing" doctrine, but only when this is understood as coming under the principle "Do not cause needless offence," a principle that can only be understood as universal and binding on all.

We must now deal with another kind of relativism that is very popular, though not so much among philosophers, and which is equally threatening to the possibility of a universal morality that is valid for all human beings. This is *subjective relativism*, or the view that morality is relative not to custom, tradition, or shared beliefs, but to purely personal belief or conviction. Whatever moral beliefs I hold, according to this view, are true for me personally, and moral reality, if there is such a thing, varies not from culture to culture but from individual to individual.

Like cultural relativism, subjective relativism is often given out in the name of liberalism. The cultural relativist may proclaim, in the name of liberalism and tolerance, that every culture has its own morality and that we should not try to impose the standards of our own culture on cultures different from our own. (We have already talked this one out in chapter 2.) The subjective relativist typically says, again in the name of liberalism and tolerance, that everybody has his or her own values, and these values, being purely personal, are not to be imposed on anyone else. In fact, there is often an attempt to combine these two views under the heading of liberalism. Unfortunately, however, the two views, which come from two completely different outlooks, are incompatible, as I shall try to explain.

Cultural relativism tells us that morality is dependent on culture, which varies from place to place and from time to time; my moral outlook, whatever it may be, is derived from the culture I inhabit or (as MacIntyre would have it) the living tradition to which I adhere. There is nothing, nor could there be anything, purely personal about it. (Even on Lovibond's view, I can only have moral views that differ from the customary morality by anticipating a future consensus, when everyone agrees with what I now believe. I cannot have my own strictly personal views.) It should therefore be apparent that cultural relativism, since it denies the possibility of morality varying from person to person, actually rules out subjective relativism. Cultural relativism derives essentially from the awareness of differing moral views at different times and places (in different societies or cultures). Furthermore, it is understood that customary or consensual morality is the only solid thing there is to appeal to, and if that is rejected there is nothing at all. Morality is quite definitely understood to be social. The possibility that anyone might have a personal or private morality is not even considered, nor could there be any room for it.

The driving force of subjective relativism, by contrast, is precisely its rejection of what is seen as socially imposed morality. Or, where moral beliefs vary from person to person – as they may do when conventional morality begins to erode – it is its rejection of what are seen as other people's personal opinions (which may be valid enough for them). It stems from the rebellion of the individual against what he or she sees as either mere convention or else mere personal opinion which, if she accepted either, would prevent her from being true to herself. (She does not need to be aware of differing conventions in other societies.) There is something essentially false, on this view, about doing the done thing. Mere convention, it is believed, is nothing but a social construct, hence morally hollow, and other people's opinions are irrelevant; one must work out one's own morality for oneself, while allowing others to do the same. On the first view (cultural relativism), society is the only possible arbiter; on the second (subjective relativism), it is the individual herself.

The first view leads inevitably to moral nihilism (the rejection of any moral truth), in spite of the attempts of people like Williams, MacIntyre, and Lovibond to salvage some real and living morality from it. (I have tried to show, in chapter 2, why these attempts fail.) This is because it leaves us with nothing but accepted beliefs to determine what is morally good or bad, right or wrong, beliefs that vary from culture to culture or from tradition to tradition and that have no justification beyond their mere acceptance within a culture or tradition. The second view denies any role for society or for consensual agreement in determining what is morally right or wrong, good or bad; rather, this becomes entirely a matter for the individual, who must, as it is sometimes put, create ("define") her own morality. Thus subjective relativism excludes cultural relativism. It is plain that the attempt to combine the two in the name of liberalism and tolerance is utterly hopeless.

Subjective relativism, unlike what I have been calling simple or naïve cultural relativism, but like the more sophisticated forms of cultural relativism we have considered, insists on there being a genuine and acceptable morality, for which there is thought to be a real need. It will not permit, as simple cultural relativism does, the immediate descent into moral nihilism (the denial that a valid morality is even possible) or *anomie* (the loss of all belief in moral value and the feeling of anchorlessness that goes with it). Yet the subjective relativist rejects any morality that he sees as externally imposed, whether by society, parents, teachers, peers, or religious authorities. He must act from his own true inner nature, from his own heart and soul.

The heart and core of subjective relativism is the rejection of any externally imposed morality, which is seen as nothing but pure convention or else mere opinion – this and the need for moral conviction and the rejection of nihilism and *anomie*. The most important source of the subjective relativists' belief that accepted morality is empty convention that has no real authority, and that there is nothing left but personal authenticity, is the so-called "death of God," the end of generally accepted religious belief in the Judaic–Christian–Islamic tradition. If you believe that God exists, then He can be seen as the authenticator of a morality that is transmitted through religious tradition and teaching. But if God is removed from the sky (leaving nothing but a hole symbolizing His absence) then we are driven back upon ourselves, as individuals, each person to create his own morality, of which he is his own authenticator. Or that, at any rate, is the view.

How many times have you heard the cry, "Who is to say what is morally right or wrong, good or bad?" Perhaps you have said it or thought it yourself. It is the cry of moral nihilism and *anomie*. It assumes – notice this – that there can be no morality without some authority; the deeply ingrained belief is that if there is no authority to decree what is morally right or wrong, good or bad, there is no authentic morality. It seems that all we have is different and conflicting opinions, and why should we accept one opinion rather than another? Obviously anything goes. "If God were dead, then everything would be permitted," as the character Ivan proclaims (in conversation with his brother Alyosha) in Feodor Dostoevsky's 1880 novel, *The Brothers Karamazov*.

In summary, all the views we have considered so far see morality as dictated by some authority or other, or else non-existent. The simple cultural relativist typically says that, because morality – as he sees it – varies from culture to culture, there is no universal moral authority, hence no valid morality at all, only different customs and practices. The more sophisticated cultural relativist says that society or tradition is the arbiter or authority and that there is a valid morality from the internal point of view of each society or tradition, although there is no valid universal morality because there is no universal authority. The religious believer says there is a valid universal morality, a morality that is authenticated by his or her God or by the religious tradition to which he or she belongs. The subjective relativist says there is a valid morality for each individual which he must work out or create for himself in accordance with his own true inner nature. Thus he himself becomes the authenticator of, or authority for, his own private morality. (He becomes, as it were, his own personal God, replacing the one now absent from the sky.) Personal authenticity becomes the only virtue. This is individualism of the purest kind. Society or culture or tradition is just not in it.

But there is a possible fifth answer to the question "Who is to say what is right or wrong, good or evil?" Why should we not answer "Nobody. It is a matter for investigation by thought and reflection"? Why couldn't it be that we just have to figure it out? Why should we not attempt to outline, for general consideration, the seeming shape and substance of a social morality, valid for all, derived from no authority, but based on understanding alone? But before we can set out on this road, we must get on with our project of defeating skepticism about the possibility of such a morality, and our task in this chapter is to defeat subjective relativism.

A number of years ago, in France, a woman charged with drowning her baby in the bathtub offered, in her own defence, the justification that she had taken a new lover and she would not have been true to herself if she had not got rid of everything in her life connected with the previous one, including the baby. She claimed she was simply following the philosophy of Jean-Paul Sartre, who had claimed, in his famous lecture "Existentialism is a humanism" and elsewhere, that the only judgment of moral fault or failing that a person could make on others was to charge them with *mauvaise foi*,[1] or failure of authenticity, failure to acknowledge one's freedom and to act upon one's own deepest convictions. This was a fault, the confessed murderess said, of which she would have been guilty had she not got rid of the baby along with everything else associated with her former lover. Needless to say, she was not acquitted! Sartre was no doubt horrified, since he had not been read, or heard, carefully. Obviously, the woman had not given sufficient attention to the following passage (and others like it) from the same lecture: "When a man commits himself to anything, fully realizing that he is not only choosing what he will be, but is thereby at the same time a legislator deciding for the whole of mankind – in such a moment a man cannot escape from the sense of complete and profound responsibility."[2] While saying that we cannot appeal to anything external in making our choices, Sartre claimed that we must nevertheless see ourselves as making decisions for humankind in general, as making or defining not only ourselves but an ideal type of humanity.[3] It is not simply a matter of always acting upon one's deepest feelings. One is free to choose and one must acknowledge the same freedom in others, but it is upon one's own ideal of a universal morality that one must act. Thus: "But in truth, one ought always to ask oneself what would happen if everyone did as one is doing; nor can one escape from that disturbing thought except by a kind of self-deception."[4] Whatever Sartre may have said in his subjective mode, this would clearly exclude some acts, including drowning one's baby in order to get rid of all traces of one's former lover because of one's powerful feelings for the new one. Whatever we think about Sartre, he cannot be charged with the straightforward subjective relativism that the woman in question took him to be advocating. Universalizability (a single morality for all humankind), however modified by the idea of personal authenticity, is an essential ingredient of Sartre's view.

We have now seen, I hope, the horrifying fault in subjective relativism that would make most people reject it on moral grounds, namely that it would permit any action whatever. Not only that, but so long as a person acted on his or her deepest convictions we would have to admire that person for his or her authenticity. Thus if Hitler believed in his heart of hearts that it was good and desirable to rid the world of Jews and gypsies because of their base nature and their corruption of true, noble Aryan culture, then we could only commend him for his efforts to do so, for he was, after all, being true to himself. And no doubt we could say the same for Charles Manson (the infamous leader of a murder cult), Leopold and Loeb (the thrill-killers who saw themselves as Nietzschean supermen[5] merely exercising their higher virtue in doing as they pleased with their inferiors), and possibly even Jack the Ripper who, some say, saw himself as simply giving prostitutes what they deserved.

We have now seen what is morally unacceptable about subjective relativism. Now let us look at the logical faults. One way of expressing subjective relativism is this: "Whatever I think, in my heart of hearts, is morally right or good, wrong or bad, *is* morally right or good, wrong or bad *for me*. For anyone else, whatever he thinks, in his heart of hearts, is morally right or good, wrong or bad, *is* morally right or good, wrong or bad, *for him*." Well, suppose I judge that killing for pleasure is morally wrong or bad. Then it is morally wrong or bad for me. But how am I to judge the action of someone who thinks it is simply the exercise of superior virtue, that it is morally good? Am I not forced to judge that it really is morally good for him or her? Doesn't his thinking it morally good make it morally good for him? And yet at the same time I have judged that it is morally wrong or bad. (That is why it is morally wrong or had for me.) Thus I am in contradiction with myself. I must judge the other person's action to be morally wrong because I have judged killing for pleasure to be morally wrong, and yet at the same time I must see it as morally right and good for that other person because that is how she has judged it. I am in an impossible position.

This is, indeed, probably just the position Sartre himself is in. In judging a certain course of action to be the right thing to do, I am not judging simply that it is the right thing for me, I am judging that it is the right thing simply, and this is enough to yield the result that it is the right thing "for all mankind" (Sartre's phrase in Mairet's translation). Thus there is no way for Sartre to avoid his universalizability claim; if one judges that a certain action is, in and of itself, right or good, wrong or bad, then this is already a universal judgment, applicable to everybody. (We do not even need to add "for all mankind" for that is already implicit.) But this inherently universal character of plain moral judgments like "As killing for pleasure, this act is wrong" does not jibe with Sartre's claim that the only moral failure of which a person can be accused is *mauvaise foi* (self-deception), or the failure to act authentically, or from her heart of hearts. It does not jibe with his claim that everyone must make his or her morality for herself or himself, that he or she must invent, there being no authority beyond one's own real feelings and the beliefs based on them (no external authority), and nothing to be discovered by reason. How can one, from one's own personal depths, create a universal morality applicable to everyone? If there is such a morality it cannot vary from individual to individual; it cannot stem from one's personal beliefs and feelings however sincere they may be! Therefore, if I think that there is nothing to appeal to beyond my own present beliefs and feelings, I cannot even make simple moral judgments for such judgments are unavoidably universal.

Very well, let us try to avoid simple and therefore universal judgments. Let us revise the formula to read: "Whatever I think is morally right, wrong, good or bad for me is morally right, wrong, good or bad *for me*. For anyone else what he or she thinks is morally right, wrong, good or bad *for him or her*, is morally right, wrong, good or bad for him or her." Notice that it is no longer being said that anything is morally right or wrong, good or bad, period, which, we have discovered, can only mean morally right or wrong, good or bad for everybody. I now only judge that it is morally right or wrong, good or bad, *for me*. In this revised version of subjective relativism. I have no views at all on what is morally right or wrong, good or bad for other people – that is their business – nor do I even consider what is morally good or bad (or right or wrong) for humanity in general, for no such question even exists. Here we have subjective relativism in its purest possible form.

According to the first kind of subjective relativism, I judge something to be morally required or morally permissible or morally good or bad, and this means judging that it is morally good or bad for all humanity. Still it is only because this judgment is sincerely made by me that the thing in question is morally required or morally permissible or morally good or bad for me. Someone else might have some different conviction which makes it good (bad) for him while, in accordance with my own judgment, it remains bad (good) for me, although the other person, like me, sees his judgment as applying to all humanity. (This is Sartre's view). According to the pure subjective relativist view, the conviction is not that something is good or bad, period, this conviction making it good or bad for me, but rather *directly* that something is morally obligatory or permissible or morally good or bad *for me*.

The point is subtle and difficult, so I shall try to make it again. Someone (e.g. Sartre) might hold that because I believe something *to be morally right*, the fact that this is my belief makes it morally right for me. But our pure subjective relativist holds not that my believing something to be morally right makes it morally right for me, but rather that I see it directly as being *morally right for me*, other people and humanity in general not being in it at all. On this pure subjective relativist view, a person cannot judge anything to be just plain morally right (hence morally right for all humanity); he or she can only judge it to be morally right for himself or herself.

"If I think it's morally right, then it's morally right for me." That was the first version of subjective relativism. Clearly it won't do, either morally or logically, for reasons that have been explained. "If I think it's morally right for me, then it is morally right for me." That is the revised or pure version. It does not get us into the logical difficulties that the first version did. You will remember that the first version gets us into trouble whenever we try to judge the actions or the character of someone whose sincere moral judgments differ entirely from our own. We must praise them because they are authentic, true to themselves – if they were not we would have to say they were moral failures – but we must condemn their actions from our own moral perspective, for we see our judgments as creating a universal morality. Nor have we any choice in the matter, as Sartre seems to imply. If I believe that something is the morally right thing, I must believe that it is the morally right thing for anyone in the same circumstances. (This is a kind of universalizability that cannot be avoided.)

The only escape from these contradictions in our moral judgments is by going the second route. There is no contradiction there. I judge only that something is morally right or wrong for me, morally good or bad for me, with no implication for others or for humanity in general. Others are similarly free to make their own judgments about what is morally right or wrong, morally good or bad, *for them*, without any universal implications. We leave one another alone, each to form his or her own "personal morality." We are all distinct individuals; morality has no social or universal dimension at all; it is strictly a private matter.

Of course, even in this case the *moral* objection remains even if the logical objection does not. Even in this revised or pure version of subjective relativism we cannot condemn the actions or the character of anyone as long as he or she is true to himself or herself, and this would include Hitler and Jack the Ripper. Of course, it is easier to imagine someone believing that if Hitler thought killing Jews was morally right, then it was morally right for him (the first version of subjective relativism) than to imagine a person believing that if Hitler thought killing Jews was morally right for him, then it was morally right for him (the second version), for it is very unlikely that that was what Hitler thought. If he thought it was morally right at all, which he probably did, he thought it was morally right, period, not just morally right for him. Although we have no difficulty in imagining someone thinking, "This is what I sincerely believe is the morally right thing to do, so it is the morally right thing for me," it is unlikely indeed that anyone ever thought or thinks "This is what I think is morally right for me, so it is morally right for me." Generally speaking, people do not say or think, first off, "This is morally right for me," they think "This is morally right," period, which, according to the first version of subjective relativism, would make it morally right for them. So there is something more than faintly unreal about this second version of subjective relativism.

We have some idea of what it would be like to believe that something is morally wrong, or morally obligatory, or the morally right thing, or morally good or morally bad, but what would it mean to say or think, right off, that it was morally wrong for me without first thinking that it was simply morally wrong? I can certainly believe that something is (non-morally) right for me or wrong for me, say a certain dress or a certain perfume or a certain job or a certain house. After all, each of us is different, and different things suit us or become us, or are to our taste, or fit our personality or our true inner nature. But *morally* right for me? Where does the word "morally" get its grip here? What could I be thinking, without first supposing that something was simply morally right, in thinking that it was morally right for me but not necessarily for anyone else?

Let us go back to Sartre for a moment. Consider the following passage:

> If, to take a more personal case, I decide to marry and to have children, even though this decision proceeds simply from my situation, from my passion or my desire, I am thereby committing not only myself, but humanity as a whole, to the practice of monogamy. I am thus responsible for myself and for all men, and I am creating a certain image of man as I would have him to be. In fashioning myself I fashion man.[6]

Now Sartre, as far as we know, never married or had children, and we have every reason to believe that this was by deliberate choice. In any case, let us suppose that it was a deliberate choice. In making this choice was Sartre thereby committing not only himself but humanity as a whole to the single life, the life without marriage or children? Was he creating a certain image of man as he would have him to be? Was he fashioning man in fashioning himself? Or was he simply deciding what was best for him, given the kind of person he was and what his aims were in life? Now it is conceivable, just barely conceivable, that in making this choice, he had decided that this was the best life for all men, or even all men and women (humanity as a whole), and that anyone who made a lifetime commitment to marriage, monogamy and children, was choosing an inferior kind of life to the freedom of the single life, perhaps with mistresses or lovers but without the responsibility of children or dependents. But it was far more likely that he was making the choice only for himself, having decided that this was right for him, allowing others to act as they saw fit. Or if he did see himself as committing humanity as a whole to the single life, wouldn't this have been incredibly pretentious? Could he not see that others might be different from himself, that others might find marriage, monogamy, and children more desirable, more congenial to their own individual personalities and their own aims in life? Why, after all, should everyone be the same? Why should one regard one's own personal preferences as best for everybody?

There is a lesson to be learned from this. We can make sense of the notion of something being (non-morally) right for me, without its necessarily being right for anyone else, when it is simply a matter of personal preference, or what one finds most congenial or comfortable or suitable or otherwise desirable for oneself. Indeed, when one's choice is only a matter of personal preference it would be presumptuous and wrong to see it as being right for everybody. It is here that "It's right for me if I think it's right for me" begins to make sense. After all, it's my life, so what right has anyone else to tell me what is best for me? They can offer advice, which I may accept or not, but in the end only I know, perhaps by trial and error, and often not without a great deal of pain, what best accords with my own individual nature. Here we have a true, genuine, and acceptable liberalism. Where matters of purely personal preference are concerned – matters that are compatible with others having different personal preferences *with no harmful effects on anyone* – no one can dictate to anyone else nor even decide what is best for him or her. This is where it makes sense to say that everyone has his or her own personal values and that no one has the right to impose her own views on anyone else. If Sartre thought that in deciding such matters of purely personal preference I am "creating a certain image of man as I would have him to be," that I am "fashioning man," then Sartre was wrong.

But *morally* right or wrong, good or bad? Surely this is something altogether different? If I judge that something is morally right or wrong, good or bad, I am necessarily judging that it is morally right or wrong, good or bad, for everybody. To suppose that it is morally wrong or obligatory or permissible or good or bad for me, but not necessarily for anyone else, simply does not make sense. And why is this? There is first of all the logical point: moral judgments are inherently universal. But why do such inherently universal judgments exist in our linguistic practice? The answer is that the questions that we call moral questions involve not just personal prefer- ences, but (1) the effect that our acts, or the kind of people we are, have on other people or the community as a whole, and (2) the effect these have, in respect of our common human nature, on our own thriving or flourishing.

Morality has to do with our life together, with our life in common, sharing the same world, with what has a bearing on human well-being as such, both individually and in community. If I preferred the life of a serial murderer I would not, for that reason, be justified in choosing it, because it has an adverse effect on other people and on society in general, to say nothing of what it does to me as a human being. While I could reject morality altogether, seeing myself as amoral, and hence free to do anything I please, I could not declare myself to be a subjective relativist and say "It's morally right for me," and that is because if morality is involved at all there is a moral objection to it; because of its social consequences, and also its effect on my humanity, it goes beyond mere personal preference. That is what distinguishes moral judgments from non-moral declarations of personal preferences, and explains why moral judgments are in their very nature inherently universal. It is in the moral area that loyalty, trust, honesty, kindness, cruelty, malice, causing needless hurt or harm, injustice, oppression, intimidation, exploitation, self-respect, personal integrity, and other serious matters like these come in, matters that affect everybody. That is why it makes no sense to say or think "It's morally good for me because I think it's morally good for me. It need not be morally good for anybody else," although one can perfectly well say, where it is purely a matter of personal preference, "It's the right thing for me because I have given it careful thought and I have come to believe that it's the right thing for me." Here no question of morality, which is universal in its very conception, need be involved.

Sartre was right in saying that in making moral judgments and choices, we are choosing for all humanity, for morality involves how people are to behave or what sort of people they should be as human beings and as members of a community. Moral questions have, of their nature, a bearing on everybody, because they have to do with the best way for human beings to live their lives. Of course, this means that Sartre was wrong in his doctrine of radical freedom where moral questions are concerned. One should be free to choose what accords with one's own special interests, talents and, in general, one's own individual nature. However, one cannot be free to make one's own morality according to one's personal preferences, for that could only result in social chaos, which would be bad for everybody, to say nothing of the strong possibility of personal misery if there really are conditions for human well-being that apply to everyone. Morality, if there is such a thing, can only be a universal, not an individual matter. We can only think of it as being the same for everybody, as Sartre himself seemed at times to recognize. There is no private enterprise where morality is concerned. In this respect the cultural relativists, who would not even consider the possibility of variation from individual to individual, have a better understanding of the nature of morality than the subjective relativists do!

Another objection to the "It's morally right for me if I think it's morally right for me" version of subjective relativism is that it would rule out the possibility of either agreement or disagreement on moral questions; there could be no moral accord and no moral disputes. Suppose that I am a subjective relativist of this kind and someone who shares this view says to me, "Drowning my baby is morally right for me because I think it is morally right for me." I can take note of what this person says but I cannot agree with her (I cannot say "You're right") because agreement would be redundant; we both believe that something is right for a person if that person believes it is right for him or her. Nor can I disagree (say "You're wrong") because that would contradict the pure subjective relativist view that we both hold. But that there can be no agreement or disagreement on moral questions is out of accord with what nearly all of us believe. Are we to suppose that it is just a mistake to believe that there can be agreement or disagreement on moral matters?

We have already seen the grain of truth in the radical or pure subjective relativist position ("It's right for me if I think it's right for me"). Where matters of simple personal preference that do not have an adverse effect on human well-being are concerned, no one can dictate to another person what is best for him or her. These genuinely are matters for purely personal decision. They need not be relevant to anyone but oneself and, while a person may give advice to another person, he or she cannot decide what is best for anyone but himself or herself. But there is also a grain of truth in the first kind of subjective relativism ("If I think it is morally right then it's morally right for me"). For if I sincerely believe that something is morally required, then, as I see it, it is morally required. (To believe anything is to suppose it to be true.) Thus it becomes a matter of conscience for me and, if I fail to act accordingly, that is a moral failure of some kind. It is, in fact, a failure to do or only to do what I think is right, a failure of conscientiousness, and who could deny that conscientiousness is a virtue?

However, thinking something to be so does not make it so. Beliefs can be mistaken, and we have been given no reason to believe that this is not true of moral beliefs along with all other beliefs. (To suppose something to be true does not make it true.) We have been given no reason to believe that conscience cannot err. Within limits (Hitler, Leopold and Loeb, Charles Manson, Jack the Ripper, and the French woman who drowned her baby would obviously be excluded), a person can be praised for his or her conscientiousness, or for having the courage of his or her convictions, even if we believe these convictions are mistaken and that the person has, in fact, acted wrongly or foolishly. Sartre saw that if a person thinks that something is morally obligatory or wrong or good or bad, then, as he or she sees it, it is morally obligatory or wrong or good or bad, from which he concluded that it is morally obligatory or wrong or good or bad for him or her. All that he was entitled to conclude, though, was that having the courage of one's convictions (conscientiousness) is a virtue. He was not entitled to go on to claim that it was the only virtue, the claim that placed him in an impossible (because self-contradictory) position when he recognized that moral judgments are inherently universal, that they can only be seen as applying to everyone.

Of course, we have not yet shown that there is such a thing as morality; only that if there is such a thing it can only be universal and applicable to everyone, which would exclude both cultural and subjective relativism. And surely we can only believe in the existence of a morality which we acknowledge to be universal in its very conception (and therefore, if it exists at all, valid for everybody) if we can show that and how it relates to human well-being generally. For only then could moral considerations give all of us reason to act or refrain from acting in certain ways or to be people of one kind rather than another.

SUMMARY

1 *Cultural* relativism is the view that ethics or morality is a *local* matter. *Subjective* relativism is the view that morality is strictly a *personal* matter. On the first view, morality is *relative to culture or tradition*; on the second view, morality is relative to *personal belief or conviction*.

2 Both relativisms, cultural and subjective, may be called forms of *ethical relativism or moral relativism*, but they are quite different. Cultural relativism sees morality as being essentially a *social* matter; subjective relativism sees it as being essentially a *personal* matter.

3 Cultural relativism, unless you are able to accept one of the more sophisticated versions of it, which gives you moral truth *of a kind*, leads inevitably to moral nihilism (the belief that there is no morality) with its accompanying *anomie* (rootlessness, anxiety), for if only customs and practices exist, and these are different in different places and at different times, there is no room for moral conviction. But we have a deep need for moral conviction, and subjective relativism tries to answer this need.

4 As the subjective relativist sees it, social morality is mere empty convention, and the God of Scripture, whose authority formerly validated morality, is dead. Therefore, there is nothing for you or me to do but fall back upon ourselves, creating our own personal morality for which we ourselves are the authority, provided we are *authentic* and do

not engage in any self-deception. This is supposed to become, for each of us, our *personal moral truth*, which implies a *personal moral reality*.

5 Cultural relativism and subjective relativism are sometimes advocated *together* in the name of liberalism and tolerance: we must be tolerant of the moralities of cultures and traditions other than our own and not judge *them* in terms of the moral values of *our* culture; at the same time we must be tolerant of the *personal* moral convictions of other people and not try to impose *our* moral convictions on *them*. But morality is either *social*, as cultural relativism claims, or it is *personal*, as subjective relativism claims. We cannot have it both ways.

6 The cultural relativist looks at other cultures and says "Hey, there is no *one* morality." The subjective relativist need not look outside her own culture. Rather she says "God is dead. Therefore what masquerades as universal morality is nothing but empty convention, lacking any real authority. I must therefore create my own morality for myself from my own, true inner nature."

7 The first form that subjective relativism can take is this: "Whatever I think is morally right or good *is* morally right or good *for me*." The trouble with this way of looking at things is that, in judging something to be morally right or good, I judge it to be morally right or good *period*. This means that I must apply the same standards to others that I apply to myself. (Moral judgments are *inherently* universal.) How then can I say that everyone is free to create his or her own personal morality? There will be a conflict in my judgments when I have to deal with someone whose sincere moral convictions differ from my own. If someone else says that something they have done is morally obligatory when I think it is morally wrong, I must see them as *good* because they are following their own authentic personal morality, but as *immoral* because they have done something that I sincerely believe to be wrong. This is an impossible situation.

8 The second form that subjective relativism can take is "If I think that something is morally right *for me*, then it *is* morally right for me." (We may call this *pure* subjective relativism.) But while we can make sense of something being *right for me*, say a certain hair style or a certain dress, or a certain sexual practice (personal preference or taste), it is hard to make sense of the notion that something might be *morally* right, but only for me. This is once more because moral judgments are inherently universal. Obviously, I should not try to impose my personal tastes or preferences on other people. (We may call this a grain of truth in subjective relativism.) But how can I help but judge them by the same *moral* standards by which I judge myself?

9 These are *logical* objections, but there is an even more serious *moral*

objection to subjective relativism whatever form it takes, which is that it would permit *any action whatever*, provided the person sincerely believed that it was morally permitted or morally required. Thus, for instance, we could not condemn Hitler for the genocide of the Jews if we believed that he did it out of sincere moral conviction, or even if he sincerely believed it was morally permissible, and desirable on other grounds.

10   Related to this, there is a second grain of truth in subjective relativism. This is that it is a good thing to have the strength of one's convictions or, in other words, *conscientiousness* is a virtue (a good quality of character). The subjective relativist, however, says, in effect, that conscience *cannot be mistaken*, and that is false. I may even reject a moral belief that I once sincerely held, in which case I can only believe I was mistaken at the time I believed it.

QUESTIONS FOR THOUGHT

1   Suppose someone were to say something like this: "Different cultures have their own morality and we should not try to impose *our* morality on another culture or judge *them* by *our* standards. Similarly, every person has his or her own moral views, which we must respect. No one should try to impose *his or her* moral views on anyone else." How would you reply?

2   "The only moral value is *authenticity*, or being true to oneself." Are there any difficulties in this view? Is there anything to be said for it at all?

3   If I believe that something, e.g. breaking promises, is morally wrong, I believe that it is morally wrong, period, any hence that it is wrong for anybody and everybody. Explain why this is so. What are the consequences?

4   Obviously I am free, within limits, to live my own life in the way I see fit. What are those limits and why are they necessary?

4

Subjectivism and Non-cognitivism

It has been argued, in chapters 2 and 3, (1) that cultural relativism, which sees morality as tied to accepted customs and practices, and subjective relativism, which sees morality as tied to individual belief or conviction, actually exclude one another, in spite of the fact that the two are often touted together in the name of liberalism and tolerance; (2) that moral questions not only are not but cannot be mere matters of accepted practice or personal conviction; and (3) that both kinds of relativism gain whatever inherent plausibility they have from a kind of confusion that we can now see is common to both: genuine moral issues are confused by the cultural relativist with matters of mere custom or tradition, and by the subjective relativist with matters of mere personal preference or what is best for me as an individual.

The sophisticated cultural relativist and the subjective relativist fail to note that genuine morality, as distinct from either custom or tradition, on the one hand, or from what is best for a person because of his or her individual nature, on the other, must be applicable to everybody, and that is because true morality can only be understood as universal. If there is nothing that is admirable or contemptible, good or bad, right or wrong, in or for anyone and everyone, regardless of custom, tradition, and individual nature, then there is no valid morality at all. The simple cultural relativist, provided he or she recognizes that the ultra-conformist "When in Rome" doctrine is a form of absolutism in disguise, is at least able to see that this is so. But the result of this realization is moral nihilism or *anomie*, with its accompanying spiritual malaise (uneasiness). If the attempts of the sophisticated cultural relativists to salvage a kind of moral truth from culture or tradition are seen to fail, nihilism again follows inevitably. The subjective relativist tries to see his moral beliefs as self-authenticating for him, but this again is an illusion even if conscientiousness (having the courage of one's convictions) is a virtue, for there is nothing to ensure that conscience cannot err. I may even come to reject the moral beliefs I once held, accepting that at the time I held them I was mistaken.

The cultural relativist says that morality can only be relative to culture; the subjective relativist says that morality can only be relative to personal conviction. We have seen what is wrong with both these beliefs. Indeed, just the contrary seems to be true: morality, if there is such a thing, can only be universal and applicable to everybody, and if it does not derive from any authority, it must (if it exists) have some rational justification. But suppose you think there could not possibly be any such justification? One possibility (a nihilist one) would be to abolish the use of moral language, to stop making moral judgments and to abandon all our moral beliefs. But another way out would be to leave our moral language in place, and to make one of the following claims. (1) Moral utterances are simply declarations or claims to the truth that one is in a certain feeling-state. They are assertions in which the speaker declares, or claims it to be true, that he or she has feelings or attitudes of favor or disfavor toward something, that he or she likes or dislikes something. These assertions or declarations do not make claims to any other truth and hence they do not refer to any moral reality, either universal or, as in the case of subjective relativism, purely personal. (2) Moral utterances make no assertions or declarations at all; that is, they do not make claims to *any* kind of truth, but rather express personal attitudes or commitments to principle in a way that does not involve asserting or affirming or declaring anything. Both (1) and (2) are meta-ethical doctrines, or doctrines about the nature of moral language: (1) is called meta-ethical subjectivism, or simply *subjectivism*; and (2), which takes two forms, emotivism and prescriptivism, is called *non-cognitivism*. These are our next and last dragons to slay.

It is important to notice the difference between these meta-ethical views and the relativisms we have been examining in chapters 2 and 3. Ethical relativism, whether cultural or subjective, makes no claims about the nature or function of moral language, to what is meant and understood when it is used in speech, writing, or thought. Cultural relativism says that moral judgments are irrevocably bound to culture or tradition, which is the only possible source of their validation; subjective relativism says that morality can only be a matter of personal belief or conviction and that each individual is his or her own authority in moral matters. Both see moral judgments as making claims to truth about what is morally good or bad, right or wrong but, as we have noted, the problem for both is that moral judgments, if they are claims to truth, can only be understood as universal, or applicable to everyone. By contrast, subjectivism claims that what look like moral judgments are really nothing but assertions or declarations that one has feelings or attitudes of favor or disfavor, assertions that make no other claims to truth at all, declarations that, unless we have reason to believe the person is lying or self-deceived, must be accepted as true, while non-cognitivism denies that moral utterances are truth claims of any kind, but are rather non-statemental expressions of attitudes (favor disfavor) or of personal commitments to principle. Meta-ethical theories of either kind would make moral utterances subjective or personal but, unlike subjective relativism, they would not see such utterances as making claims to truth about any *moral* reality, however subjective and personal.[1]

Subjectivism

Subjectivism is a theory not just about moral language, but about the language of value in general, with special attention to the word "good." Moral values, e.g. always doing what is morally right, being of morally good character, are clearly not the only values. There are also economic values, nutrition values, aesthetic values, the values things may have for their particular use (e.g. a good lawnmower), the value that professionals have if they are skilled at their particular occupation (e.g. a good teacher), the value a thing have because it is pleasant or agreeable, and so no endlessly. Crudely put, subjectivism states that any sentence of the form "*x* is good" means "I like *x*," while any sentence of the form "*x* is bad" means "I dislike *x*." Where by "good" or "bad" is meant *moral* goodness or badness, this liking or disliking takes the form of approval or disapproval, so that any sentence of the form "*x* is morally good" (or "*x* is morally admirable" or "*x* is morally right") means (*literally* means) "I approve of *x*," and any sentence of the form "*x* is morally bad" (or "*x* is morally contemptible" or "*x* is morally wrong") means "I disapprove of *x*." In no case, according to subjectivism, am I saying anything whatever about *x* itself, even though the grammar of the sentence makes it look as if I am. Rather, I am making statements about my likes and dislikes, my feelings, or my attitudes of approval or disapproval. Statements of the form "*x* is good" or "*x* is bad," the subjectivist believes, are not assertions about *x*; they are assertions about *me* – that I have a certain attitude or feeling.

Once more, it is important not to confuse subjectivism with subjective relativism. According to subjective relativism, when someone sincerely says or thinks something of the form, e.g. "*x* is morally wrong," then *x* really is morally wrong, *for her*. It is a personal moral truth. But according to subjectivism, when a person says or thinks something of the form "*x* is morally wrong," she is simply saying "I disapprove of *x*" or "I oppose *x*." There is no moral reality, hence no *moral* truth of kind, personal or otherwise (see note 1).

Since this book is an introduction to ethics, or moral philosophy, and not to the theory of value in general (axiology), you might think it appropriate, at this point, to simply forget about subjectivism as a theory about the language of value in general and concentrate on what it has to say about moral language in particular. But we must first consider it as a theory about the language of value in general because that is how it is presented. The major claims are made about the language of value in general, especially the word "good," and moral language is treated under this heading. Whatever is said about the language of value in general is understood to apply to moral language in particular. And it *is* true, after all, that moral goodness is a species of value. (Both forms of non-cognitivism, too, although prescriptivism *started out* as an account of moral language exclusively, are theories about the language of value in general, and of moral language as coming under that heading.) Furthermore, when you get to chapter 5, where we enter upon the question of reasons for choice (see especially p. 108), you will discover that questions of morality cannot be considered independently of the question of value in general. It helps to prepare the ground, therefore, to begin to consider that general question here, in our examination of subjectivism.

While subjectivism, as we shall see, does not succeed as a theory of value in general, there is, not surprisingly, a small grain of truth in it, for otherwise how could it ever have got off the ground? This grain of truth is that sometimes "This is good" really does seem to mean "I like this." If, for instance, after having bought an ice cream cone and had my first lick, I say "This is really good," I usually mean no more than "Wow! I really like this." Here "good" simply means "yummy." The theory seems to imply that we can always substitute "yummy," or some similar word such as "scrumptious," for "good," and, if we wanted to be nasty, we could call this the "yummy theory" of value.

What makes the yummy theory seem believable is that when we say something of the form "*x* is good" and leave it at that, more often than not we really do mean nothing more than that we like it, and liking something is, of course, purely subjective. But this is a relatively minor use of the word "good." More often when we use the word, we are saying, either explicitly or implicity, that something is of high or excellent quality for a thing of that kind and that means something quite different from simply liking it. It is not a mere subjective report and "yummy" or a similar word cannot be substituted. Even ice cream has its standards of excellence or quality and, of course, the standards or criteria of excellence or quality are different for each different kind of thing. Instead of saying "This is good" or "This is really good" after the first lick of our ice cream cone, we could say "This is really good ice cream" in which case we would be saying not only that we like it, but that it is good of its kind, much better than the ice cream at the other place, and we are, by implication, recommending it to others. The standards of quality in ice cream would include taste, texture, and holding its shape (not melting too quickly).

This does not mean, of course, that we might not prefer one flavor to another, or even one brand or make to another, even where both meet the basic standards of quality. But personal preferences must be distinguished from judgments of quality or value. I can say "I like this better," which is a pure subjective report with which another person can neither agree nor disagree, but that is quite different from "This is excellent wine" where I am appealing implicitly to standards of quality. I am inviting agreement, and others may agree or disagree. I am saying, or trying to say, something about the wine itself, something I am not doing when I simply say "I like this." (That report must simply be accepted.) So a distinction must be made between judgments of value, or quality, or excellence, and simple reports of personal preferences. Subjectivism as a general theory of value muddles the two, mistakenly treating value judgments as if they were reports of personal likings or preferences.

Let us take another example. Suppose I am trying to sell you a car. You like the sporty look of it, the odometer shows a very low mileage, and both the exterior and the interior are spotless. I assure you that it's a very good car. You trust me and you buy it. You then discover that it handles badly, that it's hard to start, that shifting gears is far from easy, that it has poor acceleration, that it is unstable in high winds, that the alternator belt is constantly breaking and falling off, that the brakes are unreliable, and that all this is a function of design and manufacture, not of abuse or poor maintenance. It is also perfectly clear that I must have known this. You conclude, naturally enough, that I was lying when I told you it was a good car, that I knowingly sold you a lemon. You come to me and complain. "I wasn't lying," I say, "I really like that car and that's what 'This is a good car' means. I wasn't saying anything about the car; I was only giving a report on my feelings toward it. I've been studying philosophy and I've come to realize that subjectivism is true. Don't you understand English?"

What could this be but a scam? You believe, quite rightly, not that I have achieved some deep philosophical understanding that you lack, but that I have deliberately deceived you, that I have used a bit of flagrantly false philosophy as an excuse, and that I deserve a bop on the nose. Calling a car a good car appeals implicitly to standards of value or quality in cars, standards that we both accept, standards having to do with its performance relative to normal expectations, expectations that depend on our understanding of the state of the art of design and manufacture at the time the car was made. Perhaps I thought you were an ignoramus. In any case I am a liar and a cheat and there is no doubt about it! You have been ripped off and you should never trust me again.

Notice: good *ice cream*, good *car*, not just "good" simply. We may sometimes say, especially when we are doing philosophy, things like "Pleasure is a good" or "Pleasure is the good," where "good" is being used as a noun or a substantive (see the next paragraph), but we almost never say "This is good" and leave it at that, unless we mean "yummy" or the like. We say "This is a good wrench" or "This is a good lawnmower" or "This is a really good thriller" or "He is a good teacher" or "She is a good surgeon," or carpenter or mechanic or cook or accountant or swimmer or whatever. The word "good" as an adjective rarely stands by itself. Even if we say "This is a good one" we mean that it's a good grapefruit or a good knife or a good *something*, or something good for some particular end or purpose. I might write "This is good" or just simply "good" on a student's philosophy assignment, but this is short for "good work" or "good answer to the question." In every case we are appealing either explicitly or implicitly to shared or sharable standards or criteria of worth for objects or skills of a certain kind. We really do mean to say something about the knife or the mechanic or whatever it or he or she is; we are not just talking about ourselves, our likes and dislikes.

There is another sense or use of the word "good," for we sometimes ask the question "What are the good things of life?" And in answer we may say that pleasure (the pleasant or agreeable), excitement (freedom from boredom), achievement, recognition, love, friendship, companionship, self-respect, health of body and spirit, freedom from want (a continuing supply of food, clothing and shelter adequate to one's needs), freedom from pain and suffering, freedom from fear (security), peace, prosperity, and such things as these, are goods, or genuine goods, or human goods, or simply good things. It is here that the word "good" (except in the expression "good things") is used as a noun or a substantive, rather than as an adjective (as in the examples considered so far). What we mean is that these are things that are necessary for, or that contribute to, human well-being or self-fulfillment or happiness. If I say "Health is a good thing" or "Health is a human good," I am not saying "I like health," which would simply be a report about my own positive attitude toward health. I am not, as the subjectivists claim, saying something about me; I am saying about health that it is desirable for everybody. Someone might disagree (which they could not do if I were only saying how I personally felt about health), arguing perhaps that sickness improves character or something of the sort, but disagreement of this kind about such an obvious human good as health would be strange, to say the least.

Subjectivism seems to work when "yummy" or some such word can be substituted for "good" – here "*x* is good" really does mean "I like *x*" – but to call something yummy is not to make a value *judgment*. As a general theory of value or goodness, then, subjectivism fails on all counts but this one, for it depends upon the confusion between evaluations or judgments of value on the one hand, and simple statements of personal liking or preference on the other. Genuine value judgments appeal either explicitly or implicitly to shared or sharable standards or criteria of value. They invite agreement and they may be disputed. However, simple statements of personal liking or preference may not; we can only accept them, for it would make no sense either to agree or to disagree. Therefore, true value judgments cannot be, as the subjectivists claim, mere statements of personal liking or preference.

While our expectations should not be very high, very little has yet been said about subjectivism as a theory about specifically moral judgments as distinct from value judgments in general. Remember, according to subjectivism, when a person says "x is morally good" or "x is morally admirable" or "x is morally right" or "x is morally obligatory" what she or he is actually saying is "I approve of x" or "I strongly approve of x," and when a person says "x is morally bad" or "x is morally contemptible" or "x is morally wrong" he or she is actually saying "I disapprove of x" or "I strongly disapprove of x." According to subjectivism, nothing at all, in spite of appearances, is being said about x, but rather about the speaker, about his or her attitudes of approval or disapproval towards x, whatever x may be. Thus, according to subjectivism, when someone says "Lying is wrong," he or she is only saying "I strongly disapprove of lying." It is a statement by the speaker about himself or herself, not a statement about lying. And, the subjectivist believes, when someone says "Courage is a virtue" or "Courage is a good quality in a human being," she or he is simply saying "I approve of courage" or "I admire courage" or "I regard courage with favor."

Now one thing certainly is true. If you overhear me, Ted, saying to someone (say his name is Bill), "What you are planning to do is morally wrong," then in telling someone about it you are perfectly entitled to say "Ted disapproves of what Bill is planning to do," and that is because in saying that something is morally wrong, I *am* expressing my disapproval of it in the sense of *showing* or *revealing* it. It would make no sense to say "Ted thinks that what Bill is planning is morally wrong but he doesn't disapprove of it." No more can I sensibly say, "What you are planning is morally wrong but I don't disapprove of it," unless by "morally wrong" I mean *thought to be* morally wrong, *regarded as* morally wrong, or morally wrong by the standards of conventional morality, which I personally reject. I can't judge sincerely that something is morally wrong and not disapprove of it, unless I am a Satanist (someone opposed to good and in favor of evil) and that is very rare, if we can even make sense of it.[2] I disapprove of it (unless I am a Satanist) *precisely because* I believe it to be morally wrong. Note also that just as there are many different kinds of value, and not just moral value (see above), there are many different kinds of approval or disapproval. We can approve of something because of its *convenience*, for instance. The approval or disapproval expressed in moral judgments is *moral* approval or disapproval, and you can only approve or disapprove of something *morally* if you believe it to be morally good or morally bad. This, however, is a moral *judgment*, even if it is seen as a purely personal one; it is not a declaration or avowal of one's emotional state! (see note 1).

So, believing sincerely that something actually is morally wrong (and not just said or thought or supposed to be morally wrong) does include disapproving of it. Subjectivism as a meta-ethical theory about specifically moral language has at least that much going for it. In fact, subjectivism is better off as a theory restricted to specifically moral utterances than it is as a general theory of value, for while it makes no sense (barring Satanism) to say "This is morally wrong but I don't disapprove of it," it does make sense to say, for instance, "I know this a very good painting" (perhaps pointing to the features that make it good, such as expressive power, skill in execution, and so forth), "but I don't really like it. I certainly wouldn't want it hanging in my living room." It's even possible to say "I know this music is junk but I can't help liking it anyway." Specifically moral judgments do involve the judger's approval or disapproval, but the non-moral value judgments in the examples just given, and others like them, do not necessarily imply personal liking or disliking on the judger's part.

Let us consider, then, subjectivism as a theory confined to specifically moral utterances, and let us grant the subjectivists their point that thoughts or utterances of the form "*x* is morally right," "*x* is morally obligatory," and "*x* is morally good" imply the thinker's or the speaker's or the writer's approval of *x*, and that thoughts or utterances of the form "*x* is morally wrong," "*x* is morally reprehensible," "*x* is contemptible," and so forth imply the thinker's or speaker's or writer's disapproval of *x*. Very well. When I say sincerely, "What you are planning to do is morally wrong," I am expressing my disapproval of what you are planning to do. Does this show that when I say "What you are planning to do is morally wrong" what I actually mean is "I disapprove of what you are planning to do"? This could only be true if that was what I meant when I said it and that was what you took it to mean. As part of a general theory of the meaning and function of moral language (a meta-ethical theory), it would only be true if, when they made moral statements, people meant simply to be stating their own attitudes of approval or disapproval, and this would also have to be how they were understood by others. We can't get away from the fact that the meaning of a sentence is tied to what people normally mean and understand when it is spoken, written, or thought.

But is this how moral utterances are meant and understood? Think about it for a moment. Assuming you do use moral language, is this what you mean? And whether you use moral language or not, is this what you understand other people to mean? I have a strong suspicion that the answer is "no." When I say something of the form "*x* is morally good" or "*x* is morally bad" or "*x* is a moral obligation" or "*x* is morally wrong," I mean, and you understand me to mean, something about lying, or betrayal, or whatever, namely that it is undesirable, or not to be done by anybody, or about truth-telling or loyalty that it is desirable or a good thing and that it is what everyone is to do or be. And it's no good saying that no matter what people mean and understand, all a moral statement can really amount to is "I approve of this " or "I disapprove of that." If that is what the statement really boils down to, even though something else is meant and understood, then subjectivism is not a theory of the meaning of moral language at all. Or if it is a theory of the meaning of moral language, nobody ever means what they think they mean when they form and use moral sentences and nobody understands them properly, and that, as we have seen (see the paragraph above) is impossible. Of course, if you do sincerely believe that something is morally wrong, then (barring Satanism) you do disapprove of it, and for precisely that reason, but that you disapprove of something (a statement about yourself) is not what you mean when you say, or write, or think that it is morally wrong, nor is it what you understand someone else to be saying when you hear or read it. Since it is impossible to suppose that we never mean or understand what we think we mean or understand by our moral thoughts and utterances, we must conclude that subjectivism fails as a meta-ethical theory (a theory bout the meaning of moral language).

But let us look more closely at the possibility mentioned in the last paragraph. I mean the possibility that we might reject subjectivism as a theory of the meaning of moral language (a meta-ethical theory), yet continue to hold that moral thoughts and utterances, whatever we mean and understand by them, can, in the end, only amount to declarations of personal attitudes. According to this way of looking at it we do not, as the subjectivists claim, mean or understand moral thoughts or utterances to be declarations of the thinker's or utterer's attitudes or feelings, for or against, for they are indeed intended to refer to some objective moral reality. Nevertheless, they can really be nothing but affirmations of personal approval or disapproval, since there is no moral reality.

It is, in fact, admitted by some would-be subjectivists – let us call them cognitivist anti-realists[3] – that subjectivism as a theory of moral language is false, that we really do mean to be saying something about lying, for instance (and that is what we are understood to be saying) when we say that lying without justification or excuse is morally wrong or reprehensible. But, so it is claimed, because there are no moral truths, only private attitudes, all of us who use moral language sincerely in our talk, our writing, or our thoughts, are under some kind of delusion. According to this view of the matter, we really do mean to be saying, when we say that causing needless pain or suffering, for instance, is morally wrong, that it is bad or undesirable because of what it is. According to the holders of this view, subjectivism is false as a theory of the meaning of moral language, but we are nevertheless mistaken in thinking that there is or could be any such moral reality. While we mean to be making claims about such a reality, only personal (or social) attitudes of approval or disapproval are real. The subjectivists meant to eliminate the idea of a moral reality by their analysis of moral language, but according to the view we are now considering, while the subjectivists' analysis of moral language is mistaken, their heart is in the right place, for the idea of a moral reality really is unacceptable. According to this cognitivist anti-realist view, we are not, in using moral language, declaring our attitudes or feelings for or against something, but rather we are making claims about lying, or paying your debts, etc., but these claims cannot be taken at face value because the idea of an objective moral reality is just plainly absurd. As this cognitivist anti-realist view has it, subjectivism as a meta-ethical theory is false, but we are under a systematic illusion in our use of moral language – the illusion that there is or could be a moral reality not of our own invention.

While it is strange to think that we are making a systematic error in our use of moral language, that in making moral judgments we are attempting to refer to a moral reality that does not and could not exist, nothing said so far in this book would show this to be false. The question of what a discoverable moral reality might be, and why there is nothing difficult about the idea, is taken up in part II. In the meantime, we have seen that subjectivism, since it fails as a meta-ethical theory (a theory about the nature of moral language), is no threat to this idea. It is, as we have seen, a mistake to think that the correct analysis of moral language reveals moral judgments to be statements affirming the speaker's or writer's or thinker's personal approval or disapproval, rather than statements affirming something about a person's character for instance, or lying, or paying one's debts.

Non-cognitivism: (1) Emotivism

In our discussion of subjectivism, we noted (see above): "So, believing sincerely that something actually is morally wrong (and not just said or thought or supposed to be morally wrong) does include disapproving of it. Subjectivism as a meta-ethical theory about specifically moral language has at least that much going for it." But, in spite of this, we saw that subjectivism was wrong in arguing that moral thoughts and utterances such as "Lying is wrong" were properly to be understood as declarations of the speaker's (or writer's or thinker's) approval or disapproval of some act or kind of act or of some quality of character (even if we have to agree that that approval or disapproval is implicit). We noted further that if subjectivism were true, moral utterances, as simple statements of personal approval or disapproval, could not be disputed. As the subjectivist would have it, what "This is morally wrong" says is "I disapprove of this." Given that the speaker or writer were sincere and not self-deceived, we would just have to accept such utterances as reports of his or her personal attitudes. (We can neither agree nor disagree with a person's declaration of her own attitudes.)

Obviously, we need an account of moral thoughts and utterances (spoken or written) which allows for the fact that such thoughts and utterances, assuming their sincerity and lack of self-deception, do include personal approval or disapproval of something, but one that does not reduce these thoughts and utterances to assertions of such approval or disapproval. Non-cognitivism, whatever form it takes, attempts to meet this need by claiming that while moral sentences do nothing but express personal attitudes of approval or disapproval (*emotivism*) or commitments to principle (*prescriptivism*), they are nevertheless not assertions or declarations of these personal attitudes or commitments. For the non-cognitivist, moral thoughts and utterances remain subjective and personal, but they are what we may call "non-statemental" expressions of personal attitudes or commitments. Since they are not statements or assertions (truth claims) of any kind and refer to no reality, not even to subjective states, moral thoughts and utterances, according to the non-cognitivist, are neither true nor false. The speaker or writer is not stating or affirming that he or she approves or disapproves of something or that he or she is committed to a certain principle of conduct; rather he or she is verbally but non-statementally expressing or displaying (perhaps to himself or herself) that attitude or that commitment.

The emotive theory of ethics, as it is called, first appeared in print in 1923 in a book called *The Meaning of Meaning* by C. K. Ogden (a linguist) and I. A. Richards (a literary critic and theorist). The theory is already there, complete, in capsule form:

> This peculiar ethical use of "good" is, we suggest, a purely emotive use. When so used the word stands for nothing whatever, and has no symbolic function. Thus, when we so use it in the sentence, "THIS is good," we merely refer to THIS, and the addition of "is good" makes no difference whatever to our reference. When, on the other hand, we say "THIS is red," the addition of "is red" to "this" does symbolise an extension of our reference, namely to some other red thing. But "is good" has no comparable SYMBOLIC function; it serves only as an emotive sign expressing our attitude to THIS, and perhaps evoking

similar attitudes in other persons, or inciting them to actions of one kind or another.[4]

In other words, when the word "good" is used in a moral or ethical sentence, it does not refer to ("stand for") anything in the world – this is what Ogden and Richards meant by its having no symbolic function – but has a purely emotive meaning, non-statementally expressing an attitude (of approval) and evoking or attempting to evoke a similar attitude in others, which will or may influence their actions. The subjectivist would say that the word "good" does not refer to anything beyond the subjective state of the speaker or writer (his or her attitude or feeling of approval) but, as the subjectivist sees it, it does stand for that, and what the speaker says or the thinker thinks, if he or she is sincere and not self-deceived, is true. (And, of course, if he is lying or insincere or deceiving himself, it is false.) According to emotivism, however, the word "good" (or "right" or "obligatory" or "wrong" or "admirable" or "despicable") stands for or refers to nothing whatever, not even to personal attitudes of approval or disapproval; its meaning is emotive. It has a purely expressive and evocative function and is never used to make statements or assertions (truth claims).

While the emotive theory of ethics originated in 1923 in a book jointly authored by a linguist and a literary theorist, it was quickly seized upon and developed, when they became aware of it, by the philosophers who called themselves logical positivists or logical empiricists. Logical positivism had become very influential by the early 1930s. It was essentially a theory of meaning according to which if a sentence was neither empirical (verifiable by observation) nor analytic (true in virtue of the meanings of the words used, as in "No married man is a bachelor"), it was literally meaningless. This appeared to eliminate ethics, religion, and all philosophy except the analysis of language. The logical positivists had a lot of trouble with ethics, however. It was hard to make out (although some tried) that ethical sentences were reducible to sentences that might be empirically verifiable (e.g. "A is morally good" means "A promotes happiness"),[5] yet it was difficult to maintain that ethical statements, which did appear to perform some function, were literally meaningless. The concept of emotive meaning was the answer to the logical positivists' prayer, and they adopted it as their own theory of value in general. Its first statement by a philosopher was by the then logical positivist W. H. F. Barnes in an article published in 1933 in the journal *Analysis*, which at that time was the more or less official organ of the English branch of the logical positivist movement. Here is an excerpt from that paper:

Value judgements in their origin are not strictly judgements at all. They are exclamations expressive of approval. This is to be distinguished from the theory that the value judgement, "A is good," states that I approve A. The theory that I am now putting forward maintains that "A is good" is a form of words expressive of my approval. To take an illustration: When I say 'I have a pain," that sentence states the occurrence of a certain feeling in me: when I shout "Oh!" in a certain way that is expressive of the occurrence in me of a certain feeling. We must seek then for the origin of value judgements in the expressions of approval, delight, and affection, which children utter when confronted with certain experiences.

. . . It is . . . [the] opposition between the approval of one man and that of others which lies at the bottom of controversies about value. If I maintain "A is good" against the contention "A is bad," my attempt to prove the truth of my statement is not really what it pretends to be. I point out details in A which are the objects of my approval. By so doing I hope that my opponent, when he becomes aware of these, will approve A: and so be ready to say "A is good." But what I have done is not really to gain his assent to a proposition [i.e. statement, assertion] but to change his attitude from one of disapproval to one of approval towards A. All attempts to persuade others of the truth of value judgements are thus really attempts to make others approve the things we approve.[6]

Notice how Barnes distinguishes, in the third and fourth sentences of the first paragraph above, between subjectivism and the non-cognitivist theory that he is putting forward: "A is good" is not a statement at all but a non-statemental expression of approval. (Barnes says nothing about "A is bad," but we can only suppose that he would regard this as a non-statemental expression of disapproval.) But we can't overlook the second paragraph in the quotation above. "A is good" is not said only to be an expression of approval (conveying that approval in much the same way that a smile, a clap on the back, a thumbs-up sign, or an exclamation like "Go for it!" does); it may also be used, according to Barnes, in attempting to get others to approve of what you approve of, to influence others to share your attitude of approval toward A. This second element was already present in the theory as it was first presented by Ogden and Richards in the paragraph from their book already quoted: "perhaps evoking similar attitudes in other persons, or inciting them to actions of one kind or another." This two-pronged aspect remained an essential part of the theory as it continued to be developed and made more sophisticated through the 1930s to early 1950s, the period when logical positivism was in its heyday, when it was the "with-it" philosophy of those who saw themselves as being in the know.[7] According to the theory, I am not only non-statementally expressing my approval of something in saying "A is good," I am attempting to influence the conduct of others by getting them to share that approval, and when I say "A is bad" I am not only expressing my disapproval of A, I am trying to get others to share that disapproval and act accordingly.

We must notice that Barnes treats the theory as a theory of value in general, and, as long as it deals solely with sentences of the form "A is good" and "A is bad," it is open to the objection that was raised to subjectivism as a general theory of value, namely that the words "good" and "bad", except where we may substitute "yummy" and "yucky" or some such pair, hardly ever appear by themselves and, when they do, A is implictly understood to be good or bad of its class or kind (good teacher, good basketball player, good car, good work, good painting, good peach, etc.). There is an appeal to shared or sharable standards for that class or kind of thing. But where "A is good" is taken to mean "A is morally good" and "A is bad" is taken to mean "A is morally bad," this objection does not apply, for we really do say such things, even if many people, myself included, think that even here we are appealing to sharable standards of conduct or character. And we certainly do use sentences of the form "x is (morally) right," "x is (morally) obligatory," "x is (morally) wrong ," "x is evil," "x is admirable," and "x is despicable" (or vile or contemptible).

Ogden and Richards were not academic philosophers, but Barnes was and, as a philosopher, writing for other philosophers, he is careful to distinguish his non-cognitivist theory from the subjectivism with which it might be confused. C. L. Stevenson, in developing the emotive theory, goes further and argues for the advantages of emotivism over subjectivism.[8] He points out (what we have already noted) that, if subjectivism were true, there could be no disagreement no moral questions, for if, in using moral language, I am only making assertions about my own subjective states – statements amounting, for instance, to "I have a strong positive feeling towards x" or "I disapprove of y – there is nothing for anyone to take issue with. (We also noted that there was nothing for them to agree with either.) Someone might think that I am lying, or insincere, or self-deceived, but given that I am sincere and that I am not mistaken about my own feelings, if what I am saying is that I approve or disapprove of something, that is the end of the matter. If the other person is simply saying "I have a negative feeling towards x," or "I approve of y," then she is telling me what her feelings or attitudes are. While this might result in some antagonism between us, given that each of us dislikes the other's attitude, we are not disagreeing about anything. I am stating what my attitudes are and she is stating what hers are and that is the end of the matter. Yet moral disagreement and moral disputes really do exist. Stevenson claims that his theory allows for moral disagreement but it is *disagreement in attitude rather than disagreement in belief* – a conflict in the attitudes being non-statementally expressed. No belief is involved since nothing whatever is being asserted. No statement, not even, as subjectivism would have it, a declaration of the speaker's or writer's subjective states, is being made.

If subjectivism were true, there could be no moral disagreements for if, in using moral language, all I am doing is stating my personal attitude, there is nothing either to agree or disagree with. But, as Stevenson sees it, there is genuine opposition, for what look like differences of moral opinion are really conflicts in the attitudes that it is the function of moral sentences to express in a non-statemental way. I say "x is morally bad" and you say "No, x is not morally bad," and it looks as if you are contradicting me, denying what I have affirmed. According to subjectivism, each of us is issuing a declaration of his or her own personal attitude, with which the other person can neither agree nor disagree. But, according to the emotive theory, as expounded by Stevenson, I am affirming nothing and you are denying nothing; I am expressing on attitude and you are expressing another – one which conflicts with mine – and so we are expressing a genuine opposition to one another, an opposition in attitudes. Furthermore, in saying these things, each of us is trying to get the other to adopt his or her own attitude. In my attempt to influence you, I may mention certain things about x toward which I think you will have a negative attitude, and you may mention certain things about x toward which you think I will have a positive attitude or at least not a negative one. But these facts about x, so the theory says, are not reasons supporting a judgment on which we might both agree; they are simply attempts to bring about agreement in attitude. Barnes had already said (see the quotation above) that controversies about value (including moral value) were to be understood in terms of opposition of attitudes and "All attempts to persuade other of the truth of value judgments are . . . really attempts to make others approve the things we approve," but it was Stevenson who pointed out that emotivism permits agreement and disagreement on moral questions in a way that subjectivism does not, moral agreement or disagreement being understood as agreement or disagreement in attitude as distinct from agreement or disagreement in belief.

In our examination of subjectivism above, we admitted that the subjectivist was right about one thing: when I say sincerely, "What you are planning to do is morally wrong," I *am* expressing my disapproval of what you are planning to do in the sense of *showing* or *revealing* it. But we also saw that "What you are planning to do is morally wrong" is not simply translatable into "I disapprove of what you are planning to do." When we engage in moral criticism we do not mean to be making a statement or affirmation (truth claim) about ourselves, namely that our personal attitude is one of approval or disapproval, and that is not how we are understood. It is true that I am expressing my disapproval when I say sincerely that something is morally wrong, but that is because (barring Satanism) I cannot say sincerely that something is morally wrong yet not disapprove of it. We cannot even make sense of the notion (again barring Satanism) that someone might say or think that something is morally wrong yet not disapprove of it. In saying sincerely that something is morally wrong, although I am not affirming or declaring that I disapprove of it, I am nevertheless *showing* or *revealing* that disapproval.

The emotivist rejects the subjectivist's analysis, denying that "*x* is morally wrong" translates into "I disapprove of *x*," but still claims that "*x* is morally wrong" is nothing but an expression of personal disapproval, only it is a non-statemental expression, in the same category as cries and exclamations ("Whoopee!" "Echhh!"). That is why the theory was dubbed by its opponents the "Boo! Hurrah!" theory of ethics. But emotivism is open to the most serious objection that was raised to subjectivism as a theory of moral language: that we neither mean nor understand moral thoughts and utterances simply to be expressing personal attitudes of approval or disapproval. If we object to subjectivism on the grounds that in using moral language we are not simply declaring our attitudes, it does not overcome the objection to say that in using moral language we are only verbally emoting. It is still the case that we both mean and are understood to mean by our moral utterances that something *is* morally good or bad, right or wrong, *and that is why we approve or disapprove of it*. Our approval or disapproval is *moral* approval or disapproval (see pp. 69–70 above and note 1). We are not simply talking about or own psychological states, but we are not just emoting either. Our intention in using moral language is to refer to some objective moral reality, and that is how we are understood. Whether or not there is such a moral reality is another matter.

As in the case of subjectivism, it is no good saying, in the attempt to save emotivism, that whatever we mean in using moral language, and whatever we are understood to mean, all a moral utterance really amounts to is a non-statemental expression of personal attitude. There are two possibilities here, depending upon how close we take the connection to be between the meaning of a sentence and what people normally mean and understand by it: (1) if the tie is very close, then emotivism is no longer a meta-ethical theory (a theory of the meaning of moral language), but has been turned into a form of cognitivist anti-realism (cf. pp. 71–72 above), for it has been said that it doesn't matter what we mean and understand; or (2) if we attempt to sever the tie or loosen it to the point where we can still call it a theory of the meaning of moral sentences (by saying this is what the sentences mean no matter what pepole neither mean or understand by them), it can only be concluded that people neither mean nor understand what they think they mean or understand when they think, speak, write, hear, or read sentences in moral language. But that, as we have already seen, is impossible.

Non-cognitivism: (2) Prescriptivism

In 1949 Stuart Hampshire wrote:

> It seems now to be generally assumed that to ask whether sentences
> expressing moral praise or blame are to be classified as true of false
> statements, or alternatively as mere expressions of feeling, is somehow a
> substitute for the analysis of the processes of thought by which as moral
> agents we decide what we ought to do and how we ought to behave.
> Unless this is the underlying assumption, it is difficult to understand
> why moral philosophers should concentrate attention primarily on the
> analysis of ethical terms as they are used in sentences expressing moral
> praise and blame; for we are not primarily interested in moral criticism,
> or even self-criticism, except in so far as it is directly or indirectly an aid
> to the solution of practical problems, to deciding what we ought to do
> in particular situations or types of situation; we do not normally perplex
> ourselves deeply in moral appraisal for its own sake, in allotting moral
> marks to ourselves or to other people. The typical moral problem is not
> a spectator's problem or a problem of classifying or describing conduct,
> but a problem of practical choice and decision.[9]

This insistence on the primarily practical nature of moral judgments represents a clear attack on the then prevalent emotivism. In the same paper,
Hampshire goes on to say:

> But of practical judgments one cannot say that differences which are in
> principle irresoluble are . . . in *no* sense genuine contradictions; for it is
> the distinguishing characteristic of practical judgments that they have a
> prescriptive or quasi-imperative force as part of their meaning. These is
> therefore one sense in which, when A says that capital punishment
> ought to be abolished and B says that it ought not, they are contradict-
> ing each other; their judgments contradict each other in the sense in
> which two conflicting commands or recommendations may be said to
> contradict each other.[10]

Note the words "prescriptive" and "quasi-imperative" and the reference to
commands and recommendations, for these are central to Hampshire's view.
Let us run through this. If meta-ethical subjectivism were true, then if I said
"Capital punishment ought to be abolished" I would only be saying that I
disapproved of it, and if another person said "I don't think so; I think it ought
to be retained," he or she would only be saying that she approved of it. There
would be no contradiction and nothing for either party to agree or disagree

with and there could be no moral disputes. But, of course, there are moral disputes. The emotivist thought he had the answer by saying that moral disagreement was not disagreement in belief but disagreement in attitude, with each party trying to change the other's attitude so as to agree with his own. Hampshire, by contrast, says that there is a genuine contradiction, just as it seems there is, but the two utterances "Capital punishment should be abolished" and "No, capital punishment should not be abolished" contradict each other in the same way that commands or imperative recommendations do, as in "Do this!" "No, do that!" or "Get it at store A!" "No, don't get it at store A; get it at store B." Finally, moral judgments do not describe (state facts about actions), they prescribe (tell us what to do): "In so far as we relate . . . [moral judgments] to practical deliberations and decisions, we come to recognise them as not descriptions of, but prescriptions for, actions. Practical judgments, no less than theoretical or descriptive statements, are in the natural sense of the words, literally significant, although they do not in the normal sense describe."[11] Note the contrasts: (1) moral judgments are not in the first place critical judgments of praise or blame, but practical judgments leading to decisions about what is to be done; and (2) practical moral judgments are not descriptions but prescriptions, having a "quasi-imperative" force. It was in this article of Hampshire's that the meta-ethical theory known as *prescriptivism* began.

The position was developed by R. M. Hare in his very influential book, *The Language of Morals*, published in 1952.[12] We cannot go into Hare's position in detail, but we should note the following four claims:

1   Value judgments, including moral judgments, are prescriptions and, as such, contain imperatives.
2   One cannot sincerely make or assent to a moral judgment without accepting the first-person imperative "Let me do *x*!"
3   The imperatives contained in value judgments are universal imperatives or principles, and moral judgments, especially "ought" judgments, are universal prescriptions that express decisions of principle.
4   The only ultimate justification of a decision of principle is personal commitment.

One quotation from *The Language of Morals* will suffice to make Hare's position clear:

If pressed to justify a decision completely, we have to give a complete specification of the way of life of which it is a part. This complete specification it is impossible in practice to give; the nearest attempts are those given by the great religions, especially those which can point to historical persons who carried out the way of life I practice. Suppose, however, that we can give it. If the inquirer still goes on asking "But why *should* I live like that?" then there is no further answer to give him, because we have already . . . said everything that could be included in the further answer. We can only ask him to make up his own mind which way he ought to live; *for in the end everything rests upon such a decision of principle.* He has to decide whether to accept that way of life or not; if he accepts it, then we can proceed to justify the decisions that are based upon it; if he does not accept it, then let him accept some other, and try to live by it . . . Far from being arbitrary, such a decision would be the most well-founded of decisions, because it would be based upon consideration of everything upon which it could possibly be founded.[13]

Both Hampshire and Hare see moral judgments as being essentially practical rather than critical (mere expressions of approval or disapproval), as judgments leading to personal decisions about what to do. In this respect both were opposing the then prevalent emotivism, which concentrated on approval and disapproval and had relatively little to say on the practical (decision-making and advice-giving) aspect of moral judgments.[14] It remained for Hare, however, to argue that these personal decisions were, as decisions of principle, inherently universal or universalizable – not just what I am to do, but what anyone in my circumstances is to do. "To ask whether I ought to do A in these circumstances," says Hare, ". . . is to ask whether or not I will that doing A in such circumstances should become a universal law."[15] In other words, I am not just prescribing for myself. I cannot prescribe for myself without prescribing for humankind in general and *therefore* for myself. I can only will to do myself what I can will as a principle, and principles, as universal imperatives, apply to anyone in the same circumstances.

Now Sartre had nothing to say about imperatives, or about moral language in general – he did not engage in meta-ethics, being content to leave moral language unexamined – but the resemblance here to Sartre (a resemblance which Hare himself recognized), should be instantly apparent.[16] Yes, my decisions involve only my personal commitments, both say, but at the same time I am making decisions for humanity in general; anyone in my circumstances is to do just this. In this respect Hare is open to the same major criticism that we levelled at Sartre: what am I to say when I sincerely advocate one thing and someone else sincerely advocates another? (Note the key emphasis on the word "sincerely.") On the one hand, I must say she has made her personal commitment, which for her is universalizable, so she is in the clear, but, on the other hand, because she opposes the principles to which I adhere, principles which I see as universal and applicable to everyone, I must say that she is in the wrong! But we cannot have it both ways. Either my decision is purely personal, a decision about what *I* ought to do, having no necessary relevance to anyone else, or else it really is a decision for all humanity, crying out for consensus, and requiring me to say that those who disagree with me are wrong. Hampshire appears to opt for the first alternative, but Hare, like Sartre, wants to have his cake and eat it too.

We have found grains of truth in all the doctrines we have examined before this one. (*Cultural relativism*: morality is social, not personal, and custom, if there is no moral objection, is to be respected. *Subjective relativism*: different people find different things valuable or worthwhile, and these differences are to be respected so long as no moral questions are involved. *Subjectivism*: "*x* is good" does mean "I like *x*" where "yummy" or a similar word is substitutable for "good." *Emotivism*: Sincere moral judgments, whatever else they may do, really do express attitudes of approval or disapproval, although in making them we do not affirm that we have these attitudes.) Is prescriptivism to be the only exception? We have been given reason to believe that no theory is able to get off the ground unless there is some truth lurking in it somewhere. It is time to ask some pertinent questions.

We must first of all ask whether it is true, as the prescriptivists claim, that moral judgments are primarily concerned with choice and decision, and only secondarily with appraisal, that they are first of all practical rather than critical, that they are more directly connected with deciding what to do than with assigning praise or blame. To begin with there is no doubt about how to assess "This is what, all things considered, I morally ought to do." Such a judgment comes at the end of a particular kind of deliberation, namely considering moral reasons for and against a certain course of action, or for and against two or more different alternative courses of action, and it normally results in the decision to do the thing in question. That is because we would not bother to engage in deliberation unless we were trying to come to a decision about what to do, and if we don't, at the end of our deliberation, do what we have come to think we ought to do, then the whole process will have had no point. Because the whole point of deliberation, including moral deliberation, is action and choice, it is clear that the judgment "This is what I ought to do," when it comes at the end of deliberation, is primarily practical. It is also true that emotivism, in its early stages, overlooked this aspect of moral language, concentrating on the appraisal of conduct and character as good or bad, right or wrong (e.g. "He is a good man for what he did"). It did take into account the attempt to influence the attitudes, and hence the conduct, of others through the use of moral language, but it overlooked the role of moral language in deliberation.[17] But is the fact that moral language is used as a means of making practical decisions enough to justify the claim that moral language is first of all practical and that all other uses of moral language are subordinate to this? Are the other uses of moral language understandable, as Hampshire claims, only in their relation to this primary practical use?

Non-cognitivists, of both kinds (emotivists and prescriptivists) tended to concentrate on the use of a few moral words, such as (morally) "good," "bad," "right," "wrong," and "ought." Emotivists tended to concentrate on the first four, prescriptivists on "ought." There certainly does seem to be a direct connection between "ought" and decision-making ("I ought to go to my class this morning"), though this is less obvious with the other four words, especially (morally) "good" and "bad," which do seem to belong primarily to appraisal ("He is a good husband because he helps with the housework"). But to give some idea of the variety of moral judgments, consider the following list, which I borrow from a paper of my own:[18]

1   Some professors behave irresponsibly toward their students.
2   That picture is obscene.
3   Elmer is the school bully.
4   You are a liar.
5   That was a very selfish thing to do.
6   How thoughtful and considerate of you.
7   Greed is a base motive.
8   That guy is a real creep.
9   Hitler was a moral monster.
10   You deserve to be flogged for that.
11   There is no denying the heroism of Susan B. Anthony.
12   Capitalism (communism) is an abomination.
13   One should always respect the sincerely held ideals of others.
14   He is nothing but a layabout (couch-potato).
15   She is a wholly admirable human being.
16   There is a moral obligation to aid the distressed.
17   That was an act of treachery.
18   What you did was execrable.
19   Torture is morally wrong.
20   There is nothing wrong with sex outside marriage.
21   Prudence is a virtue.
22   They were guilty of an atrocity.
23   Kindness should be received with gratitude.
24   Clearly this is what I morally ought to do.
25   Non-human animals have rights.
26   It was a case of rampant sexism.
27   Justice requires equality before the law.
28   Violence is justified only as a last resort.
29   It is nobler to forgive small injuries than to seek to return them.

30   The more fortunate have an obligation to help those who have fared less
well.

Now some of these, such as nos 1–3 and 26, have the form of simple
reports. Others, like nos 4, 5, 17, and 18, are direct accusations. No. 6 is a
kind of moral congratulation. Nos 8–11, 14, 15, and 22 bestow praise or
blame on a particular individual or group. Nos 7, 12, 13, 16, 19, 20, 21, 23,
25, and 27 through 30, are general, as distinct from particular moral statements. Only no. 24 is directly tied to deliberation and choice. I may say that
I did not do this on purpose. I was not even thinking of the question of
whether or not moral judgments are fundamentally practical when I composed
this list; I was only trying to display the scope and variety of moral judgments.
It just turned out that only one of the 30 was a first-person particular "ought"
judgment of the kind we make at the end of moral deliberation and which is
supposed to lead to action.

And what of the others? Well, the general ones, especially the statements
of principle (nos 13, 16, 19, 20, 23, 25, 28, 29, and 30) can appear in the
context of deliberation, as principles that we may appeal to in trying to decide
what we morally ought to do, here and now. (These are the kind of thing
that, according to Hampshire and Hare, can be *reasons* supporting a practical
"ought" judgment, though both agree that what are reasons for me need not
be reasons for you, because of our different commitments or ways of life.)
They can also be simply stated as general moral principles to be used as a guide
to conduct (reasons for action) whenever an appropriate occasion should arise.
The general statements that are not statements of principle – nos 7, 12, 21,
and 27 – can easily be seen to relate to practical matters. If greed is really a
base motive and I want to think well of myself, then I will not do this greedy
thing. If capitalism (or communism) is an abomination, then perhaps I should
cooperate with it as little as possible and, in the right circumstances, perhaps
do what I can to help bring it down. If prudence really is a virtue, then, since
I want to be a person of good character, and so admire rather than despise
myself, I should cultivate the virtue of prudence. If justice requires equality
before the law, then perhaps I should do what I can to oppose the injustice
of, say, racial bias, in criminal proceedings. In every case the moral judgment
has some bearing on present or future action.

Dead or non-existent characters, however, are a different matter. It is
difficult to see how praise or blame of historical individuals or fictional
characters for their deeds can have practical implications, since there is no
hope of reforming them. Neither do simple reports of moral misdeeds seem
in any obvious way related to practical matters. But if we look carefully, even
at the more dubious cases, we can see that something practical is involved,
even if indirectly. If I say that some professors behave irresponsibly toward

their students (1), then the chance that I deplore that fact is about 90 percent. And if I do deplore it, the chances are strong (unless I am a total cynic) that I think something should be done about it. If I declare that picture to be obscene (2), the chances are equally strong that I think it should not be exhibited. If Elmer is the school bully (3), I no doubt think that something should be done about Elmer (and others like him). If I say that Hitler was a moral monster (9), it is pretty clear that I think he is not to be emulated. If I accuse you of being selfish (5) or a liar (4), I am not merely criticizing you, I am calling for you to reform and threatening to have no more to do with you if you do not change your ways. Even if I am complimenting you on, or thanking you for, your thoughtfulness and consideration (6), am I not implying that thoughtfulness and consideration are always desirable and hence to be shown, even if they can't always be expected?

Must we not conclude from this review that all moral judgments have practical import, that some ought judgment is implied? Must we not agree with the prescriptivists that all moral judgments have implications for action, even if explicit ought judgments do not have the primary role that Hampshire claimed they had (see above)? One way of putting it, and one way the prescriptivists did put it, was that moral judgments all contain a *gerundive* element, which means they all imply or suggest, even if they do not state, that something is to be done or that something is to be avoided (not to be done). This is why the prescriptivists claim that moral judgments contain an imperative element (or command) that takes them out of the realm of statements and makes them incapable of being true or false. ("Go to bed!" is neither true nor false.) The prescriptivists' further assumption is that these imperatives, since they affirm nothing and hence can be neither true nor false, must come from within, expressing personal commitments (acceptance of imperatives). This is true, they claim, whether these commitments do (Hare), or do not necessarily (Hampshire), have universal implications, i.e. whether or not they are seen as imperatives (prescriptions) that apply to everyone. The emotivists may say that we are trying, in using moral language, to get others to share our attitudes, and hence to act as we do or would do, but Hare thinks that because we are making personal commitments to principle – something he thinks we cannot avoid – we must, when we make ought judgments for ourselves, judge that this is how anyone and hence everyone is to act in the same circumstances. We have already considered the difficulties in this position (pp. 81–82 above).

There are, as we have seen, very good reasons for saying that all moral judgments carry implications for action, either direct (as in the case of present-tense ought judgments) or indirect, where some ought judgment is implied. Does this compel us to say that they contain, as part of their meaning, an imperative element of personal commitment, and that therefore they are not statements and can be neither true nor false? (see p. 80 above). A hint of the answer appeared in our discussion of emotivism: "It is still the case that we both mean and are understood to mean by our moral utterances that something *is* morally good or bad, right or wrong, *and that is why we approve or disapprove of it*" (p. 78 above). The emotivists insisted that because moral utterances were expressions of approval or disapproval (which some of them certainly are) yet were not statements of that approval or disapproval, they must belong in the same category as grunts and screams and hoots of joy. but it makes more sense to say that when we call something morally good, for instance, our approval is expressed *in* calling it morally good. For in thinking of something as morally good, we are in that very thought thinking well of it, and that means approval. It does not follow that thinking something morally good amounts to no more than personal approval, or that saying something is morally good amounts to no more than non-statementally expressing that approval. Isn't it far more likely that we approve of it *because* we think it is morally good? Our thinking it morally good does not reduce to our simple approval; it is what accounts for that approval, which is *moral* approval (see pp. 69–70 and 80 above and note 1). And, of course, one cannot think of something as morally good without approving of it, nor can one say that something is morally good without thereby expressing that approval. An important point is here made clear: the emotivist analysis is not necessary in order to account for the attitudes implicit in thinking something good or bad, right or wrong. No more is the prescriptivist analysis necessary in order to account for the implications for action (the gerundive element) that all moral judgments have. These implications for action, either particular (here and now or there and then) or general (statements of principle) are direct in moral "ought" judgments as well as in judgments (particular or general) that something is wrong, obligatory or permissible (not wrong), and indirect in other moral judgments, where some ought judgment is implied. There is no need to speak of imperatives and there is no need to deny that moral judgments are capable of being true or false. If I come to the conclusion that I morally ought to do something, perhaps it *really is* what I morally ought to do, and for the very reasons I think it is. Contrary to what prescriptivists believe, this in no way lessens or reduces or eliminates the practical aspect of such a judgment.

Conclusion

What subjectivism, emotivism, and prescriptivism all have in common is the belief that there is something irreducibly subjective or first-personal in moral judgments, which excludes the possiblity of their being true or false. And their influence is very strong, for how many times have you heard an exchange like the following. A: "Gays should not be discriminated against; they have the same rights as everybody else." B: "Ah, but that's a value judgment!" B's response is supposed to put an end to any further discussion of the matter. Don't we all know, B is implying, that value judgments are subjective, so why should I pay any attention to your opinions? In this respect, subjectivism and non=cognitivism are like subjective relativism. However, they are unlike cultural relativism, which sees morality as being inherently shared rather than purely personal or individual.

Then there is the important matter of universality. We saw, both in our examination of cultural relativism and in our examination of subjective relativism, that moral judgments are inherently universal and intended to apply to all of humanity. Sartre at least recognized this, and we saw the trouble that this got him into (chapter 3, pp. 53–54). Hare, coming at it from a different angle (meta-ethics), also recognizes this inherent universality, and we saw how this, combined as it is with his insistence on the irrevocably personal nature of moral judgments, lands him in a similar pickle (pp. 81–82 above). Of course, it does not follow from this that there is or even that there could be a universal morality, one applicable to all humanity, regardless of time or place. What does follow is that either there is such a universal morality or there is no morality at all, that morality is nothing but an illusion. That a universal morality is, after all, an intelligible notion, and not even a difficult one, will be the argument of part II.

SUMMARY

1   The theories dealt with in this chapter are *meta-ethical* theories; that is, theories about the nature, function, and meaning of moral language. *All of* them say that moral sentences mean something different from what they appear to mean, and all of them claim that moral thoughts and utterances are irreducibly *subjective* or contain an irreducibly subjective element which takes them out of the realm of objective truth and falsity. We may therefore say that all these views are *anti-realist*.

2   Meta-ethical *subjectivism* claims that "*x* is good" means "I like *x*" – that and nothing more. In the moral case, this liking takes the form of approval or disapproval. As a general theory of value, based on the analysis of moral language, subjectivism fails miserably. "*x* is good" only means "I like *x*" where we can substitute some such word as "yummy" for "good." Otherwise, when we say that something is good we mean that it meets certain acceptable standards for things of a certain class or kind, or for various occupations, skills, social roles, and professions. Or if

we say that something, such as pleasure, for instance, is a *good*, we mean that it is a contribution to human well-being generally.

3   What look like *moral judgments*, according to subjectivism, are really nothing but declarations of personal approval or disapproval of certain actions or qualities of character.

4   Now when we sincerely make a moral judgment, we *are* expressing our approval of some conduct or some aspect of character, but we are not *declaring* that approval; we are not *stating* that we approve or disapprove of it; rather that approval or disapproval is *implied*. That is because if we believe that something is morally wrong, for instance, we *do* disapprove of it. What the subjectivist fails to notice is that we disapprove of it *for that reason*. (If we think that something is morally wrong, our disapproval is *moral* disapproval.) That is why we can say that our disapproval is *expressed* in our saying that something is morally wrong, although that is not what we are *saying*.

5   The most serious objection to meta-ethical subjectivism is this: when we used moral language to say such things as "Lying is wrong," we do not understand ourselves, nor are we understood by others, to be simply declaring that we personally disapprove of lying. Yet if the use or function or meaning of moral language were to declare or make known our attitudes of approval or disapproval, we would have to understand that this was what we were doing in using moral language and this is how we would have to be understood by others. It is absurd to suppose that we can all be mistaken about what we mean to say when we say such things as "Lying is wrong," and that others misread us in the same way as we misread ourselves.

6   It is possible to suppose – this would be another form of anti-realism – that whatever we mean or are understood to mean, all we could possibly *convey*, and all that we could be understood to convey by our moral utterances, was our personal approval or disapproval of some act or aspect of character. But this would mean that we were all under another kind of permanent delusion, something that it is very hard to believe.

7   A final objection to subjectivism is that, if it were true, there could be no moral agreement or disagreement. If I am simply telling you what I approve or disapprove of, and you are simply telling me what you approve of or disapprove of, then that just has to be accepted. There is nothing to agree or disagree about.

8   Non-cognitivism is the view that moral utterances are not statements at all and therefore cannot be true or false. It takes two forms – emotivism and prescriptivism.

9   Emotivism is the view that moral language is used not to *declare* what one's attitudes are, but to express them in a non-statemental way. Moral

utterances are expressions of approval or disapproval of conduct or character, but they do not *state* anything at all. Rather, they are like shouts and cries and whoops of joy, or exclamations such as "Whoopee!" or "Echh!" Lying is wrong turns out to mean something like "Down with lying!"

10   Emotivism was supposed to have an advantage over meta-ethical subjectivism in that it allowed for moral disagreements, except that they are disagreements *in attitude* rather than disagreements in belief (Stevenson).

11   Much of what was said about subjectivism applies equally to emotivism. Most importantly, when we use moral language, we do not understand ourselves to be merely emoting, nor are we so understood by others. And how can we not mean what we think we mean and what we are understood to mean when we use moral language? Secondly, yes, moral utterances *do* express attitudes of approval or disapproval, as was said before, but that is not because the use of moral language is mere shouting. It is because if we sincerely believe that lying is wrong, *we disapprove of lying for that reason* – our disapproval is moral disapproval – and that disapproval is *implied* when we say, sincerely, that lying is wrong.

12   Again, some anti-realist – we may now call him a *cognitivist* anti-realist – might declare that no matter what we *think* we are saying when we use moral language, all we are *really* doing is emoting. But again, how could we explain such a universal delusion?

13   Prescriptivism began by opposing emotivism, saying that emotivism overlooked the *practical* aspect of moral thoughts and utterances. According to prescriptivism, moral judgments are essentially practical – moral ought judgments are taken as basic or fundamental – and they all imply *personal commitments to principle*. They therefore contain an imperative element ("Always do this," "Never do that") which means that in spite of all appearances they are not really statements at all and are not capable of being objectively true or false.

14   Now all moral judgments *do* have practical or *gerundive* (to be done or not to be done) implications as well as *attitudinal* ones of approval or disapproval, but this is in no way surprising, since they really are supposed to "guide conduct," as the prescriptivists go to such great pains to show us. But these practical implications do not show that moral utterances are not statements and are not capable of being objectively true or false. Even if something *really were* what you morally ought to do – in other words, even if it were objectively true that you morally ought to do it – the practical implications would not be any the less; indeed, they would be even more stringent.

Chart summary for chapter 4 Meta-ethical theories:* a comparison

Questions	Subjectivists	Emotivists	Prescriptivists	Cognitivist anti-realists
1 Is there a universal moral reality to refer to when we use moral language?	There is no universal morality	There is no universal moral reality	There is no universal moral reality	People *mean* to refer to a universal moral reality but they are deluded, since there can be no such thing
2 Is there a personal reality referred to when we use moral language, e.g. my beliefs, my feelings, my personal morality?	Yes. In using moral language one is referring to one's personal attitudes of approval or disapproval, e.g. "*x* is morally bad" means "I have a feeling of disapproval towards *x*."	No. *Nothing* is referred to. One is only emoting or exclaiming ("Lying is bad" means something like "Down with lying" or "Lying, ecchh!")	No. There is no personal reality referred to (one is only showing a personal *commitment to principle*)	No. There is no personal reality referred to or meant to be referred to
3 What limitations are placed on our existing moral language?	Our existing moral language can be used only to declare or state what our feelings or attitudes are. It has no other use	Our existing moral language can be used only to emote or exclaim or to clarify to oneself what one's own feelings or attitudes are. (Its function is basically emotive or exclamatory)	Our existing moral language is used in practical reasoning, but all reasons come back in the end to personal commitments to principle. Our moral language cannot be used to refer to any moral reality	There are no limitations. Moral language means just what it seems to mean. But moral statements are all false because there is no moral reality
4 What is the primary function of moral language?	The primary function of moral language is to declare the speaker's personal attitudes (to state what they are). The terms of moral language signify the speaker's approval or disapproval	The primary function of moral language is to express one's feelings or attitudes non-statementally (without making claims to truth of any kind) and to get others to share those feelings or attitudes. The terms of moral language have an emotive function only, expressing, showing, expressing, without declaring, the speaker's approval or disapproval	The primary function of moral language is to express one's (explicitly or implicitly) personal commitments to principle (in Hare's case seen as universal principles), without making any claims to truth. This means that moral thoughts or utterances must contain imperatives or commands (in Hare's case, *universal* imperatives)	The primary function of moral language is to make (impossible) truth claims about a universal moral reality. (Still, this may be a socially useful game to play to keep people in line)
5 What moral words or terms does the school of thought concentrate on?	It concentrates on "good" and "bad"	It concentrates on "good" and "bad"	It concentrates on "ought" and "should." (This connects with the understanding of moral language as essentially practical)	It does not concentrate on any particular word or words

6 What is the stance on moral agreement and disagreement? (A: "I think capital punishment is wrong." B: "Well, I think it's right.")	There is nothing to agree or disagree with. It is impossible to agree or disagree with a person's statement of his or her own feelings or attitudes, e.g. "I disapprove of lying."	Agreement and disagreement exist, but only in attitude, not in belief. (To believe something is to think it true. One just *has* a feeling or an attitude)	Agreement and disagreement exist, but they consist in sharing or failing to share the principles to which the parties are personally committed	People do agree and disagree, just as they appear to do
7 (a) What is (are) the central flaw(s) in their position? (b) What is (are) any secondary flaws?	The central flaw is that when people make moral statements they neither mean nor are they understood to mean to be declaring their personal attitudes or stating what they are. They *mean* to refer to a moral reality. Their personal attitudes are *shown* or *revealed* (not stated) in moral utterances of the form "x is morally good" or "x is morally bad"	The central flaw is that when people use moral language they neither mean nor are they understood to mean to be expressing their attitudes by emoting or exclaiming. They both mean and are understood to mean to be making claims to moral truth. Another flaw is that emotivism overlooks the *practical* function of moral language in making decisions and giving advice. (The emotivists concentrate on "good," and have little or nothing to say about "ought")	The central flaw is that when people use moral language in making moral judgments they both mean and are understood to mean to be making claims to moral truth. Furthermore, they understand their moral judgments to be true for everyone	The central flaw is that there appears to be no way to account for the universal delusion among sincere users of moral language that there is such a thing as moral truth (that there is a moral reality)
8 What is (are) the grain(s) of truth which give(s) credibility to the theory?	(1) The theory works as a general theory of value where "yummy" can be substituted for "good." (Here "x is good" does mean "I like x.") But these are statements of personal preference or liking. They are not judgments of value which involve an appeal to shared or sharable standards. (2) In making moral judgments, we *do* express our attitudes, not in the sense of *declaring* them or *stating* what they are, but in the sense of *showing* or *revealing* them. (One cannot think that something is morally wrong or bad without disapproving of it *for that reason*)	The emotivists are right in pointing out that in making moral judgments we are expressing, without stating or declaring, our feelings and attitudes. (Our attitudes are expressed in the sense that they are *shown* or *displayed*. One cannot judge that something is morally good or bad without approving or disapproving of it)	The prescriptivists are right in saying that moral judgments *do* have implications for action (practical import). However, they are wrong in supposing that moral language must contain imperatives or commands in order to account for this	The grain of truth (a rather large grain) is that moral language means exactly what it seems to mean (but see the central flaw above)

★Meta-ethical theories are theories about the nature and function of moral language. Examples of some terms of moral language considered by these theorists: "good," "right," "ought," "should," "bad," "wrong," "ought not," "should not"

QUESTIONS FOR THOUGHT

1   "There is no way in which you can eliminate the subjective element in moral and other value judgments." How would you respond to this?

2   "You say that capital punishment is wrong, but what you mean is that you don't like it. Well, I do. So there." Is there any disagreement here?

3   "Moral judgments are action-guiding and therefore contain imperatives, and this means that they cannot be true or false." How might a realist (believer in the truth or falsity of moral judgments) respond to this?

4   "When I say that something is morally good, I am expressing my approval of it." What makes this true? Must this be *all* that I am doing?

Recommended Reading

Chapter 1 Psychological Egoism

Thomas Hobbes, *Leviathan* (1651), part I, ch. 14.
Joseph Butler, *Fifteen Sermons on Human Nature* (1726), sermon XI.
Joel Feinberg, "Psychological egoism," in *Reason and Responsibility: Readings in some Basic Problems of Philosophy*, ed. Joel Feinberg, 7th edn (Wadsworth, Belmont, Calif., 1989), pp. 489–500.
Ronald D. Milo (ed.), *Egoism and Altruism* (Wadsworth, Belmont, Calif., 1973).
Thomas Nagel, *The Possibility of Altruism* (Clarendon Press, Oxford, 1970), ch. 9 ("Altruism: the intuitive issue").
Richmond Campbell, "Egoism," in Lawrence C. Becker (ed.), *Encyclopedia of Ethics* (Garland, New York and London, 1988), pp. 294–7.

Chapter 2 Cultural Relativism

For simple cultural relativism, see the books by Sumner, Benedict, Westermarck, and Mead listed in chapter 2, note 1. For sophisticated cultural relativism, see the books by Williams, MacIntyre and Lovibond referred to in the sections on these authors. For other defences of cultural relativism, see:
Gilbert Harman, "Moral relativism defended," *Philosophical Review*, 84 (1975), pp. 3–22.
Gilbert Harman, *The Nature of Morality* (Oxford University Press, Oxford, 1977), pp. 57–133.
Stephen Toulmin, *An Examination of the Place of Reason in Ethics* (Cambridge University Press, Cambridge, 1950), pp. 144–6.
Bernard Williams, "The truth in relativism" (1975), reprinted in Bernard Williams, *Moral Luck* (Cambridge University Press, Cambridge, 1981).
D. Z. Phillips and H. O. Mounce, *Moral Practices* (Schocken Books, New York, 1970).

Criticisms of cultural relativism are to be found it:

Bernard Williams, *Morality: an Introduction to Ethics* (Harper, New York, 1972), ch. 2.

David Lyons, "Ethical relativism and the problem of incoherence" (1976), reprinted in Micael Krausz and Jack W. Meiland (eds), *Relativism Cognitive and Moral* (University of Notre Dame Press, Notre Dame and London, 1982), pp. 209–25.

Geoffrey Harrison, "Relativism and tolerance" (1976), reprinted in Micael Krausz and Jack W. Meiland (eds), *Relativism Cognitive and Moral* (University of Notre Dame Press, Notre Dame and London, 1982), pp. 229–43.

E. J. Bond, "Could there be a rationally grounded universal morality? (Ethical relativism in Williams, Lovibond, and MacIntyre)," *Journal of Philosophical Research*, 15 (1990), pp. 15–45.

Chapter 3   Subjective Relativism

Although it is a very, very common belief, no philosopher, as far as I know, has argued for subjective relativism in its pure form. Of course, you should read Sartre's "Existentialism is a humanism" (reference in chapter 3, note 1). See also:

D. H. Monro, *Empiricism and Ethics* (Cambridge University Press, Cambridge, 1967), ch. 10. A defence of a kind of subjective relativism.

Chapter 4   Subjectivism and Non-cognitivism

First of all see the references in the notes. In addition, there are the following:

P. H. Nowell-Smith, *Ethics* (Penguin Books, Harmondsworth, 1954). An influential, much-quoted and much-discussed book, presenting a theory that is a blend of emotivism and prescriptivism.

D. H. Monro, *Empiricism and Ethics*, (Cambridge University Press, Cambridge, 1967). An elaborate defence of subjectivism.

J. O. Urmson, *The Emotive Theory of Ethics* (Hutchinson, London, 1968).

Philippa Foot, "Moral arguments" (1958) and "Moral beliefs" (1958–9), both collected in *Virtues and Vices* (Oxford University Press, Oxford, 1979). Important early criticism of non-cognitivism.

Chart summary for part I Moral skepticism:* a comparison

Questions	Psychological egoism	Cultural relativism (simple)	Cultural relativism (sophisticated)	Subjective relativism
1 What is the theory a theory of?	A theory of motivation (a psychological theory, not a moral theory)	A theory about the nature of morality	A theory about the nature of morality	A theory about the nature of morality
2 What is the main thrust of the theory?	All human acts are self-regarding and *could* not be anything else	Morality is entirely a matter of custom, which varies from culture to culture. There are no moral truths	There are genuine moral values but they are real only from within the perspective of a culture or tradition	God is dead and convention is empty so I must create my own authentic morality for myself
3 Does the theory allow for any moral reality (any moral truths?)	Universal ethical egoism is an option (otherwise there is none)	There is no moral reality or moral truth – only various customs, practices, and beliefs	Yes, there is a moral reality but it is *internal to* (true only from within) a culture or tradition	Yes. There is a private or personal moral reality (there are private or personal moral truths)
4 Is there an authority for moral judgments? If so, who or what?	There is no authority. (You don't need an authority to tell you to be as clever as you can at pursuing your own advantage)	One's culture or tradition is *seen from within* as authoritative, but there is no real authority	Yes. The authority is the culture, the tradition, or consensus	Each person, as the creator of his ow her own private morality, is his or her own authority
5 Does this view inevitably lead to moral nihilism and *anomie*?	No. Not if you're happy with it	Yes. No moral beliefs are seen as valid	No. Not if you can accept it	No. Not if you can accept in
6 What is the main flaw in the theory?	It confuses "Every act is done to satisfy some desire of the agent's own", which *is* certain and necessary, with "Every act is done to satisfy a self-regarding desire," which is not	It makes the false assumption that morality consists in following accepted customs and practices	These theorists fail to note that we need not, and often cannot, appeal to a culture or tradition in defending our moral claims	This theory fails to note that morality has a social function which a purely private morality could not have
7 What is the grain of truth in the theory?	There really is no such thing as altruism, if by that is meant selflessness. In acting for the sake of something other than yourself you are still doing what is most important or what matters the most to you	Moral beliefs and practices really do vary from culture to culture (but no moral conclusions can be drawn from that)	These theorists at least recognize that there is a moral reality, even if is a different reality from within each distinct culture or tradition	Conscientiousness really is a virtue, as is being true to yourself

*These are all forms of skepticism that would cast in doubt the possibility of an objective, universal, and non-egoistic morality

Subjectivism	Emotivism	Prescriptivism	Cognitivist anti-realism
A meta-ethical theory: a theory of the meaning and function of moral language (and the language of value in general)	A meta-ethical theory: a theory of the meaning and function of moral language (and of the language of value in general)	A meta-ethical theory: a theory of the meaning and function of moral language (and the language of value in general)	A theory of value, including moral value
Moral judgments are declarations of personal feelings or attitudes. ("Lying is bad" means "I hate lying")	Moral judgments are exclamations (non-statemental expressions) of personal feelings or attitudes. ("Lying is bad" means "lying boo!")	Moral judgments are prescriptions for action based on commitments to principles	No moral beliefs are true (all moral believers are in error). Morality is simply a useful social invention
No. There is no moral reality (there are no moral truths)	No. There is no moral reality (there are no moral truths)	There is a personal morality based on commitments to principles, but there are no moral truths	No. There is no moral reality (there are no moral truths)
No. There is no authority because there is no morality – only feelings and attitudes	No. There is no authority because there is no morality – only feelings and attitudes	I am the authority for my own personal morality, for the commitments to principle that I make	No. Moral beliefs are simply accepted. There is no authority because none of them is true (there is no reality for them refer to)
Yes	Yes	No. Not if you can accept it	No. Not if you can accept the "socially useful invention" story. Otherwise yes
We neither mean nor are we understood to mean to be simply declaring our personal attitudes or feelings when we make moral judgments	We neither mean nor are we understood to mean to be merely shouting or emoting when we use moral language sincerely	We neither mean nor are we understood to mean simply to be expressing our personal commitments to principles when we use moral language	It is impossible to accept that we are simply deluded in having any moral convictions or making any moral claims
In making moral assertions one is also expressing the implicit attitudes that go with the moral beliefs	In making moral assertions one is also expressing the implicit attitudes that go with the moral beliefs	Moral judgments do have a practical aspect (but we do not need prescriptivism to account for this)	There are no non-natural facts

Part II
A Rational Basis for Ethics

5

Practical Reason and Value

We have finished a careful examination of five views which, if we accepted any one of them, would mean either that there could be no morality valid for all humanity regardless of time and place (no universal morality), or no morality that involved ever acting for the sake of other people or the community as a whole (the common good). These five views are (1) psychological egoism, (2) cultural relativism, (3) subjective relativism, (4) subjectivism, and (5) non-cognitivism in both of its forms – emotivism and prescriptivism. There is a danger, however, in simply listing these views, for it might seduce you into thinking that they compete at the same level, which they do not. Unlike all the others, (1) is a theory of *motivation*. According to (2) and (3), there is such a thing as morality, but it is relative. None of the first three has anything to say about language or meaning, but (4) and (5) are meta-ethical doctrines or theories about the nature and function of moral language.

Psychological egoism, if it were true, would mean that it was psychologically impossible to do anything that was not self-regarding, hence impossible to act for the sake of others of the community as a whole. The only ethical theory it would permit would be ethical egoism which, in its simplest form, means trying to get as much as you can for yourself without regard to anyone or anything else, or being clever or smart at pursuing your own interest – understood as your own material wealth, power, status, and pleasure. Even if you have to compromise with others, this would only be because it would be the best deal you could get for yourself. The reason for this is that if psychological egoism were true, you *could* not care about anything besides yourself. But we saw that, as a supposedly necessary truth, psychological egoism failed because what is necessarily true is not that all acts are self-regarding but that all acts are done to satisfy some desire of the person's own, and a person's desire need not be self-regarding simply because it is hers. In simple terms, psychological egoism confuses the owner of the desire and its object. That I must act to satisfy some desire of my own says nothing about the object of that desire, and I may genuinely desire, for instance, the good of another person.

Cultural relativism – the view that morality is entirely relative to culture or tradition – was seen to fail because it is based on a confusion between (a) accepted social practices, or the moral beliefs that are held by those within a particular evaluative perspective or historical tradition, and (b) what actually is good or bad, right or wrong. In considering whether something is good or bad, right or wrong, we may, and often do, as we discovered in chapter 2, appeal to considerations not based on what is accepted within our own culture or tradition, and without simply adopting the moral perspective of some other culture or tradition. Accepted or traditional practices can be queried or questioned, and on moral grounds.

According to subjective relativism, it is up to each individual to make up or create his or her own morality, and since any self-made morality is valid for the person whose creation it is, it is to be respected by others. This fails because in judging something to be right or wrong, good or bad, I judge it to be right or wrong, good or bad, period, and I must judge others by the same standards by which I judge myself. I cannot, therefore, respect other people's opinions when they differ from my own. Morality can only be understood as being for everybody, at least for everybody here and now. Sartre recognized this fact, which got him into serious conflict with the subjective relativism he also wished to advocate (see chapter 3, pp. 53–54). "It's morally right for me if I think it's morally right" may cash out as "Follow your conscience," but while conscientiousness is a virtue, conscience can still be mistaken. (There is such a thing as erring conscience.) That conscience is not infallible is shown by the fact that I may change my mind on a moral question, perhaps regretting something I once did in good conscience, in which case I can only believe that I was mistaken in my original judgment. The temptation is to change tack and switch from "It's right for me if I sincerely believe it's right" to "It's right for me if I think it's right for me." This makes some sense if we are talking about personal tastes and preferences ("personal values"), but it seems to be outside the realm of morality altogether. "It's morally right for me if I think it's morally right for me" seems to make no sense at all and that is for the reason that (as Sartre recognized) I cannot think that something is *morally* right but *only for me* (see chapter 3, pp. 55–57).

Let us turn now to the meta-ethical theories: the theories about the meaning of moral words and sentences and the nature and function of moral language. These are subjectivism and both kinds of non-cognitivism (emotivism and prescriptivism). The trouble with all of them is that they could only be true if people both meant and understood by their moral thoughts and spoken words to be declaring their personal attitudes (subjectivism), or expressing them in some other way (emotivism), or issuing prescriptions for action (prescriptivism), and nothing more. But it is quite clear that this is not what people mean and understand by their moral thoughts and utterances even though being for or against something (which has implications for action), really is implied in having a moral view. That we are for or against a thing, however, is *explained* by the fact that we think that it is good or bad, right or wrong (see chapter 4, pp. 78, 86). Indeed, it is impossible to think something good or bad, right or wrong, and not for that reason be for or against it. When people make moral judgments, of whatever kind, they mean to be referring to some universal moral reality (stating some objective moral truth) and that is how they are understood (see chapter 4, pp. 70–71, 78).

We have now thoroughly reviewed the failings of the five theories we examined in part I. But, as has already been pointed out (chapter 3, p. 60; chapter 4, pp. 72, 87), even if these criticisms succeed, we will not yet have shown that there are any moral truths and hence that there is a moral reality. But if there are no moral truths and hence no moral reality, this could only mean that everyone who sincerely uses moral language is deluded. According to the English philosopher J. L. Mackie, this is true. They are deluded. He believed that ethics and value in general are nothing but useful social inventions, useful because they make it easier for us to live together in harmony. According to Mackie, non-cognitivism is false as a theory of moral language; in making value judgments, including moral judgments, people *do* intend to refer to an objective realm of real values. But since such a realm could not possibly exist – according to Mackie it is an absurd fiction – all sincere value judgments are mistaken. He called his view the "error theory of value."[1] This is a form of the cognitivist anti-realism that we considered as a postscript to our examinations of subjectivism (chapter 4, pp. 71–72), and of emotivism (chapter 4, p. 78).

Needless to say, Mackie's claim has serious implications. If we believe, as he does, that there are no moral truths because there is no moral reality (of any kind) for our moral judgments to refer to, we have only two choices: (1) we may believe that people, no matter what they think they mean or how they are understood, are really only emoting or otherwise expressing their personal attitudes or commitments; or (2) we may, with Mackie, believe that thinking and acting as if there were a moral reality – a game of "Let's pretend" – is just a useful social invention. Neither of these choices seems satisfactory, so we are left asking whether, after all, there could be objective moral truths and therefore *in some sense* a universal moral reality. This is the question we must now investigate.

Fact and Value

A serious threat to the possibility of there being objective moral truths and hence a universal moral reality, is the so-called "fact/value distinction." This is the belief that whereas factual claims can be objectively true (facts exist), value judgments, including moral judgments, however they might be arrived at, cannot. The fact/value distinction is standardly appealed to by the non-cognitivists (beliefs *v.* attitudes, truths about the world *v.* commitments to principle) and implicitly by cognitivist anti-realists like Mackie, and so we must deal with it now. (We must remember that non-cognitivism, too, is a form of anti-realism; if the non-cognitivist analysis of moral language – in either of its forms – is right, there is no objective moral reality, and the claim that there is and could be no objective moral reality is precisely what anti-realism is.)

As it was latched on to by the non-cognitivists, the fact/value distinction is this. Facts, if they are genuine facts – how things are, or what is so – must be objectively determinable either by observation or experiment (empirical verification) or some other related means. (Here are some facts: 49.4 percent of the voters in the referendum held in the Canadian Province of Quebec on October 30, 1995 voted in favor of separation from the rest of Canada. Today is Tuesday. Birds do not have teeth.) Facts, as such, it is said, are *value-neutral*. What makes value judgments distinct from facts, the non-cognitivists say, is that they are not objectively determinable in the way that facts are, and this is *for the reason that* they contain an emotive or imperative or gerundive element which (a) a real fact does not contain and (b) which is irreducibly subjective or personal. (Some typical value judgments are: "this is a good car." "Patience is an important virtue." "What that man did was wicked in the extreme.") Thus, according to the non-cognitivists, "Patience is an important virtue" either expresses an attitude of favor or approval or admiration toward patience or a commitment to patience as a guide to conduct, something which a simple statement of fact could not possibly do. Whereas facts are objectively true, value judgments all contain an unavoidably subjective element of attitude or commitment. (Cognitivist anti-realists like Mackie would say that since there is and could be no realm of objective values to refer to, value judgments could not possibly state facts, and therefore some other account of them must be given.)

Not all schools of thought, however, subscribe to the fact/value distinction. It is possible to hold the view that there *are* truths involving value and that they are just a kind of empirically verifiable fact. This is called *naturalism* (see chapter 4, note 5). It is also possible to hold – G. E. Moore is an example as we shall soon see – that in addition to *natural* facts, there are *non-natural* facts. The view that there is a non-natural realm of values or, in philosophers" jargon, that values are non-natural objects, properties, or relations, is often *called* "moral realism." Anti-realists of the non-cognitivist variety like to say that we have two choices: either value judgments contain an element (emotive, imperative, gerundive) which is unavoidably subjective, or they refer to a non-natural realm of values, and no one could seriously believe *that*. (The third possibility – naturalism – is excluded.) Cognitivist anti-realists like Mackie also say that we have two choices: either value language, including moral language, refers to a "queer" non-natural realm of values, or value is an invention that serves a useful social purpose. (Again, naturalism is excluded.)

The important thing to note is that what is being said in both of these cases is: you must be either a realist or an anti-realist, and realism, defined as the belief in a non-natural realm of values, is not a serious option. The position that will be argued for in this chapter is that yes, value judgments may be determinably true or false, but this does not imply any reference to a "queer" non-natural realm of values. Furthermore, to understand this point it is only necessary to have a clear understanding of what value is. If by "fact" is meant "empirically verifiable fact", then to claim that value judgments are facts would be to advocate naturalism, to which there really are overwhelming objections. To extend this sense of the word "fact" to include non-natural facts is obviously of no help. But by "fact" we can mean simply any truth, of whatever kind ("It's a fact that you acted very badly yesterday; there's no getting away from that") and I shall be arguing that moral truths are a species of fact in this broad sense. This is an alternative – other than naturalism – to the two choices offered by either kind of anti-realist. *It is realist in the sense that it claims there are objective moral truths and falsehoods, and in that sense a universal moral reality, but it is not realist in the sense of claiming that value judgments refer to a non-natural realm of values.* If this argument succeeds, it will have been shown that, at least in one sense of the word "fact" (i.e. "anything that is true"), there is no fact/value distinction. But now we must get on with our detailed examination of the issue.

The non-cognitivists made much of something called the "naturalistic fallacy." As they saw it, this consisted in treating value judgments as if they were factual claims, failing to notice what they regarded as the hard and fast distinction between the two. The expression "naturalistic fallacy," however, originated with the early twentieth-century English philosopher G. E. Moore, who claimed that good (the quality or property supposedly denoted by the adjective "good") was a simple, unanalyzable, non-natural property, the nature of which could not be understood in terms of any natural property (such as being pleasant, or conducive to happiness, for instance). For Moore, this meant the same thing as saying that the *word* "good" is indefinable. Any attempt to define the word was, according to Moore, to commit the naturalistic fallacy.[2]

Moore made his case very persuasive with what is called the open-question argument: whatever we declare good to be, other than simply itself, we can always legitimately ask the question "Is that good?" Thus if we try to say that a thing's being good is the very same thing as its being conducive to happiness, for instance, or that the word "good' means the same as the phrase "conducing to happiness" (Moore made no distinction between these two), we fail, for it still makes sense to ask the question "Is what conduces to happiness really good?" or, as Moore would understand this, "Does what conduces to happiness really possess the property of being good?" This is what is meant by saying that the question is still open, and it obviously could not still be open (still sensibly askable) if being good and being conducive to happiness really were the very same thing or if the word "good" and the phrase "conducive to happiness" had the very same meaning. To make the point absolutely clear, consider this example. A duckling *just is* a baby duck. Agreed? Furthermore, the correct definition of the word "duckling" is "baby duck." This being understood, it would *make no sense* to go on to ask the question "Is a duckling really a baby duck?" Or, in Moore's terms, the question would no longer be open. The question, however, whether something is really good always is open (always makes sense). Therefore, Moore says, we cannot say that good (the property denoted by the word "good") is identical to any other property, or that the word "good" can be defined in other terms, which, Moore thinks, could only be naturalistic terms.[3]

Now, if we were to offer a definition of the word "good" in terms of some natural property or properties (see note 2) such as "pleasant" or "conducive to happiness," for instance, this would make value judgments (at least in principle) empirically verifiable and hence in no way distinguishable from ordinary, value-neutral observable facts (naturalism) (see chapter 4, pp. 85–6). This genuinely is unacceptable because it would leave out the gerundive implications (something to be done or not to be done) of value judgments, as well as their implicit expression of attitude, both of which we have seen (chapter 4, p. 74) to be really there. Moore, however, was not at all concerned with the gerundive implications or the implicit expression of attitude in value judgments; in fact, he thought that if something was good, that was a *non-natural* fact (the possession of the non-natural property of goodness), something which could only be *objectively true* (not subjective in the least). He therefore was not concerned with the fact/value distinction as we presently understand it, the claimed existence of which is used by the non-cognitivists to argue for the irreducible *subjectivity* of value judgments (chapter 4, pp. 86–7), and the existence of which cognitivist anti-realists like Mackie take to be implied by the *impossibility* of there being any non-natural facts.

The fact/value distinction, as we know it, is traced back to the eighteenth-century Scottish philosopher David Hume who claimed, famously, that one could not derive an "ought" from an "is."[4] This has been treated by twentieth-century philosophers as meaning that one cannot *logically* derive an "ought" from an "is," or that no "ought" conclusion can follow logically from "is" premises. Hume did notice the gerundive implications of value judgments, and believed that, because of those implications (something is to be done or not to be done), value judgments had to be tied to some object of desire. (Remember how, in our examination of psychological egoism in chapter 1, we saw that, necessarily, every act of every person is done to satisfy some desire of that person.) Thus, according to Hume, I cannot sincerely say "I ought to do x" (believe that I ought to do x) unless I want to do x for its own sake or doing x will achieve something else I desire. And no one can believe that they ought to do x (which implies that x is something they are to do) unless either they want to do it or doing it will bring about (or help to bring about) some other end they desire. Otherwise, he thought, we could not account for the fact that, if accepted, value judgments, in particular ought judgments, had the power to motivate action. (It is true that if we believe we ought to do something and hence see it as a thing to be done, we will have *some* motivation, hence some desire to do it, even if that desire can be overcome by some stronger opposing desire. If there were *no* motivational power in a judgment that we ought to do something, such judgments, since they are supposed to lead to action, could have no point.) The belief that sincere value judgments must be tied to something already desired or wanted is called *internalism*. The belief that they are independent of desire, but can still motivate, is called *externalism*.

The similarity between Hume's internalism and the non-cognitivism we have examined (chapter 4) is not difficult to see. The non-cognitivists, in order to account for the ability of sincere value judgments to motivate, and the fact that they seem not to be empirically verifiable, argued that value judgments (including moral judgments) constituted non-statemental expressions of personal attitudes or commitments (together with an invitation to share those attitudes or commitments). To have such an attitude or to have made such a commitment clearly implies (because some motivation exists) that something is wanted (to be done or not to be done, to have or not to have, to exist or not to exist), at least at the time the judgment is made. Hume seemed to think that a moral judgment must be tied to something already wanted, whereas non-cognitivism, at least the prescriptivist variety, seems to leave open the possibility that the want or desire comes into being *at the same time as* the judgment. But we may still call non-cognitivism an internalist view because it plainly implies that the element of desire (necessary for motivation) is contained within the sincerely held judgment itself (because of its practical import). Hume was not a non-cognitivist for he did not deny that moral utterances were genuine statements, or even that they could be true or false, but the support given to non-cognitivism by Hume's view is not difficult to see.

Now we have agreed with the non-cognitivists that value judgments (including moral judgments) do express attitudes or commitments, that they do, whether directly or indirectly, have implications for action (see chapter 4, p. 86). We have only denied, what the non-cognitivist claims, that this is the *only* function of moral sentences, that this is what they *mean*. Instead, we have offered the view that if someone sincerely says or believes that something is good or bad, right or wrong, or that something ought or ought not to be done (even if these specific words are not used), they do approve or disapprove of it, or they are committed to some principle of action, and that is precisely *because* they believe the thing to be good or bad, or that it ought or ought not to be done, etc. (see chapter 4, pp. 78, 86). Yes, value judgments (including moral judgments) do carry with them an attitude of approval or disapproval or a commitment to principle. But, as we have seen, that is easily understood without resort to the claim that this is what moral sentences mean (that this is their function), or that, because they express attitudes or commitments, they contain an element of subjectivity that cannot be eliminated.

To illustrate this point, suppose, just for the sake of argument, that telling lies simply for the sake of personal advantage and without any other justification or excuse, really were morally wrong. If this were true – in which case it would be universally applicable (chapter 3, pp. 53–4, 55, 57–9; chapter 4, p. 87) – and I *recognized* its truth, I would have a negative attitude (con attitude, attitude of disapproval) toward it and be committed to the principle that one ought not to tell lies simply for the sake of personal advantage. What this shows is that, in order to account for the attitudes and implications for action implied in moral judgments, we do not need to claim that they do not come to *anything more* than having (and possibly expressing) these attitudes or making or having made these commitments to principle. Notice I am not claiming here and now that lying without justification or excuse really is wrong, I am only saying that *if* it were wrong *and* we recognized it, the attitudes and the implications for action would be there, and that we do not need to resort to subjectivism or non-cognitivism in order to account for them. We would have those attitudes and our value judgments (including moral judgments) would have implications for action *even if value judgments were genuine statements that were objectively either true or false*.

Still these attitudes and these implications for action would not be there if all value judgments (including moral judgments) were reducible to ordinary, empirically verifiable or falsifiable statements of fact (naturalism), which would be one way of avoiding the fact/value distinction. They are not that. Moore's "open question" argument does work against all forms of naturalism, not because (as Moore thought) "good" is an unanalyzable non-natural property, but rather because the practical (gerundive) and attitudinal import of value judgments is simply eliminated in any naturalistic account. Moore's non-naturalism does not help here, for it no more accounts for the attitudinal and gerundive (practical import – to be done or not to be done) implications of value judgments (including moral judgments) than a naturalist account of value does. It is because of the inescapable attitudinal (approval, disapproval) and gerundive (to be done, not to be done) implications of moral judgments that naturalism fails, not, as Moore alleges, because goodness is a non-natural property. Still this does not, as we have just seen, force us to say that value judgments are *merely* attitudinal and gerundive, and therefore irrevocably subjective. They would have these implications even if they were genuine statements that were either objectively true or objectively false, or, to put the same thing in philosophers' jargon, even if they had a truth-value.

This understanding of the matter is the key to the solution of the internalism/externalism question (see above). Internalism claims, you will remember, that since there can be no action without motivation and no motivation without desire (we may call this "Hume's principle"), you cannot sincerely assent to an ought judgment, which has implications for action, unless you have some desire to do the thing you have concluded you ought to do. Externalism, on the other hand, claims that the truth of ought judgments is objective and cognizable, and therefore independent of any desires you may now happen to have. The solution seems to be this. If you come to understand, after deliberation, that you ought to do something, then that recognition, *because of* its practical or gerundive implications, *creates* a desire to do the thing in question. In this way externalism and internalism are reconciled. (This point should become clearer after our examination of value and reasons for choice in the next section.)

What are we now able to conclude about the fact/value distinction and its importance to the issue of whether value judgments can be objectively true? First of all, we must recognize that naturalism is false because it does not account for the gerundive or attitudinal implications in value judgments, including moral judgments. Value judgments, then, are not simply statements of empirically verifiable facts such as, for instance, "The sun will set at 7.30 p.m. tonight" or "George is wearing a red shirt," facts that in themselves have no attitudinal or gerundive implications. In this sense there is a fact/value distinction. But the fact that value judgments do, as value judgments, have attitudinal and (direct or indirect) gerundive implications (to be done, to be had, to be kept or preserved, not to be done, to be avoided or prevented, to be eliminated), does *not* imply, as the non-cognitivists claim, that their validity is dependent upon purely personal or subjective attitudes and commitments, and hence that they are not real statements and so cannot be objectively true or false. We have not been given sufficient reason to believe that a fact/value distinction claimed on this basis exists. Value judgments could be genuine statements, capable of being objectively true or false (of having a truth-value), and still carry attitudinal and gerundive implications. Moral truths, as expressed in moral value judgments, would then be a species of fact, though not of the purely empirical or, for that matter, the non-natural kind. (Remember, "fact" can mean "anything capable of being true or false.") The value element, which straightforwardly empirical statements lack, would lie precisely in those attitudinal and gerundive implications.

If we can make out a case for the existence of moral (and other evaluative) truths and falsehoods, then the fact/value distinction of the non-cognitivists and (implicitly) of Mackie, a distinction which would exclude the possibility of moral truth and objectivity, will have been eliminated. All that will remain will be a harmless distinction between statements which do and statements which do not have gerundive or attitudinal implications. It has been claimed in this chapter (p. 103) that the meaning of the word "fact" need not be restricted to what is in principle empirically verifiable, or verifiable by intuition (as Moore claimed non-natural facts to be). In observing that "fact" can be taken to mean simply "anything that is true," we will have at least disarmed the fact/value distinction as a weapon against the possibility of there being objective moral truths *provided we can show how moral claims can be made out or rationally justified.* If we succeed in showing, as will be attempted in the rest of this chapter and in chapter 6, that there are moral truths, and how they can be known to be true, we will thereby have succeeded (in accordance with this broad definition of "fact") in showing that there are moral facts. We may for the present, therefore, set the fact/value distinction aside (see figure 5.1) and turn to the question of what can ground or justify value judgments, including moral judgments, or show them to be true.

I am going to argue that value judgments, including moral judgments, when they are true, are *grounded in, or justified by, practical reason.* (You don't need to worry now about what that means. It will be made clear in what follows.) Since moral judgments are a species of value judgment, we can only get at what makes *them* true by considering the question of what makes *any* value judgment true, and since non-moral value judgments are easier to handle, we should begin there. If we can determine what it is that makes a non-moral value judgment true, especially in the context of decision-making, then we can look at moral judgments and see how they fit the pattern, if indeed they do.

VALUE JUDGMENTS
(including moral judgments)
e.g. "She is a good teacher"
e.g. "Lying is wrong"

No FACT/VALUE distinction
(value judgments are objectively "true" or "false")

FACT/VALUE distinction
(used to argue for the subjectivity of value judgments)

Naturalism

Argument
1 Value judgments that are true are simply empirical facts. They can be verified by observation, experiment, or measurement. They are objectively true or false.

Weakness
2 Naturalism is false because it does not account for the gerundive or attitudinal implications in value judgments, including moral judgments. "Lying is wrong" is not a simple statement of an empirically verifiable fact like "The sun will set at 7.30 tonight."

The non-naturalists (Moore)

Argument
1 Moore used his "open question" argument to defeat naturalism and its claim that there is *no fact/value distinction*.
2 He did not himself introduce a fact/value distinction as one would have expected. Instead, Moore said value (goodness) belongs to a *non-natural realm* (transcending nature) so that *truths of value are a species of "non-natural" fact*.

Weakness
3 We do not need to invent a non-natural realm for values to belong to. Moore's argument for this realm is not convincing.

The non-cognitivists

Argument
1 A distinction must be made between empirical facts and values. Value judgments have attitudinal and gerundive implications. Straightforward empirical statements do not.
2 The validity of value judgments (including moral judgments) must be dependent on *personal and subjective* attitudes. *Value judgments cannot be objectively true* – unlike empirical facts.

Weaknesses
3 The non-cognitivists are wrong in thinking that empirical facts (verifiable by measurement or observation) are the only kind of facts. This assumption leads them to state that value judgments must be *subjective* because empirical facts (which they believe to be the only objective facts) do not and cannot have attitudinal and gerundive implications. They overlook the possibility that there might be a kind of fact that *has* gerundive or attitudinal implications.

The cognitivist anti-realists (Mackie)

Argument
1 A distinction must be made between empirical facts and values. Value judgments, which are not empirically verifiable, are intended to refer to a non-natural ("queer") realm of values. They are supposed to be a funny, non-empirical kind of fact. But this, says Mackie, is absurd. These alleged facts are mere inventions (pretend facts) and their purpose social control. These pretend facts cannot be objectively true. Mackie mocks the whole idea that value judgments could be objectively true.
2 The belief, for example, that lying is wrong, may if accepted, be useful for social control, but it cannot, like an ordinary factual belief, be true or false.

A new look at the fact/value distinction

Argument
1 *Empirical facts are not the only kind of facts. By "fact" we can mean any one of the following:
   (a) empirical facts: anything which is empirically verifiable, and for that reason capable of being objectively true. This sense of the word may be extended to include:
   (b) non-natural facts: facts which belong to a non-natural realm (Moore/non-naturalism) and are supposed to be objectively true. However "fact" can mean:
   (c) "anything that is objectively true."
2 Moral truths, expressed in moral judgments like "Lying is wrong", are facts in the sense of (c) above. They *are* facts – though *not of the empirical kind*. These facts are not verified by observation or measurement but are *justified by practical reason*.

Conclusion
There is no fact/value, distinction when "fact" means "anything capable of being objectively true." Thus, value *judgments* such as "Lying is wrong" can have *an objective and universal validity*.

Figure 5.1 The fact/value distinction as it relates to the objectivity or subjectivity of moral judgments

Reasons for Choice

Practical reason is concerned with reasons for choice (reasons for choosing a certain course of action), and so everything turns on our understanding of exactly what a reason for choice is. Let us look at the question of reasons supporting ought judgments in the hope that it may get us where we want to go. A reason supporting an ought judgment *is* a reason for choice. This is how we move from thought to action in our lives, and it explains the practical import or gerundive aspect of ought judgments, leaving aside other kinds of value judgments for the moment. What is a reason for choice? The following is clear. To say that one ought to (or should) do, or have something, or try to be or to become a person of a certain kind, is to say that there is a reason or that there are reasons for doing it or having it, or for trying to be or to become that kind of person. To say that one ought not to (or should not) do something, or have it, or be or become (if one can avoid it) a person of a certain kind, is to say that there is a reason or that there are reasons for not doing it or having it, or for not being or becoming that kind of person. In both cases one must be able to specify precisely what that reason is. Thus:

1   "You really ought to see that play." "Why?" "you would really enjoy it and you do need to get out of the house once in a while."
2   "I really shouldn't have such a big house." "Why, if you like it?" "The upkeep is just too expensive and trying to keep it clean wears me out."

The conclusion in (2) is that I should sell it and get something smaller, even though I have a reason for keeping it, namely that I like it. It is important to notice that *any* reason for (or against) a certain course of action (or inaction) implies that one ought (or ought not) to do it, *other things being equal*. Thus if I liked the house and there were no reasons against keeping it (in this case if I could afford the upkeep and get some help in keeping it clean), I could only conclude that I should keep it, which would mean that keeping it (not selling it) was the thing to do. But in the present case other things are not equal (I cannot afford it and it is too much work), and so the final, practical ought judgment – the judgment arrived at after weighing and balancing the reasons for and against – is that I ought to sell it and get something smaller.

When is there a reason for choosing or not choosing a certain course of action (or inaction)? The obvious answer is that there is something of value or worth to be gained from that choice, or something bad or undesirable (something of negative value) to be avoided, prevented, or eliminated. And if there is *sufficient* reason for choice, leading to the conclusion that *this*, of all the courses of action open to me, is the one I should choose, this means that, all things considered, there is more value to be gained (or less to be lost) by this course of action than by any other that is open to me. Ought judgments, then, are supported by reasons, reasons for choice, and to give the reason is to specify the value to be gained by the choice in question. This applies to general, other-things-being-equal ought judgments, as well as final, all-things-considered ought judgments. In both cases, given that the reasons are genuine reasons (the values genuine values, i.e. the ends to be achieved genuinely worthwhile) and, in the case of final ought judgments, that everything has been taken into account and the balance-sheet correctly drawn up, we can say that the judgment is *grounded in reason*. In the case of final ought judgments, we can say that the judgment and hence the choice (if we follow reason and make that choice) is *fully justified*.

Notice that we are speaking here of *practical* reason, or reasons for choice, as distinct from *theoretical* reason, or logic, where conclusions *follow logically* from premises. In logic, given that one accepts the premises, one must accept the conclusion on pain of contradiction. As an example of theoretical reason, consider the following. "All men are mortal. Socrates is a man. Therefore Socrates is mortal." A piece of practical reasoning, by contrast, might run as follows. "It would be a lot of fun, and there's no reason why I shouldn't do it, so I'm crazy if I don't" (i.e. I ought to do it, or I'm irrational if I don't). Here we cannot speak of a conclusion following logically from premises. Rather, we say that this choice is justified because there is more to be gained and less to be lost by this course of action than by any other course of action open to me. Grounding in (justification by) practical reason is quite distinct from grounding in (justification by) theoretical reason, and the two must not be confused. Thus, what is being argued here does *not* commit the version of the naturalistic fallacy (pp. 104–5 above) which claims that an ought judgment, which is a practical judgment, can *follow logically* from non-practical premises.

Notice that in none of the examples so far introduced are the reasons for or the reasons against a choice or course of action *moral* reasons. (The reasons for: "You would enjoy it," "You need to get out once in a while," "I like it," "It would be fun." The reasons against: "I can't afford the upkeep," "Keeping it clean tires me out and takes up too much of my time.") Thus the ought judgments in these examples are not moral ought judgments. Since reasons for choice are tied to value or worth achievable by action (or inaction), we can say that the values in question, whether the positive values of pleasure (enjoyment), new experience (novelty and excitement), and simple liking (finding agreeable), or the negative values (disvalues) of boredom, depression, drudgery, and poverty, are not moral values. Thus not all reasons for choice are moral reasons, not all ought judgments are moral ought judgments, and not all values justifying choice are moral values. This is an important point that is often overlooked. And there is something else that should not be overlooked: the positive values are all contributions to the well-being (happiness) of the person whose choice it is, and all the negative values are contributions to his or her ill-being (unhappiness).

It is time to consider some moral examples for a change, and here are three:

1   "You really ought not to do it." "Why not?" "You promised you wouldn't."
2   "I really ought to do something for him." "Why?" "It's only fair, after all he's done for me."
3   "You should stop doing that." "Why?" "It is cruel and unnecessary. You are simply being a brute."

The same analysis applies as before. These are ought judgments implying that there are reasons for doing or not doing the thing in question. This in turn implies that there are values to be gained, or not to be lost, values important enough to determine choice. The question "Why?" is legitimate and the maker of the judgments must be able to state what he or she believes to be the reasons for or against. It is simply that in the case of moral ought judgments, the reasons upon which these judgments rest must be moral reasons and the values to be gained (or not lost) moral values. Notice that such things as "It would be kind," "It would be generous," "It would be the courageous thing to do," are standardly offered as moral reasons for doing a thing, and such things as "It would be cruel", "It would be brutal," "It would be unfair," "It would cause needless offence," are standardly offered as moral reasons against doing something.

Now, what are we to say about these values, both moral and non-moral? And remember, we are concerned with values achievable by action and choice. Consider: if I am persuaded by someone whose opinion I trust that I really would enjoy the play, and I really do need (to avoid depression) to get out of the house once in a while, and there are no reasons against, such as lack of money, or having previous commitments, or not being able to afford the time, or not having anyone to go with and never enjoying things when I go by myself, then (assuming tickets are still available on an evening I am free), I *really do* have sufficient reason for going and I *really ought*, all things considered, to go. In other words, it is really *true* that I should go, or it is a *fact* that I should go. This *is* the right thing for me to do.[5] Is this because I have an attitude of favor toward acting this way in these circumstances (emotivism), or because I am personally committed to some principle or other (prescriptivism)? No. It is because doing what one enjoys doing (pleasure) really has value, and depression is a bad thing, a thing to be avoided or overcome. Is this bit of practical reasoning valid only for me, because of my personal attitudes or commitments? No. It is clearly valid for anyone in the same circumstances and this is how I understand it. *It is objectively determinable by an appeal to practical reason that I should go and that anyone in the same circumstances should do the same thing.* And what I say here applies equally to the second non-moral example. (You can work it out for yourself.)

What we learn from these examples is that value or worth or desirability is not, in an important sense, something purely subjective (something that exists only for me). Although different people find different things enjoyable, pleasure or enjoyment in activities or experiences is a good or a value for everyone, even if we sometimes ought not to do what we would enjoy the most, because there are other, over-riding reasons for not doing it or for doing something else. (It might be injurious to myself, for instance, or it might cause hurt to others.) And similarly, even though different people like different things, everyone should keep what they like if they have no reason for giving it up. Again, things like not having enough money, or enough time, or being over-burdened, or being depressed, are bad things, and provide universal reasons against making certain choices.

This is an important point, and so we must be clear about it here, although it is taken up again at the beginning of the next chapter. Consider what we called in chapter 3 (pp. 56–8) personal preferences. These do (obviously vary from individual to individual. I like one thing and you like another. I like period furniture; you like modern furniture. I like my hair long; you like your hair short. You like the south; I prefer the north. You prefer marriage and children; I prefer the single life. You are homosexual; I am heterosexual. And so on and so forth, endlessly. It is clear that, in an important sense, these values are personal and subjective. *Yet having, getting, and doing what one likes, or finds agreeable, or to one's taste, is, as such (hence objectively), a universal value – a good for everyone. And similarly having, getting, and doing what one finds unpleasant or disagreeable, what one hates or radically dislikes, is, in itself (hence objectively), an evil (a bad thing) for everyone. Pleasure or enjoyment in things (objects, experiences, activities) is one of the universal human goods, just as unpleasantness is one of the universal human evils.* (For other universal human goods see chapter 4 and chapter 6, p. 119.)

We are now at the point where we must ask the question just what value is, in particular value achievable by action and choice (which is the kind of value that concerns us here), and the answer should be clear. *It is that which is worth having, getting, or doing, or, on the negative side, what it is desirable to avoid, prevent, or eliminate.* This is not a matter of purely personal or subjective attitude or commitment. (Do I just happen to have a favorable attitude toward doing what I enjoy doing?) Things (such as the pleasant and the unpleasant) just are desirable or undesirable as the case may be, as contributions either to my well-being or my ill-being, and it is difficult to see, at least in cases such as these, how this desirability or undesirability could fail to be recognized, with attitudes and commitments following accordingly (e.g. do what you enjoy doing if you can and there is no over-riding reason against). *That my thriving, flourishing, or happiness is a good for me and yours a good for you does not need to be argued for. Nor is there any need to postulate any queer, non-natural objects, properties, or relations to account for the objective reality of these values or of the values dependent on them.*

Let us look at the moral examples. If "you promised you wouldn't" is a reason against doing something, that can only be because promise-keeping is a genuine value, and if "it would be cruel and unfair" is a reason against doing something, that can only be because cruelty and unfairness are bad or undesirable things. And similarly for brutality and causing needless offence. Now in the non-moral examples given above, and other non-moral cases, e.g. "You ought to wear your winter coat today because it's really nippy and if you don't you'll be cold and you might catch something" (values: health and comfort), the reasons can hardly help but be recognized as reasons, it being perfectly clear that the values appealed to are genuine values, and hence that the ought judgments based on them are objectively true. But on moral values, as we all know, there are seemingly unresolvable disagreements, so we are not going to have the same clear sailing that we had in the non-moral cases we looked at.

Let us take a brief preliminary look at the difficult question of moral reasons now. We have eliminated moral relativism of both kinds, cultural and subjective (chapters 2 and 3), so there is no falling back on those. We can therefore only conclude that either there is a valid universal morality (as our understanding of moral language implies) or there is no morality at all. We have no choice, then, but to try to show that there really are valid moral reasons for choice and, in order to do this, we must make an attempt to show what it is that makes them reasons. In other words, we must try to present an acceptable moral theory. And if we succeed, we will have shown that there is a universal morality grounded in reason. To say that morality is grounded in reason (rationally grounded) – and remember it is practical reason we are talking about, not theoretical reason – is simply to claim that genuine moral reasons do exist. This, as we have just seen, comes to the same thing as saying that *there are genuine moral values – things that are both plainly moral and genuinely desirable, hence worthy of anyone's choice.* Furthermore, if morality is not grounded in reason, this means simply that there are no moral reasons, and that can only be because there are no genuine moral values. If that is true we can just forget about morality.

Finally, in order to claim that there are genuine moral values, there is no more need to postulate their real existence in a funny, non-natural realm than there is to suppose that real existence in such a realm is required for there to be non-moral values. We need only show that there are genuine moral ends that really are worth our pursuing, possessing, or preserving. *If we can make out a case for this, then we will have shown that there is such a thing as objective moral truth and, in that sense, that there is a universal moral reality.* That is what will be attempted in the next chapter.

SUMMARY

1   The three meta-ethical theories that we examined in chapter 4 seek to show, by the analysis of moral language, that moral utterances contain an unavoidable element of *subjectivity*, which makes it impossible for them to be objectively true or false.

2   We have seen that all of these analyses fail, but one might *still* try to claim that moral utterances were unavoidably subjective, or at least that they were not capable of being true or false. This is cognitivist anti-realism, and its chief exponent is J. L. Mackie. Mackie holds that moral language means just what it appears to mean, and that its users are attempting to assert objective moral truths. But, he says, since there are not and could not be any objective moral truths, users of moral language are under some sort of delusion. There could not be any objective values, and that includes moral values. Mackie called his theory "the error theory of value."

3   Mackie believed that there could not be any objective moral truths because this would imply the existence of a "queer" realm of objective values outside the natural world. We will have to show that the belief in objective moral truths and *in that sense* an objective moral reality does not imply any such foolish belief.

4   Anti-realists, both non-cognitivist and cognitivist, make much of something rather confusingly called "the fact/value distinction." This is basically the claim that there can be no logical inference from fact to value. It takes two main forms – the so-called "naturalistic fallacy" and the "is/ought" distinction.

5   Talk of naturalistic fallacy began with G. E. Moore, who claimed that "good" was a unique and unanalyzable non-natural property. (Obviously Mackie would have no truck with him.) Moore claimed, on the basis of the so-called "open question" argument, that "good" could not be defined: whatever we define good to be, the question "Is that really good?" always stays open, which it could not do if our definition were correct. Moore believed that any offered definition of "good" would have to be in terms of some *natural* property or properties. This is the view he called "naturalism" and naturalism would include any theory that treated moral truths as facts about the natural world.

6   Now the open question argument really does defeat all forms of natural-
     ism, but Moore's claim that "good" is a simple, unanalyzable non-
     natural property (non-naturalism) is of no help. This is partly because it
     is hard to believe in the existence of any non-natural property, but also
     because what distinguishes value judgments from value-neutral state-
     ments of fact is precisely, as the non-cognitivists pointed out, the attitu-
     dinal and practical (gerundive) implications that value judgments have
     and that value-neutral factual statements do not have. If there really is
     a fact/value distinction, this would have to be its basis.

7   The "is/ought" distinction goes back to David Hume (in the eighteenth
     century), who claimed that one could not logically derive an "ought"
     from an "is." This was because ought judgments have implications for
     action and therefore must, as Hume saw it, be tied to desires. (The view
     that moral judgments are necessarily tied to desires is called *internalism*.)

8   We have agreed with the non-cognitivists that value judgments, includ-
     ing moral judgments, do have both attitudinal and gerundive (practical)
     implications. But we also saw that this, in itself, did not prevent them
     from being statements that were objectively true or false. If by "fact" we
     mean simply "anything that is true," and if we could show that value
     judgments, including moral judgments can be true, then the fact/value
     distinction would be disarmed as an argument for a necessarily subjec-
     tive element in value judgments, including moral judgments. We would
     be left with a harmless distinction between facts which do and facts
     which do not have attitudinal and gerundive implications.

9   What is claimed in this chapter is that ought judgments, to which we are
     willing to give priority of place, are supported by *practical reason*.
     Theoretical reason moves logically from premises to conclusions, but
     practical reason is based on *values that can be achieved by action and
     choice*.

10   To say that one ought to do something is to say that there is a *reason* for
     choosing that course of action, which in turn means that there is some-
     thing of value to be gained (or not to be lost) by doing it.

11   All non-moral ought judgments can be seen to be justified in terms of
     certain universal values (values for any and every person) to be gained,
     all of which contribute to an individual's thriving, flourishing, happiness,
     or well-being.

12   If there is such a thing as an objective and universal morality, then we
     must be able to show that there are genuine moral values and that they
     provide genuine reasons for action; in other words, we must be able to
     show that moral judgments, like other value judgments, are *grounded in
     practical reason*. If we can do this, and especially if we can show
     that moral ought judgments are ultimately grounded in a single all-

embracing value, as non-moral ought judgments are grounded in the single all-embracing value of personal well-being, then morality will also be shown to be grounded in practical reason. This is what it would mean to say that morality has a rational foundation.

QUESTIONS FOR THOUGHT

1   "Value judgments are purely personal. They cannot, therefore, be objectively true or false." How would you respond to someone who said this?

2   "Value judgments could not possibly be objectively true, for this would imply that there there were 'queer' non-natural properties such as 'good' and 'wrong,' which obviously there could not be." The truth and objectivity of value judgments does not imply any such thing. Why?

3   How are we to understand ought judgments (practical judgments)? How can they be justified?

4   What would or could it mean to say that morality was grounded in reason?

6
Moral Value

In chapter 5 we established the following.

1   To say that one ought (or ought not) to do something, or to say that one should (or should not) do it, is to say that there is a *reason* for (or against) doing it, a reason that can always be spelled out.
2   To give the reason is to specify the *value* (thing of worth) that is to be gained (or preserved) by the choice in question.
3   In non-moral cases, genuine values are values tied to the well-being of the chooser.
4   Where the value is a genuine value, the ought judgment is rationally grounded, hence objectively true.

(These four points apply to other-things-being-equal as well as all-things-considered ought judgments: whenever there is *a* reason for a certain course of action, then one ought to take that course of action unless there is some over-riding reason why one should not. In the case of final or all-things-considered ought judgments, given that we have taken all reasons, both for and against, into account, we may say that there is *sufficient* reason for choosing a certain course of action, that this choice is fully justified. It is *true* or a *fact* that *this*, all things considered, is what we ought to do here and now.) These four points show us how ought judgments, which are a species of value judgment, are *grounded in practical reason*. Our task in this chapter will be to consider how *moral* ought judgments (and other moral judgments) might also be grounded in practical reason, and in order to do this we must examine the question of what a *moral value* might be.

We have seen that the non-moral values (things of worth) achievable by action or choice are, in an important sense, not subjective. For they are not, as the non-cognitivists claim, a function of the attitudes that one just happens to have or the commitments that one just happens to have made. (These values include the avoidance, prevention, or elimination of things that are bad, as well as the doing, getting, having, keeping, and preserving of things that are good.) Because of individual differences, personal preferences vary from person to person, and one style of life may be best for one person but not for another. Nevertheless, the value of thriving, flourishing, or happiness (in the sense of well-being) is a good for everyone. This state of being and the things that make it possible or otherwise contribute to it – health, protection from the elements, comfort, security, prosperity (material well-being), pleasure (if it is not harmful to oneself or to others), achievement, recognition, self-esteem, friendship, love and affection, etc. – are values for everyone (universal values). I do not just *happen* to like *these* things or mysteriously have a pro-attitude toward them. They are actual goods (good things) for me just as they are goods for everyone else, and this does not need to be argued for. Equally their absence or their opposites are evils for everyone (universal evils).

You might think that personal preferences (likes and dislikes), and pleasure/unpleasantness (the enjoyment or finding disagreeable of various activities and experiences), because these vary from individual to individual, are an exception to this universality of value. But even here we can say that liking and disliking (no matter what we happen to like or dislike) and pleasure or unpleasantness (no matter what we happen to enjoy doing or experiencing, or find unpleasant or disagreeable) are objective values, positive or negative, for everyone (universal values). (These may be called *hedonic* values, after the Greek word for pleasure. The word *hedonism* is used for the doctrine that hedonic values – positive and negative – are the only values there are.)[1]

We can say, then, that the non-moral values attainable by choice are all related to one thing – the thriving, flourishing, happiness, or well-being of the person whose choice it is. The ancient Greeks had a name for this state of being. They called it *eudaimonia*. (We shall be using this term often.) This is the all-embracing value to which every non-moral value contributes. But what of *moral* values? What, if anything, makes them genuine values? If there are no such values – and to be values for us they must be worth *our* pursuing – we can forget about morality. If there are genuine moral values, how do we explain their exist ence? These are the questions we must now consider.

Eudaimonia (Well-being)

All non-moral values of the kind that are worth a person's having, getting, or doing, are related to that person's thriving, flourishing, happiness, or well-being (*eudaimonia*).[2] In purely abstract terms, x is a value for A if and only if x is a contribution to A's *eudaimonia*. Notice that it is not because a person *wants* a thing that it is a value for him or her. One can want something desperately yet be disappointed or even damaged when one gets it. The famous nineteenth-century English writer, Oscar Wilde, who was known for his wit, is reported to have said: "Life contains two kinds of serious disappointment: the first kind is not getting what you want and the second kind is – getting it." Desiring or wanting is necessary to motivate, but it cannot be the source of value. No more can one, by an act of will, decide to value something or, as the saying has it, "place a value on it." (Some recent philosophers have even adapted the economic term "valorize" to signify the non-existent and impossible act of making something valuable by willing it to be so.)[3] We do not *place* a value on something, we *find* it valuable, or we are in some other way persuaded of its value – maybe Mommy or Daddy told us it was valuable – and thus we value it. We can only value a thing if, for some reason, we believe it to be valuable or worthwhile, and if we do believe it to be valuable or worthwhile (desirable), then we value it. (Thus a good definition of "to value," in this sense, would be "to believe valuable.")[4]

So much, then, for the non-moral values that determine what courses of action we ought to choose. We may conclude that they are all contributions to the *eudaimonia* of the chooser. And what of moral values? We already know (chapter 5, pp. 113–14) that these, like all values attainable by choice, must be things worth having, getting, or doing, or, on the negative side, what it is desirable to avoid, prevent, or eliminate. Let us go back and consider the things that we said in chapter 5 were typically offered as *moral* reasons for or against a particular course of action:

1　Q: "Why not?" *A*: "You promised you wouldn't."
2　Q: "Why?" *A*: "It's only fair."
3　Q: "Why not?" *A*: "It is cruel and unnecessary."
4　Q: "Why not?" *A*: "It would cause needless offence."
5　Q: "Why?" *A*: "It would be kind of you."
6　Q: "Why?" *A*: "It would be generous of you."
7　Q: "Why?" *A*: "It would be the courageous thing to do."

We already know (chapter 5, pp. 110–11) that all *reasons* for or against a particular course of action stem from *values* (things worth having, etc.) to be gained or not lost, and the reasons given in these examples, since they are *moral reasons*, can only be related – if they really are reasons to *moral values* (chapter 5, p. 112). We saw that non-moral values achievable by action and choice are all tied to the *eudaimonia* (thriving, flourishing, happiness, well-being) of the chooser. If there really are moral values, then their (a) each one of them is an independent value in its own right; or (b) they too, like non-moral values, are tied to some one all-embracing value. If this were so, and we could determine what that value was, we would have the foundation of a moral theory. It is time now to examine these possibilities.

The Basis of Moral Values

Notice first that if values of any kind are to provide reasons for *me*, they must be worth *my* having, getting, or doing. There was no problem where non-moral values were concerned, for we saw that these were all tied to my own happiness or well-being (*eudaimonia*). But what are offered as moral reasons do not relate in the same obvious way to my own *eudaimonia*. Indeed, most of them seem to have more to do with the good of others or with the social good in general. Let us look once more at the examples in the paragraph above of things that are typically offered as moral reasons, and let us ask, for each example, first what the value in question might be, and second what, if anything, makes it a value for everyone, myself included.

(1) "You promised you wouldn't." The value here, if it is a genuine value, is the value of keeping promises made. In other words, it is the value of doing what we have solemnly agreed to do, thereby leading the person with whom we made the agreement to count on us to do it. Well, supposing we don't keep our promise, what are the consequences? To begin with, the person to whom we made the promise is let down by us and, unless we have a real justification or excuse which the other person can acknowledge, any *trust* there may have been between us is destroyed. Perhaps we don't care, although we may, if the relationship is one that matters to us. But if promise-breaking without justification or excuse is, in its own right, something not to be done, then promise-keeping must be a value to be honored whether we care or not in a particular case. So the value in question (the value of promise-keeping) cannot relate exclusively to *my own* happiness or well-being (*eudaimonia*).

Let us look more closely at promise-keeping as a moral value. Suppose that no one ever honored his or her promises made if it was to his personal disadvantage to do so. The result would be a general breakdown of trust, and trust is something that is absolutely necessary (not merely desirable) if we are to *live together* in peace, amity, cooperation, and good will, with a minimum of adversarial conflict − a state of affairs that is desirable for *everybody*. I cannot will that *others* be allowed to break their promises whenever they think it is to their advantage because (a) I might be the one who is let down, and (b) this would be a cause of social breakdown where everyone is a loser. Furthermore, if *I* were to break my promises whenever it was to my personal disadvantage to keep them, I would be contributing, however slightly, to that breakdown.

How then can I make an exception in my own case? Or, to put it another way, how can I claim a moral *right* for myself if I am not prepared to grant the same right to other people? How can I say that I am allowed to break my promises if it is to my personal advantage to do so, while denying that others have the right to do the same? Moral language, we must remember, is universal in its import (see chapter 3, pp. 53–4, 55, 57–59; chapter 4, p. 87; chapter 5, p. 106). Of course, I could declare myself to be *amoral*, denying that there is such a thing as morality, hence denying that there is such a thing as a moral right (a position that would force me to give up the sincere use of moral language). But if there is such a thing as a moral right, the right to break my promises when it is to my advantage to do so cannot be one of them.

What, then, makes promise-keeping a value (something worthwhile) for everyone? The answer is as follows. A good social environment is desirable for everyone and I must do my part in maintaining it, even if it is to my immediate advantage to let down another person who has trusted me, which would contribute (in however small a way) to social breakdown. Remember that the well-being of society, or the community, is an essential part of the well-being of each individual member. This does not mean that the reason I have for keeping my promises – a moral reason based on a moral value – is egoistic. It is not. In understanding why the reason is a reason I am not thinking only of my own purely personal good – if I were I would break my promise if it were to my immediate advantage – I am thinking (a) of the other person (who could, on another occasion, be me) and (b) of the importance for everybody, including myself, of having and keeping good social relations. That is why being trustworthy, or honest, is honorable and hence admirable and good. And if you recognize this fact, you will judge both others and yourself accordingly. You will also recognize that honesty (trustworthiness) is a higher value, even for you, than your immediate advantage, and therefore that there is no ultimate self-sacrifice or self-denial in being honest and trustworthy. The same reasoning that we applied here to promise-keeping (not breaking promises) can also be applied to the honesty-related values of not telling lies[5] and not stealing or cheating unless you have a justification or excuse that others could acknowledge. I will leave you to work out the case for these other honesty-related values on your own.

(2) "It's only fair." This must be handled quite differently. In our example (chapter 5, p. 112), it is only fair that I do something for him because he has done an awful lot for me. This is not simply a case of tit for tat or "I'll scratch your back if you scratch mine," which would merely be an exchange of favors, the first being a deposit in the favor-bank and the second its withdrawal. In the tit-for-tat sort of case I do you a favor on the *understanding* that you will return it when you can. It may be unspoken, but I make it plain

that I am putting myself out for you, and so I expect that when I call for it, you will put yourself out for me. Thus we will both profit. If you don't return the favor when I call for it, you have broken an explicit or implicit agreement. I suffer a net loss and I have a genuine grievance against you. This is what is called breach of contract. It is very much like breaking a promise and it can be handled in the same way. In this sort of case I would not do the favor unless I expected a favor in return, and we would not normally, in such cases, speak of *unfairness* if the favor is not returned, although we might describe not returning the favor – something we had explicitly or implicitly agreed to do – as *unjust*. But in our example ("It's only fair") we are entitled to assume that the favors have been freely given and that the recipient is not expecting or demanding a favor in return. Perhaps it was done out of simple kindness, but I think (and so, perhaps, do you) that I should show my gratitude to the other person by doing something for him. This would not be a favor *returned* as a contractual obligation, but again one freely granted. He has been kind to me, so it is *only fair* that I should be kind to him.

Why is his having been kind to me a moral reason for my being kind to him? What does it mean to say that not being kind to him would be unfair? He has treated me well so I should treat him well. Don't you agree? But why is this? What is the value to be gained (or not lost) *for me*? It is certainly not that it profits me personally; in fact it profits *him*. Indeed, *my* profiting him by doing him a kindness is the whole point of it. It is, after all (if it is a reason at all) a moral reason, and hence the value (if there is one) a moral value. Well, we can say, he has been kind to me, so he *deserves* my kindness. (Fairness and justice are very closely related.)

There are three things here. First, because he deserves my kindness it would be unfair of me if I did not show kindness to him. Secondly, not to show him kindness would be ungrateful. Finally, kindness is in itself a good thing, for it contributes to our living together happily, and is therefore to be encouraged. If I am not kind to those who have been kind to me, this will, because it is unfair and ungrateful, cause resentment, which would tend to inhibit further kindnesses, not just to myself, but to other people. It is better to live in a society or a community (the family included) where people are kind and considerate to one another. Kindness should therefore be met with kindness, in the common interest. But this is mainly about kindness – kindness breeding kindness, which is a shared good. The offered reason in our example, however, was "It's only fair."

Let us take another example of unfairness. You have taken your turn and you are about to take another one. "No," I say, "it's my turn." "Tough," you say. "But that's unfair," I say. And it is unfair, as I'm sure you will agree. "Unfair," like "brutal" and "bully" (chapter 2, p. 27), is already a moral term and so, if we use it sincerely, we are already committed to making moral judgments. Unfairness is a negative moral value (something to be shunned, prevented, or eliminated). But there really is such a thing as unfairness. Didn't you just agree? So morality exists. But what is it about unfairness that makes it a negative moral value and hence a reason against doing something? The answer is plainly that it interferes with friendly relations and creates adversarial competition and conflict, something that is bad for everybody – bad for the community and therefore bad for me as a member of it. Again, the common good is part of the good of each and every individual member of the community, and if we don't show concern for it everybody suffers, including ourselves. This does not mean that we should only show concern for the community, the common good, out of concern for ourselves; we should show concern for the community for its own sake. This means going beyond narrow self-interest, yet in acting for the common good we do benefit ourselves, for the good community is good to live in and the bad community, full of adversarial conflict, is bad, with everyone at risk. That is why being concerned for the community and acting accordingly is good and honorable, while having no concern for the community (caring only about ourselves) is ignoble and bad. Perhaps we can now see why.

(3) "It is cruel and unnecessary." Here a reason has been given to prevent or stop an action. Two things: someone suffers but for no good reason, and you are the willing cause. This is bad for the person who suffers (with no compensating good) and it reflects badly on you. I will think ill of you as heartless and so will anyone else who knows what is going on. "Cruel," like "brutal," "bully" and "unfair," is a moral term – a term of condemnation. To say cruelty is bad is redundant, for cruelty itself is a negative moral value (something to be shunned, avoided, or prevented, and on moral grounds). Do you believe that there is such a thing as cruelty? If you do you are committed to the making of moral judgments. But what makes cruelty a negative moral value? First of all, it is built into the concept of cruelty that someone, perhaps more than one, suffers as a consequence, and suffering is an evil for the sufferer. Furthermore, cruelty breeds cruelty, hatred, resentment, and adversarial conflict. It is therefore a social evil, contributing to a bad situation for everybody, for it brings on the continuing lust for vengeance (getting even), and perhaps wars and ethnic hatreds extending indefinitely into the future. (Think of Ireland, the former Yugoslavia, or the Middle East.) It is therefore in everyone's interest not to be cruel, to discourage acts of cruelty, and to prevent them, if possible, regardless of the momentary joy that may be found in doing harm to those whom one hates. That is why an act's being cruel is a moral reason against doing it. That is why the disposition (tendency) to be cruel, which is reinforced by every act of cruelty, is an aspect or dimension of character that is ignoble (a vice), and to be discouraged or expunged.

We have established that cruelty is a negative value for everyone, something to be avoided or shunned, and so we have dealt with "cruel." What about "unnecessary?" Well, to begin with, it is clear that if something is done because it is necessary and for no other reason, it cannot at the same time be cruel. I may have to inflict an evil on a person to prevent a greater evil, as when I hit someone hard to save him from drowning, or to put an end to a fit of hysterics, or when I justifiably punish him. But such acts are not cruel; they hurt, but they are necessary. I need not and normally do not *want* to hurt the person, as I do when I am cruel, but I have to hurt him in order to save him from something worse, or to prevent some greater evil for others. Of course, if I do want to hurt him, that is an exhibition of the disposition to be cruel regardless of the evil I am preventing, and that, as such, is to be condemned.

(4) "It would cause needless offence." As in the previous example, this is offered as a reason for *not* doing something. An offence is a bad thing – a hurt – for the person offended. But if causing needless offence is a moral reason against doing something, then it must be bad for the offender as well, a thing which he must be able to see as not to be done and which, if he does do it, reflects unfavorably on his character. Why is this so? Before we attempt to answer this question we should look at the word "needless." It is quite impossible to go through life without innocently offending other people, often unavoidably. Many people take offence easily and there is nothing we can do about it. The evil of the offence given is often less than the measures that would have to be taken in order to prevent it (perhaps not saying something that should be said). But sometimes the offence is avoidable and at no cost, in which case it is to be avoided. Why? Because it is causing an unnecessary evil, which is not only bad for the sufferer, but leads (once more) to resentment, bad feeling, and adversarial conflict, and that is (once more) a social evil which everyone has reason to avoid. Need any more be said?

(5) "It would be kind of you." This is another example, like (1) and (2), in which a reason is offered *for* doing something. We talked about kindness under (2), where we talked about meeting kindness with kindness. But now we must talk about simply being kind – performing acts of kindness and being disposed to be kind, not necessarily in response to the kindness of another. It has already been said that kindness is a good thing because it contributes to our living together happily, and that it is therefore to be encouraged. The reference was, of course, to *being* kind, but while a kind act is normally a benefit to the *receiver* of the kindness, we must argue, if we are to show that kindness is a moral value and hence that being kind is a moral reason for choice, that it is a value for the *giver* of the kindness as well as for the receiver. Why do we have reason to be kind? Sometimes kindness is inappropriate; we may have to be harsh (within limits) when we are combating evil, or when

we are embattled and have to defend ourselves. But harshness is antagonistic and, for that reason, undesirable if it is not necessary. Not to be kind is not necessarily to be harsh or unkind, but it is to be cold and uncaring, to shut people out, and that is a source of misery. Furthermore, in a cold and uncaring social atmosphere people are isolated, lonely, and tend to be hostile to one another, which is once again a social evil from which everybody suffers. Kindness, apart from creating good feeling for both the giver and receiver, tends to create social harmony, friendliness, and good social relations generally, which benefits everyone. That is why everyone has reason to be kind and to cultivate kindness, and because kindness is directed to others, it is a moral reason for choice. This also explains why a kind or kindly disposition, or aspect of character, is praised and a cold one disdained. It explains, in other words, why to possess a warm and kindly disposition is a virtue.

(6) "It would be generous of you." Once more this is offered as a reason *for* doing something. An act of generosity, too, creates good feeling for both giver and receiver. Generosity also tends to create good social relations generally and, for that reason, is to be encouraged, for everyone benefits. The stingy person may, as she sees it, be looking out for herself, but lack of generosity has a tendency to produce adversarial competition, isolation, and bad feeling which, if it is widespread, creates a bad social atmosphere for everybody. Fortunately (in the one case), and unfortunately (in the other), both generosity and stinginess, like kindness and coldness, are contagious, each act of generosity and each refusal to give tending to produce more of the same. The stingy person in the land of the generous receives a net material gain, the generous person in the land of the stingy a net material loss. So, if others are stingy, I will be stingy too, and if others are generous that will encourage me to be generous. And which is the happier land, the land of the generous or the land of the stingy? Where would you prefer to live? I leave you to answer that one for yourself. Generosity is clearly a virtue (to be admired and encouraged), stinginess clearly a vice (to be deplored and discouraged). Of course, in the land of the stingy you have to be stingy and otherwise unfriendly if not downright hostile in order to survive, but can't we all agree that this is an unhappy state of affairs, one to be overcome if possible?

(7) "It would be the courageous thing to do." This is a little different. We admire courage and we are contemptuous of cowardice. In fact, "brave" and "cowardly" are already moral terms. It is easier to run away from danger, or the unpleasant, than to face it, even if it means abandoning the pursuit of an obvious good. But this is also an obvious weakness, and to run away habitually from danger or unpleasantness, even if it needs to be faced, is a weakness of character. Because there are often dangers and things which are unpleasant to be faced, we need a courageous disposition, both to achieve our own ends,

and to be able to do what is morally required of us. That is why cowardice is a weakness or a vice and why courage is a strength or a virtue. And we need not only our own courage but the courage of others as well; their cowardice can be the cause of our suffering. Courage, and some other virtues, such as self-discipline, are directly beneficial to the possessor, as well as to others who may be affected by her choices. Thus, anyone has an immediate reason of personal benefit to be able to show courage when it is called for. This personal benefit is in addition to the benefit it gives to others who may, on some occasions, depend upon our choices for their well-being. This benefit to others is what makes the cultivation of courage (like the other virtues we have been considering) a contribution to the common good, to be cultivated for the sake of that good, which is a good for everybody.

Conclusion

We have only examined a small selection of things standardly offered as *moral reasons* for choice, but it should be enough to allow us to draw some important conclusions. *Non-moral* reasons are directly tied to values related to the happiness, well-being, or *eudaimonia* of the person who is making the choice. *Moral* reasons are characteristically tied to values related to the well-being or *eudaimonia* of the community or society as a whole. Moral values are necessary for the establishment and maintenance of good social relations, a good that is of value to everybody. Moral reasons are reasons for the person making the choice because a good community, constituted by good social relations, is an essential part of the personal good (*eudaimonia*) of each and every individual member. That is because we are social creatures by nature, living in mutual dependence, and we are better off as cooperating and contributing members of a community or communities, where friendliness, willing mutual support, and good feeling prevail, than we are as mere individuals, each isolated and in competition with others for the goods of the world. Given our social nature, and the reality of our social relations, we cannot achieve *eudaimonia*, the fulfillment of our own individual natures, all on our own, but only as participating members of a good community. It is therefore in the interests of anyone and everyone to ensure that such a community, with its good social relations, so necessary for happiness, come into being and be sustained.

In acknowledging the existence of moral reasons, and acting for the sake of moral values, we are not acting for our exclusively individual or personal self-interest; if we were all doing this we would be in perpetual competition with one another, something that leads inevitably to hostility and adversarial conflict, a bad thing which *everyone* has reason to avoid. Rather, by being good members of the community or communities to which we belong, we are acting for the common good, a good which is of profound importance for our own personal well-being. This may mean abandoning the perpetual quest for power, status, wealth, and leisure time for the pursuit of pleasure (and for more of these than others), a quest which is unavoidable when every individual is acting in competition with others for his or her own exclusive self-interest. (This is a competition that is certain to become adversarial.) In acting morally, I may well be acting for the sake of others, but in doing so I am acting in a way that will help to preserve or sustain the common good or the good of the community, as constituted by good social relations. In the absence of this good, I am essentially in isolation and unable to achieve true individual self-fulfillment, which is something that, because of my social nature, I can only achieve as a participating member of a good community, one where good social relations prevail.

The source of *all* value, then, both non-moral and moral, is *eudaimonia*. By this is understood flourishing, thriving, well-being, or happiness, whether through what has personal value for an individual, or through the common good or the good of the community or communities to which she or he belongs (moral value). And what, indeed, could give us reasons for choice, other than some connection with *eudaimonia* (thriving, flourishing, well-being)? I think you will see, on reflection, that the answer is: nothing whatever. Thus it is only by connecting moral value with *eudaimonia*, which is what we have just attempted – in outline – to do, that it is possible to show that morality has a grounding in reason (which here, of course, means *practical* reason). The spelling out of a substantive moral theory (an account of what morality is, what ends it serves, and how it may be justified or grounded) will be the business of parts III and IV.

SUMMARY

1   All the non-moral values that are worth a person's having, getting, or doing, are related to that person's thriving, flourishing, happiness, or well-being, which we shall call, after the Greeks, *eudaimonia*.

2   We want to show that morality is grounded in practical reason. Because reasons for choice are tied to values achievable by action, if there really are *moral* reasons, they must be tied to *moral* values achievable by action.

3   If values of any kind are to provide reasons for *me*, they must be worth *my* having, getting, or doing. Non-moral values were no difficulty here, since they were seen to be tied to *my own* happiness or well-being (*eudaimonia*). But moral values seem to be tied to the good of others or to the social good in general. How, then, can they be values *for me*?

4   Looking at some things typically offered as moral reasons, we discover that the values in question usually relate to the good of the community as a whole, or what we may call the *common good*.

5   Moral reasons, tied to moral values, are *values for everybody*, because the common good is part of the good of every individual member of the community. This is because of our inherently social nature. It is impossible to achieve real personal *eudaimonia*, real self-fulfillment, except in the context of a good community.

6   Moral reasons are not egoistic, but they are not altruistic either, since we all share in the common good.

7   The source of *all* value, then, is *eudaimonia*. By this is understood flourishing, thriving, well-being, or happiness, whether through what has personal value for an individual, or through the common good, the good of the community or communities to which he or she belongs.

8   Reflection shows that nothing else but *eudaimonia* could be the ultimate grounding for ought judgments. Nothing else could be the ultimate source of reasons for choice. It is only by connecting moral values with *eudaimonia* that it is possible to show that morality has a foundation in reason, which here must be understood as *practical* reason.

QUESTIONS FOR THOUGHT

1   If a moral value is to provide *me* with a reason for action, then it must be a reason *for me*. How is this possible? Does that mean it must be of direct benefit to me?

2   *Eudaimonia* (thriving, flourishing, well-being, happiness) has been described as the all-embracing value. Could anything else provide the ultimate ground for action and choice? Explain.

3   How might we justify a moral claim (e.g. "One ought to keep one's promises" or "Kindness is a genuine virtue")?

4   "In addition to purely personal goods there is a *common* good." Do you agree? What is the importance of this for morality?

Recommended Reading

The Fact/Value Distinction

There is a great deal written on the fact/value distinction. For the primary source of the "naturalistic fallacy" and of non-naturalism, you should read the first chapter of Moore's *Principia Ethica* (reference in chapter 5, note 1). Have fun! For the primary source of the "is/ought" distinction, you should first have a look at Hume (reference in chapter 5, note 2). Also:

W. K. Frankena, "The naturalistic fallacy" (1939), reprinted in J. Margolis (ed.), *Contemporary Ethical Theory* (Random House, New York, 1966), pp. 141–56.

John Searle, "How to derive 'ought' from 'is'," *Philosophical Review*, 73 (1964), pp. 43–58.

Alan Gewirth, "The 'is-ought' problem resolved," *Proceedings and Addresses of the American Philosophical Association*, 47 (1974), pp. 34–61.

W. D. Hudson (ed.), *The Is/Ought Question* (MacMillan, London, 1969).

E. J. Bond, *Reason and Value* (Cambridge University Press, Cambridge, 1983), pp. 93–5.

Internalism and Externalism

David Hume, *A Treatise of Human Nature* (1737–40), book II, part 3, s. 3, and book III, part 1, s. 1.

W. D. Falk, "Ought and motivation" (1947–8), reprinted in W. D. Falk, *Ought, Reasons, and Morality* (Cornell University Press, Ithaca, NY, 1986). This is where the term "internalism" is first introduced.

W. K. Frankena, "Obligation and motivation in recent moral philosophy," in A. I. Melden (ed.), *Essays in Moral Philosophy* (University of Washington Press, Seattle, 1958). Frankena considers the internalism/externalism debate, pointing out the merits and demerits of each position, without coming down firmly on either side.

Thomas Nagel, *The Possibility of Altruism* (Oxford University Press, Oxford, 1970), pp. 7–14. Nagel advocates an internalist position.

Bernard Williams, "Internal and external reasons" (1979), reprinted in Bernard Williams, *Moral Luck* (Cambridge University Press, Cambridge, 1981).

E. J. Bond, *Reason and Value* (Cambridge University Press, Cambridge, 1983), ch. 2 ("Motivating reasons and grounding reasons'), and ch. 4 ("Objective value: I").

Practical Reason

Aristotle, *Nicomachean Ethics*, book VI.

Stephen Nathanson, *The Ideal of Rationality* (Open Court, Chicago, Ill., 1994). A thorough and first-rate examination, with plenty of references.

Joseph Raz (ed.), *Practical Reasoning* (Oxford University Press, Oxford, 1978).

Douglas N. Walton, "Practical reason[ing]," in Lawrence C. Becker (ed.), *Encyclopedia of Ethics* (Garland Publishing, New York and London, 1992), pp. 1000–2.

Philippa Foot, "Morality as a system of hypothetical imperatives" (1972), reprinted (with additional material) in Philippa Foot, *Virtues and Vices* (Blackwell, Oxford, 1978), pp. 157–72. In this widely read paper, Foot argues that moral reasons are *not*, as such, reasons for everybody.

Realism and Anti-realism in Ethics and the Theory of Value

Moral realism is essentially the view that there are moral truths or moral facts, and that moral knowledge is possible. It is therefore always cognitivist in its meta-ethics, although one can be a cognitivist without being a realist (e.g. Mackie). Moral realism can take a number of forms. It can be either naturalist or non-naturalist, or in the case of Bond (see reference below), neither. Non-cognitivist anti-realism has been taken care of in chapter 4, and readings on that subject appear in the Recommended Reading for that chapter.

J. L. Mackie, *Ethics: Inventing Right and Wrong* (Penguin Books, Harmondsworth, 1977). The strongest statement of the cognitivist anti-realist position, and the origin of much current controversy.

Ted Honderich (ed.), *Morality and Objectivity: a Tribute to J. L. Mackie* (Routledge, London, 1985). A collection of essays, most of them critical of Mackie.

Mark Platts, *Ways of Meaning: an Introduction to a Philosophy of Language* (Routledge, London, 1980), ch. 10 ("Moral reality").

S. W. Blackburn, "Moral realism," in John Casey (ed.), *Morality and Moral Reasoning* (Methuen, London, 1971), pp. 101–24.

John McDowell, "Virtue and reason," *The Monist*, 62 (1979), pp. 331–50.

Peter Railton, "Moral realism," *Philosophical Review*, 95 (1986), pp. 163–207.

Jonathan Lear, "Moral objectivity," in S. C. Brown (ed.), *Objectivity and Cultural Divergence* (Cambridge University Press, Cambridge, 1984), pp. 135–70.

E. J. Bond, *Reason and Value* (Cambridge University Press, Cambridge, 1983), ch. 5 ("Objective value: II").

Part III
What Morality Is

7

Three Different Approaches to Ethics

We have seen that moral values, and hence moral reasons, are tied to the common, social, or communal good, which is a good for everyone and a necessary part of the *eudaimonia* (thriving, flourishing) and self-fulfillment of each individual person with his or her own unique nature. This has, as promised, shown the rational grounding of morality, which is a grounding in *practical* reason, and thus has given us the foundation for a moral theory.

In the examples we considered, we saw that there were two kinds of moral reason:

1 Reasons for or against a particular kind of *action* as such; for example, promise-keeping and causing needless offence.
2 Reasons for or against having a certain *disposition of character* (being a person of a certain disposition or tendency); for example, honesty or dishonesty, courage or cowardice (being an honest or a courageous person and not being a dishonest or a cowardly one).

The first kind of reason determines that an act is morally required or morally obligatory (e.g. promise-keeping), unless there is some excuse or justification for not doing it that others can accept, or that it is morally wrong or morally required not to do (e.g. causing needless offence) unless there is some excuse or justification that others can accept (which there cannot be in the case of causing *needless* offence) for doing it. The second kind of reason is a reason for developing, preserving, and encouraging a certain morally desirable state or disposition of character, or for discouraging, preventing the development of, or attempting to get rid of, a certain morally undesirable state or disposition of character, both in oneself and in others. The desirability or undesirability which makes these reasons genuine reasons is, for both kinds, the social good

or the social evil of the acts (morally required or morally wrong) or dispositions (desirable or undesirable) in question. This includes the breeding and
reinforcing of good by good and of evil by evil, and it is, in every case, a
contribution to the well-being (*eudaimonia*) or ill-being (including misery and
suffering) of all the members of a community *as* members of that community
and having the ties that that involves.

It is time now to begin the spelling out of a substantive moral theory that
was promised at the end of chapter 6. Remember that a substantive moral
theory is an account of what morality is, what ends it serves, and how it may
be justified. We must begin by observing that there are three different ways
of looking at morality, ways that are quite different. Two of these ways of
viewing morality are familiar to all of us, even if we need to have our
attention drawn to the differences. These two ways have already been hinted
at in chapter 6 and the paragraph above, but now it is time to come clean.
(The third way will be considered briefly at the end of this chapter and
examined in detail in chapter 12.)

Two Aspects or Dimensions of Morality

I am going to present the view that these two ways of viewing morality, often
seen as rival conceptions of what morality is, are really two different *aspects* or
dimensions of morality. There is first of all that aspect or dimension concerned
with the moral requirement to do certain things and not to do others, which
I shall call the *deontic* aspect of morality, after the Greek word for duty. The
second aspect or dimension is that concerned with the states or dispositions of
character that are desirable or undesirable, strong or weak, admirable or
contemptible, noble or base (ignoble). I shall call this the *aretaic* dimension,
after the Greek word for virtue or excellence. In the first case (deontic), we
speak of the moral requirement to perform *acts* of a certain kind and not to
perform others; and in the second case we speak of the aspects of character in
respect of which a *person* is morally good or morally bad (admirable on the
one hand, despicable or contemptible on the other). The admirable aspects of
character are called *virtues*; the despicable or contemptible aspects of character
are called *vices*. Deontic moral judgments are judgments on acts (as wrong,
obligatory, or permissible); aretaic judgments are judgments on people, in
respect of their having a certain disposition of character (virtue or vice). Either
kind of judgment may be general, as "Promises should be kept" or "Courage
is a virtue," or particular, as in "You broke your promise" or "That was a
cowardly act." In short, the deontic dimension of morality is concerned with
the avoidance of wrongdoing (whether by doing something or failing to do
something), while the aretaic dimension is concerned with goodness or
badness of character.

Prior to the late eighteenth century, when Kant published his *Groundwork for the Metaphysics of Morals* (1785), philosophical ethics dealt with morality almost exclusively in aretaic terms. This philosophical tradition began with Plato (*c*.430–347 BC) and his pupil Aristotle (384–322 BC), both of whom spoke exclusively in terms of virtues and vices. This was true even of Kant's immediate predecessor, Hume, the third part of whose *A Treatise of Human Nature* ("Of morals") appeared in 1740, and whose *Enquiry Concerning the Principles of Morals* appeared in 1751. Kant's approach to ethics, however, was exclusively deontic – he said that the only thing that had moral worth was obeying the moral law because it was the moral law – and his influence was overwhelming, not only with philosophers, but with people generally. (You will still find people who think that morality is exclusively concerned with whether acts are right or wrong.) It is only recently that philosophers and, through their influence, non-philosophers, have taken up once more the aretaic (virtue) approach to ethics.[1]

Aretaic *v.* Deontic Morality

I have just spoken of *approaches* to ethics, but it really does seem plain that the deontic and the aretaic are two different *aspects* or *dimensions* of morality, the existence of which emerged naturally in our examination of moral reasons and the values to which they are attached (chapter 6, pp. 121–7). Still, Plato, Aristotle, and their successors considered morality exclusively in terms of virtues and vices, while Kant and those who succeeded him (until very recent times) considered morality exclusively in terms of duty, obligation, or moral require-ment (right and wrong). This is what justifies us in calling the aretaic and the deontic different approaches to ethics. Furthermore, in recent times, many have argued either that the aretaic can be understood in terms of, or eliminated in favor of, the deontic, or that the deontic can be understood in terms of, or eliminated in favor of, the aretaic. We must ask now whether either of these things is possible, or whether, in fact, an adequate moral theory must take account of both, attempting neither to eliminate one dimension in favor of the other, nor to explain the aretaic in terms of the deontic or vice versa.

We shall begin with a reminder. The deontic dimension is concerned with the avoidance of wrongdoing whether by doing something understood to be morally wrong (e.g. causing needless hurt) or failing to do something under-stood to be morally required (e.g. aiding the distressed when our help is needed). The aretaic dimension, by contrast, is concerned with the qualities of character that are admirable or deplorable, strong or weak, noble or base (ignoble) – the qualities of character in respect of which a man or a woman is thought to be praiseworthy (e.g. courage, honesty) or to be despised (e.g. laziness, selfishness).

The first thing to be noticed is that the model or paradigm for deontic morality is *law*, the idea of moral law, as distinct from positive law (the law of the land) originating for our culture in the moral (as distinct from ritualistic) component of the Biblical Law of Moses, which was said to have been given to him by God. I am referring to the last five of the Ten Commandments (Exodus 20: 13–17), and the moral laws in the book of Leviticus (Leviticus 19: 9–18).[2] Side by side with the aretaic tradition, there existed, at least from the time of Cicero (106–43 BC), the tradition of what is called "natural law." Cicero was inspired to invent this term by the Greek Stoics' (third and second centuries BC) notion of virtue as the wisdom of following the order of a rational nature. (He saw natural law as the moral foundation of Roman law.) The idea was notably taken up by (St) Thomas Aquinas (ca.1225–74), one of the most important philosophers of the Middle Ages and a major influence on the Roman Catholicism of today. Thomas, being profoundly influenced by Aristotle, related (or attempted to relate) the idea of natural law to that of virtue and vice or, in other words, he saw the deontic as an aspect of the aretaic. In any case, the notion of moral requirement to do or not to do certain things (deontic morality) owes its origin, in our culture, first to the recognizably moral parts of the Law of Moses, and second to the natural law tradition.

We must never forget the fact that the key to the idea of moral require-ment (or obligation) to do certain things, and not to do others, is the idea of law from which it derives. This is to be found – obviously – in the notion of a moral *code* (a deontic concept), which might contain such items as "Never tell lies" and "Always keep your promises." Ordinarily, law implies some authority – the lawgiver – and Thomas Aquinas saw natural law as part of Divine law, although he also said that it was available to natural human reason, even that of a pagan. But Cicero, and also Kant, who was strongly influenced by Cicero, saw reason itself as the lawgiver – there was no other authority – and this accords nicely with what was said in chapter 3 (pp. 51–2).

Let us take a further look at the notion of a moral code, which we could call the simplest form deontic morality can take. This is nothing but a set of do's and dont's: you must always do this and you must never do that. (The relationship to law is very clear.) A moral code consists of a set of rules, and what it does is lay down a number of lines that must not be crossed, on pain of moral transgression (wrongdoing), which carries with it guilt, blame, and, perhaps, just punishment, just as the law of the land lays down a number of lines that must not be crossed on pain of legal transgression (law-breaking) which, if you are caught and convicted, carries with it legal guilt and legal punishment. Now real and justified deontic morality could not consist simply in a moral code, if only for the reason that we might have an excuse or justification for breaking a rule, an excuse or justification that others could accept.[3] Thus I might be morally (if not legally) excused for stealing a loaf of bread if I or someone close to me is starving and we neither have the money to buy it nor anything else that will be accepted in exchange for it. We might even say that stealing bread in these circumstances is morally justified. (We are doing it to prevent a greater evil which is otherwise unavoidable.) Or I may, because of unforeseen circumstances which I can do nothing about, be unable to keep a perfectly valid promise. And so on and so forth. But notice two things: (1) if stealing and promise-breaking are morally wrong or, in other words, if the rules against stealing and promise-breaking are valid moral rules, then *having to* steal or break a promise is morally regrettable, and I am still under an obligation to make amends if and when I can; (2) that if an act is morally wrong that can only be because it (unjustifiably) violates some valid rule or principle,[4] perhaps "Do not steal" or "Keep your promises" or, to take two other likely examples, "Do not bear false witness" (i.e. tell damaging falsehoods about others) or "Do not cause pain or suffering to others." What this shows is that deontic morality *is* inherently legalistic and, like the law, it sets limits to what one may or may not do at one's pleasure.

Now let us consider aretaic morality. Whereas deontic judgments are judgments applying to acts, or kinds of act, as being (or not being) morally required or morally wrong (morally required not to do), and are judgments on people only when someone is thought to be inexcusably guilty of some moral transgression, aretaic judgments are judgments applying to people in respect of some aspect of their character, an aspect or dimension which is understood to be virtuous or vicious (admirable or contemptible, noble or base, strong or weak). The general practical question for aretaic morality is not "What am I, and others, morally required to do and what not do?" or "By what moral rules should I and others limit their choices?" but "What kind of a person am I to be (or try to be) and admire others for being and what kind of person should I and others not be?" or "What qualities of character am I to encourage and attempt to develop and preserve in myself and others, and what qualities should be absent?" or "What qualities of character make a person an admirable human being, and what qualities of character make a person deserving of contempt or disdain?" or simply "What qualities of character are moral virtues and what qualities are vices?"

The Aretaic as Deontic: a Mistake

Can we, as others have argued, give an account of moral virtues and vices in terms of being morally required to do some things and not to do others? Or can we give an account of wrongdoing, whether by action or inaction, in terms of moral virtues and vices? Let's give it a try and see what happens.

Suppose we start with the virtue of courage. In terms of what moral rule or rules could we understand this? What first comes to minds is "There is a moral requirement to perform courageous acts." But obviously this will not do? How often? All the time? Twice a week? Five times a year? Or we could try, "You morally ought always to be courageous unless you have some justification or excuse." Always? But your present situation need not call for or require courage. Courage is only called for when you have to face a danger or a fear for the sake of a good. Justification or excuse? What would be a justification or an excuse for not being courageous when courage is called for? "I didn't do the brave thing because I was afraid." That is not a justification or an excuse; that is cowardice. I may not have it in me to do the courageous thing, but that shows weakness of character. But then I cannot *choose* to be brave. Either I have it in me or I do not.

By contrast, none of this is true of "Never tell lies" or "Always tell the truth." I can *choose* not to tell a lie, or not to break a promise, or not to cause hurt or harm to others, or at least that is the assumption in describing these as moral rules. Otherwise what would be the point? If I cannot choose not to break my promise and thus avoid wrongdoing, what is the point in saying I am morally required to? We are *held responsible* for our wrongdoings, but can I be held responsible for something if I really can't help doing it? Some actions (keeping or breaking a promise, lying or telling the truth, hurting someone or not hurting him or her) can be chosen at will, or that is what deontic morality assumes. If doing something is morally wrong, because it would be telling a lie or breaking a promise, for instance, then it is *not to be done* without justification or excuse. It is assumed, therefore, that one is able to choose not to do it. However, to look on the aretaic side, one cannot simply choose to have a certain state of character. Either one has it or one does not. All one can do is try to develop that state of character by forcing oneself to do what a person who had that state of character would do in the relevant circumstances, until it becomes a disposition or a habit. If one succeeds then one will have *acquired* that state of character, but this will take time and effort and determination and there is no *guarantee* that one will succeed.

It has sometimes been suggested that we can succeed in bringing aretaic morality under the umbrella of deontic morality through the notion of *supererogation*. (This term comes from the Latin literally meaning "above the call.") To do what is supererogatory is to do *more than* what is morally required. The most familiar examples of supererogation are to be found in the Sermon on the Mount, given by Jesus to his disciples:

> Ye have heard that it hath been said, An eye for an eye, and a tooth for a tooth: But I say unto you, That ye resist not evil: but whosoever shall smite thee on thy right cheek, turn to him the other also. And if any

men will sue thee at the law, and take away thy coat, let him have thy cloke also. And whosoever shall compel thee to go a mile, go with him twain. Give to him that asketh thee, and from him that would borrow of thee turn thou not away. Ye have heard that it hath been said, Thou shalt love thy neighbour, and hate thine enemy. But I say unto you, Love your enemies, bless them that curse you, do good to them that hate you, and pray for them which despitefully use you, and persecute you. . . . (Matthew 5: 38–44)

Now we are only under a moral obligation or a requirement to do (or not do) something to or for somebody, if that person has a moral *right* to our doing it (or not doing it). Let us suppose that we are morally required to repay our debts (unless we have some valid justification or excuse). Then, if I owe you five dollars, I have an obligation to repay you, and you have a moral right to claim that five dollars from me. Notice that because this is required of me, it is *expected* of me, and if I renege on the debt, I have done wrong, you have a genuine moral grievance against me (you have been wronged by me), and I am rightly blamed or condemned. I do not earn any moral Brownie points for repaying my debts, for I am morally obliged to do this, and everyone is expected to do what is morally required of them. They are to be blamed if they fail, but they do not merit praise for doing what they are morally required to do, or for not doing what they are morally required not to do. (This is built into the concept of moral requirement.) However, suppose that, out of Christian charity I, knowing you need the money badly, give you ten dollars instead of the five I owe you, then I have done more than is morally required of me, that is I have performed *an act of supererogation*, and for that I do earn moral praise. I didn't *have to* do it, but I did it anyway, if not from Christian charity, then out of the generosity of my heart.

If we take the Sermon on the Mount as central, then we can say that Christian morality is a morality of supererogation. But notice that Jesus is *commanding* us to perform supererogatory acts, and if we go the second mile in order to obey Christ's commandment or instruction, we are not doing it out of the goodness or the kindness of our hearts; we are doing it in order to be obedient to Christ's teachings, perhaps to ensure our place in the Kingdom of Heaven. It is only if we do it because we are *moved by kindness*, and not because we are commanded to do it, that it can be said to exhibit the *virtue* of kindness. We can choose to do what Christ tells us to do, e.g. go the second mile, but we cannot choose to possess a virtue. Performing a super-erogatory act *under instruction*, although we can choose to do it, does not flow from any virtue. A virtue is something we may or may not have, but we cannot *decide* to have it. We can try hard to develop it by acting as we *would* do *if* we possessed it, but that is all. Perhaps we are *morally better* if we act as a person who possessed the virtue would act, and so we should do it. Thus Shakespeare's Hamlet to his mother (who has, according to Christian ortho- doxy, commited incest by marrying his father's brother): "Assume a virtue if you have it not" (*Hamlet*, Act III, Scene 4) which means "Act as the person who possessed the virtue (here chastity) would, even if, because you don't possess it yourself, you are disinclined." (This, by the way, shows how the aretaic as distinct from the deontic conception of morality was prevalent in Shakespeare's time.) Hamlet goes on to advise his mother:

> . . . Refrain tonight; [i.e. from going to her new husband's bed]
> And that shall lend a kind of easiness
> To the next abstinence: the next more easy;
> For use almost can change the stamp of nature.

Hamlet is repeating the view, first put forward by Aristotle, and which has been put forward again here (p. 140 above), that one can try to acquire a virtue (in respect of which one would be a better person) by acting as the person who possessed the virtue would act, until, through habit, no matter what your *natural* inclinations are, acting in this way becomes a fixed disposition.

The fact that an act of supererogation can be performed in response to a command or a directive or by simply *deciding* to do it, whatever one's inclination, shows that performing acts of supererogation cannot be the correct account of what it is to possess a moral virtue. For one does not possess the virtue of kindness, for instance, unless it is part of one's character, a fixed disposition or tendency to perform acts of kindness, without having to work at it, that is without having to battle any contrary inclinations, and the same is true of courage and the other virtues. It is even more obvious that the concept of supererogation could not account for the vices – for vicious, base, or ignoble dispositions. To begin with we would need here, to do the job, not a concept of supererogation (going beyond the call of duty), but one of "suberogation" (doing *less* than one's duty)! But to do less than one's duty could only mean to fail to do something that one was morally required to do, and that no more accounts for what a vice is, than supererogation, *as such*, accounts for what a virtue is, and for the same reasons: having a vice, like having a virtue, is a fixed disposition of character. Single acts, whether of a virtuous or a vicious kind, need not flow from such a fixed disposition.

Now one might attempt to argue that this makes no difference. The fundamental notion, one might try to say, is an *act* of a certain kind, say a courageous act or a cowardly act, and the corresponding virtue or vice is simply the disposition or tendency to perform acts of this kind, so that they are performed without strain. The disposition, it might be claimed (the virtue or the vice), can only be understood in terms of the *kind of act* that the person said to possess the virtue or the vice has a fixed disposition to perform; the disposition, it might be argued, is defined in terms of the kind of act, and not vice versa. This seems at first to be reasonable enough, but on closer examination it seems not to be true. We observe what we can only call a courageous act, and we say "It took a lot of guts to do that!" Or we observe an act of kindness and we say "That was very kind of you." In both cases we are commenting on the character of the person; we are observing what we take to be an act that flows from an aspect of character, a disposition to show courage or to be kind, and we are praising the person for having this aspect of character, this disposition. The person could say, in reply, "I'm not really a kind person; I forced myself to do that because I thought I couldn't live with myself if I didn't," or "I'm not really a courageous person you know; I was really scared and I wanted to run away, but I was even more afraid of what would happen to me if I didn't do what I did." (Perhaps he would have been shot for desertion under fire.) Driven by fear, was this an act of courage? With this new information, we would want to withdraw our claim that it took a lot of guts. And the other act; if there was no *impulse* of kindness, would we still want to say it was a kind act? I do not think so.

It looks as if in describing an act as kind or courageous we are attributing the *disposition* of courage or kindness to the person who did it – we are attributing an aspect of character, an attribution that we would quickly and decisively withdraw if we found that he or she did not have that disposition after all. So it seems that the kind of act is to be understood in terms of the disposition rather than the disposition in terms of the kind of act. To understand what a kind act is, is to understand what it is for an act to flow from a kindly disposition or aspect of character. To understand what an act of cowardice is, is to understand what it is for an act to flow from a cowardly disposition or aspect of character. Being a kind person comes first in our understanding; performing an act of kindness has to be understood in terms of this. Being a coward comes first in our understanding; a cowardly act can only be understood in terms of this. Aretaic words like "kind" and "cowardly" (virtue and vice words) are used *primarily of people and only secondarily of acts*, and even when they are used to describe acts, they are also a comment on the person. Deontic words like "right," "wrong," and "obligatory" are used primarily of acts and reflect on the person only when he or she is guilty of some wrongdoing. (We do not praise people for doing what they are morally required to do or not doing what they are morally required not to do.) "Supererogatory," which is also in the deontic category (doing *more* than is morally required), is different from these in that it does assign moral merit to the person who performs a supererogatory act, and is in that respect like virtue words, but it is still primarily a description of acts and not of people.

Leaving these objections aside for the moment, we said above that possessing a virtue could not amount to the same thing as performing acts of supererogation for the reason that one could simply, by an act of will, do something supererogatory, regardless of one's actual disposition or inclination. Still an act that is really done out of kindness or of courage, and not just willed or forced, may *also* be a supererogatory act, that is in acting virtuously one *may* be doing more than is morally required. One might still try to argue, on this basis, that supererogation is the key to virtue. But this won't do for a virtuous act *need not be* supererogatory. One might, for example, need courage in order to do what one is morally required to do. So the virtues still cannot be defined in terms of supererogation nor, more obviously, can the vices be defined in terms of suberogation, its shadow opposite. We must conclude that the aretaic cannot be understood in deontic terms.

The Deontic as Aretaic: Again a Mistake

We have considered whether aretaic morality can be understood in deontic terms and our answer has been in the negative. We must now ask whether deontic morality can be understood in aretaic terms, although the answer has largely been given already. Deontic morality, you will remember, lays down lines that cannot be crossed (either by action or inaction) unless there is some justification or excuse that is acceptable to others. It says that there are some kinds of act and some kinds of abstention that are morally required or, to put the same thing in other words, that there are some kinds of act that we are morally required not to do and others that we are required not to abstain from doing.

Two things are important here: (1) we must be able to specify just what these acts or abstentions are; and (2) we must understand that, without a valid justification or excuse, we are *always* required to do or abstain from doing them. We must never, by act or omission, be guilty of any wrongdoing. It is clear that (2) depends on (1) for we can never resolve always to do A, or never to do B (without a valid justification or excuse) unless A and B can be precisely specified *as acts* – the doing or not doing of one kind of thing or another, e.g. lying or doing what you promised you would.

Can acts, because they are describable as acts of courage or kindness, then, be morally required, or can acts, because they are describable as cowardly or cold-hearted acts, be morally required never to do without a valid justification or excuse? The answer is "no." This is because whether an act of a certain kind is also describable as courageous or cowardly, kind or cold-hearted, varies from time to time according to the circumstances. This is not true, however, of the acts prescribed or proscribed by deontic morality. If something is a lie, or the breach of an agreement that was solemnly entered into, or the rendering of aid to someone who needs it from us, or the causing of hurt or harm to another person, then it is just that. It can be instantly recognized as such, and consequently done or not done. "Always do what is kind," "Never do what is cold-hearted," "Always do what is courageous," and "Never do what is cowardly" do not tell us in the same way exactly what we are supposed to do or or not do. And what can we make of "Never do what is cowardly without some justification or excuse"? The answer is nothing at all. It does not even make sense. Deontic judgments are quite distinct from aretaic judgments and cannot be understood in terms of them. We can only conclude that deontic morality cannot be understood in terms of aretaic morality. (Some of these considerations also help to explain why aretaic morality cannot be understood in terms of deontic morality.)

Can We Dispense with either the Aretaic or the Deontic?

We have just considered the questions (1) whether aretaic morality can be understood in terms of deontic morality; and (2) whether deontic morality can be understood in terms of aretaic morality. The answer in both cases has been "no." It is now time to consider whether we can dispense with either one or the other; that is, whether an account of morality in either exclusively aretaic or exclusively deontic terms would be adequate or satisfactory, whether it would tell all the story that needs to be told about morality.

Let us first consider the question whether a virtue and vice account (an aretaic account) of morality is adequate in itself, or whether we do, after all, have to bring moral requirement (deontic morality) into our account. The answer is quite simple. While it is good and desirable, from every point of view, for people to have the virtues and not to have the vices (assuming them to be such), there are also certain things that are, on moral grounds, not to be done without justification or excuse, such as lying, or causing hurt or harm to others, and other things, such as keeping one's promises, giving aid to the distressed when our aid is required, and doing what is expected of us in our social roles (parent, friend, teacher, doctor, etc.),[5] that are, on moral grounds, to be done. And, furthermore, it is understood that these things are to be done or not to be done *regardless of any disposition or inclination we may have to choose otherwise*, that is regardless of whether or not we possess some relevant virtue, or have some relevant disposition of character (some vice) that would hinder us. We have, in other words, to make these choices, whatever our inclination or disposition is, and we must be able to do so by a sheer act of will, based on the understanding that they *are* morally required of us. The extent to which we possess the virtues, therefore (whether or not every moral requirement can be related to some virtue or vice), cannot be relied upon to ensure that we are never, whether by act or omission, guilty of any wrongdoing. If there really is such a thing as wrongdoing, which we have every reason to believe there is, then the mere recognition or understanding that a certain choice (to do or not to do something), would be morally wrong has to be sufficient to motivate us, regardless of our dispositions or our inclinations. (Otherwise moral rules and principles would be useless in guiding conduct.) There are certain lines that, in the common interest, must not to be crossed, and there is no way to avoid this. We therefore cannot dispense with deontic morality and adopt a purely aretaic approach.

We must now ask whether we can dispense with the notions of virtue and vice (aretaic morality), and deal with morality exclusively in terms of moral requirement and supererogation. In other words, is the deontic approach, leaving out any reference to virtues and vices (states of character), adequate in itself in dealing with questions of morality? The answer itself is a huge "no," for how can one leave out such matters as courage and kindness, laziness and heartlessness, in considering the question of what it is to be morally good or bad? Being of good or bad character — what it is to be morally strong or weak, noble or base, admirable or contemptible, *as a person* — is an essential part of our understanding of what morality is. An acceptable moral theory, therefore, must take account of both the deontic and the aretaic dimensions.

A Third Approach: Morality as a Complete Guide to Conduct

Finally, there is a third approach to morality, one first assumed by the nineteenth-century English philosopher John Stuart Mill (1806–73), and adopted by many philosophers since. This is the understanding that morality provides a complete and general, cradle-to-grave guide to conduct, dictating to us on every occasion just exactly what we are to do, or telling us just exactly what is *the morally right thing* to do on any occasion of choice whatever. It is perfectly obvious that deontic morality, where the model is law, does nothing of the kind. Deontic morality, like law, lays down certain lines that are not to be crossed unless there is some valid justification or excuse, and otherwise it leave us alone to do as we please. Aretaic morality would also seem *not* to provide a general guide to conduct. "Always be virtuous" is an instruction that cannot be followed because we cannot choose to have a virtue. "Always do what the virtuous person would do whether you possess the virtue or not" won't do because we have no reason to suppose that all our choices are to be based upon moral considerations. Some acts may be *morally neutral*. (Should I buy the yellow toothbrush or the red one?) The belief that morality provides a complete and general guide to conduct, common as it is, seems to be simply a mistake. This will be discussed in detail in the final chapter of this book (chapter 12).

SUMMARY

1   There are three different ways of looking at morality.

2   Two of these emerged in our discussion of moral reasons in chapter 6.

3   These are (1) the *aretaic*, and (2) the *deontic*. (For the third, see item 18 below.)

4   These have often been seen as *rival* conceptions of morality.

5   Nevertheless, it is best to construe them as different *aspects* or *dimensions* of morality.

6   The aretaic is concerned with the qualities in respect of which a person is of good moral character (*virtues*) or bad moral character (*vices*). The deontic is concerned with certain kinds of *act* (or abstention) which are said to be morally required or morally obligatory.

7   Until very recent times (late eighteenth century), the aretaic conception of morality dominated. It has only been seriously revived in the second half of the present century.

8   The model for deontic morality is *law*, which declares that there are some things that must be done and other things that must not be done. Deontic morality says the same thing.

9   The simplest form of deontic morality is a moral *code*, or a set of do's and dont's. It has its origin, for Judaic-Christian culture, in portions of the Law of Moses in the Old Testament.

10   There did exist, from the first century BC, a tradition of "natural law", another source of deontic morality, but until the time of Kant (late eighteenth century) an attempt was made to assimilate this to the aretaic conception of morality.

11   Natural law was seen as available to natural human reason and, while Aquinas (in the thirteenth century) saw it also as an aspect of Divine law, it nevertheless carried the authority of reason.

12   Deontic morality cannot consist simply in an inviolable moral code because we may have a legitimate justification or excuse for breaking a moral rule.

13   Still deontic morality is inherently legalistic and, like the law, it sets limits to what we may or may not do at our pleasure. (It may therefore be called an ethics of *limitation*.)

14   Deontic morality asks "What things must I do and what things must I not do?" By contrast, aretaic morality asks "What kind of person am I to be (or try to be) and admire others for being, and what kind of person should I and others not be?"

15   Some have argued that aretaic morality (or the aretaic dimension of morality) is to be understood in terms of deontic morality. But this is not possible for the following reasons:

(a) Deontic morality prescribes and proscribes. In other words, it says that there are some things one must *always* do (unless there is an acceptable justification or excuse) and other things one must *never* do (without an acceptable justification or excuse). We can recognize instantly whether an act comes under a moral rule or principle. "Always keep your promises" is an instruction that can be followed but "Always do the brave thing" is not.

(b) One can *choose* not to break a promise, but one cannot *choose* to be brave. Either one possesses the disposition (virtue) of courage or one does not.

(c) Supererogation, or doing *more* than is morally required of you, will not account for the virtues since one may *choose* to supererogate whether one possesses a virtue or not.

(d) The disposition (virtue or vice) is not defined in terms of the kind of act, but rather vice versa. (To call an act an act of kindness is to say something about the character of the doer.)

16 Others have argued that the deontic can be understood in aretaic terms, but this too is mistaken for similar reasons: moral rules or principles rule out certain clearly defined acts or abstentions, regardless of one's dispositions or inclinations otherwise; the virtues are fixed states of character which one may or may not possess.

17 Some have argued that we can dispense with either the aretaic or the deontic dimension of morality. However, we need them both. The deontic is necessary because there are certain lines that must not be crossed, whatever our inclinations. Nor can we leave out such matters as courage and kindness, laziness and heartlessness (states of character) in considering what it is to be morally good or bad. Being one kind of *person* and not another is an essential part of our understanding what moral goodness is.

18 The third conception of morality sees it as being a *complete and general guide to conduct*. But deontic morality, like law, lays down certain lines that are not to be crossed and otherwise leaves us free to do as we please, and not every act exhibits a virtuous or a vicious character (or is what a virtuous or vicious person would do). Some acts are *morally neutral*. (Detailed discussion of this question is reserved for chapter 12.)

QUESTIONS FOR THOUGHT

1 Deontic morality is modeled on *law*. What is the significance of this?

2 "You're a lazy son-of-a-bitch. You've been doing nothing but lie around

and watch TV for the last week." Laziness is a weakness of character (a vice), but has this person necessarily done anything morally wrong?

3   "He really is a person of good character; he always goes the second mile." Will this do? Explain.

4   Would you be happy with a exclusively aretaic or an exclusively deontic conception of morality? Explain.

8

Goodness of Character (Aretaic Morality)

A lot has already been said about aretaic morality in chapter 7, so a brief recap is perhaps all that is needed here by way of introduction. Aretaic morality, or the aretaic dimension of morality, as it is less misleadingly called (chapter 6, p. 137), is concerned with good and bad qualities of *character*, the fixed dispositions or tendencies in respect of which a *person* is said to be morally admirable or contemptible, strong or weak, or, in the traditional and now somewhat old-fashioned language of aretaic morality (often called virtue morality), noble or base. (For "base" we can substitute "ignoble" if we wish.) These qualities of character are traditionally called virtues and vices, and while these terms, like "noble" and "base", sound a little old-fashioned, we will continue to use them, for they are traditional and in common use among philosophers. Honesty (trustworthiness), dishonesty, kindness, cold-heartedness (indifference), laziness, courage, and cowardice are some of the virtues and vices we have already looked at, directly or indirectly, and, as you will soon see, there are a great many more.

You will remember that the aretaic dimension of morality (henceforth "aretaic morality" for short), which is concerned with the good or bad character of persons, is to be contrasted with the deontic dimension, to which the aretaic dimension, as we saw in chapter 7 (pp. 139–44), cannot be assimilated. The deontic dimension of morality (henceforth "deontic morality" for short), unlike aretaic morality, derives from the concept of law. It consists of rules or principles which prescribe (require) or proscribe (forbid) acts of certain kinds (e.g. promise-keeping, causing hurt or harm to others) unless there is a valid justification or excuse – one that could be consensually agreed upon – for not doing it in the one case or for doing it in the other. Otherwise, it leaves us free to do or not do as we please (the morally permissible). Aretaic morality, by contrast, gives us a (not necessarily denumerable) set of virtues and vices (fixed dispositions or tendencies) any one of which contributes to a person's being of good or bad moral character.

It has been seen that we may defend a claim that a certain disposition of character is a virtue or a vice by showing how it contributes to the production or maintenance of *eudaimonia* (flourishing, thriving, happiness, or well-being) (see chapter 6, pp. 124–7). This virtue or vice may be either social/communal (e.g. justice, friendliness, and their opposites, injustice and unfriendliness), or purely individual (e.g. prudence, self-discipline, and their opposites, foolishness and self-indulgence), or both (e.g. courage, patience, and their opposites, cowardice and impatience). It has furthermore been argued that, given our social nature, the well-being of the community is an essential ingredient in the well-being of each individual member of that community (see chapter 6, pp. 127–8). This explains why the good of the community – the common good – is a value for each and every member of it, and therefore why anyone's possession of a social virtue – and that includes possessing it oneself – is a value for everyone, oneself included. Thus, possessing a social virtue is a value or a good for me, which means that I have a reason for possessing it (see chapter 6, pp. 126–8). Indeed, it is difficult to imagine what else, besides this *eudaimonia*, communal and individual, could make the possession of a certain disposition or quality of character a value for anyone and everyone, or what else could make the possession of some other disposition or quality of character undesirable for anyone and everyone, as must be the case with anything that genuinely is a virtue or a vice. We must remember that a good quality (virtue) or a bad quality (vice) must *by definition* be something that is either desirable or undesirable for anyone and everyone to possess. (If it isn't desirable, then it's not a virtue, and if it isn't undesirable, then it's not a vice.) If we could not defend the claim that a certain aspect of character was a virtue by showing how it is conducive to *eudaimonia* (common or individual), or a vice by showing how it contributes to its prevention or destruction, how else could we defend such a claim? What other kind of value could it possibly have? What else could make some qualities of character noble and admirable and others contemptible and base, both in oneself and in others?

Aretaic Words and Phrases

It is time to produce another list, this time of aretaic terms, many of them colloquial. The list contains a number of words simply ascribing bad character to a person without denominating any particular virtue or vice. Some of these words are gendered, but there is nothing we can do about that. None of them, so far as I know is sexist. (We cannot call a woman a bastard – in the colloquial sense – nor can we call a man a bitch, except in the gay world, but to use these words does not necessarily mean we are anti-man or anti-woman.) Many of the words, including those naming more specific qualities, are nouns. Virtue and vice terms need not be adjectival, as we have already seen in the case of "liar" and "bully" (chapter 2, pp. 26–7). Here is the list:

really nice person	likeable	disagreeable
dear (*n*.)	agreeable	unpleasant
great	real	nasty
terrific	horrible person	rotten-to-the-core
super	monster	good guy
nice	beast	great guy
sweet	animal	decent chap
good-hearted	awful	good egg
decent	terrible	bastard
good-natured	vile	son-of-a-bitch
lovable	disgraceful	creep
endearing	no good	asshole
swine	friendly	malicious
shit	sociable	uncaring
darling	considerate	boastful
bitch	polite	arrogant
harridan	pleasant	conceited
shrew	thoughtful	vain
battle-axe	responsible	petty
incorruptible	layabout	stuck-up
straight	malingerer	narrow-minded
hard-working	procrastinator	pig-headed
dedicated	pinchpenny	selfish
open-minded	tightwad	self-centered
broad-minded	liar	materialistic
kind	fraud	shifty
generous	glutton	devious
thoughtful	pig	crafty
caring	thief	on-the-make
warm	coward	can't be trusted
honest	chicken	sly
sincere	bully	deceitful
frank	brat	corrupt
modest	lazy	depraved
fair-minded	shiftless	gross
courageous	rude	two-faced

has guts	inconsiderate	treacherous
enterprising	cruel	vicious
wise	brutal	shameful
loyal	vicious	mean
trustworthy	bad-tempered	crooked
self-possessed	irascible	twisted
disrespectful	insincere	ungrateful
cheeky	phony	cold
impertinent	greedy	sullen
dishonest	stingy	sleazy

You will first of all notice that the expressions "good man," "good woman," "bad man," "bad woman," "good person," "bad person" do not appear on the list. Unlike "good boy" and "bad boy", "good girl" and "bad girl,"[1] which we may use when we talk *about* children as well as when we are praising or condemning them, these expressions ("good man", etc.) are used to refer to adults only when we are talking *to* children. The (gendered) terms like "creep," "bastard," "son-of-a-bitch," "asshole" (all masculine!) and "bitch" – is there another feminine term for "bad woman"? – are the ones that are likely to be used in adult speech (even when used by adolescents among themselves) to refer to people regarded as mature. The next thing you should notice is that these are all *moral* terms – terms ascribing goodness or badness to a person's character as a whole or some aspect of it and thereby conveying moral praise or condemnation. What this shows is that aretaic morality – the morality of character – is deeply embedded in our ordinary ways of thinking and talking about people.

Next, there is obviously no claim for the completeness of this list. One could go on adding (or deleting) words endlessly. I'm sure you could add many of your own – some of them no doubt words that I don't know – and you could delete many that are unfamiliar to you. Related to this, we should remember that, in a language like English, vocabulary is changing continuously. Thus, if we were living in the nineteenth century, the list of words we would come up with would be quite different, even if they signified the same thing (had the same use).[2] Again, words can change their meaning over time, thus "bitch" originally meant a sexually loose woman, and "son-of-a-bitch" meant "son of a whore," which was intended as an insult to the man's mother.[3] (We still have "slut" which, being a remnant of this excessively puritanical attitude toward females, is not included in the list. Perhaps "prude" should have been included.)[4]

Finally, some words, like "thrift" and "thrifty," "chaste" and "chastity," "humble" and "humility," "knows his (her) place," once undoubtedly denominating virtues (and their opposites vices), have, at least for many people, lost their positive moral content. (Do we have a hint of moral disagreement here?) There are also words like "tough," "firm," "aggressive," "ambitious," "assertive" which signify virtues for some but not for others. (More on these – what I call the *macho* virtues – later.)[5]

Very well, our aretaic moral vocabulary changes, virtue and vice words change their meaning, what was once regarded as a virtue or a vice may no longer be regarded as such, the cultural atmosphere changes, and people may disagree over what qualities of character are vices and what qualities of character are virtues. Does this not suggest cultural relativism (chapter 2)? What Bernard Williams (chapter 2, pp. 25–6) calls the "thick" moral concepts (which we have now seen to be aretaic concepts), even the "thick" concepts of our own culture, change over time, and with these changes our "evaluative perspective" changes. Does this not suggest that Williams may be right after all about the relativity of morality to such a perspective? I shall argue that we do not need to draw this conclusion.

Real Virtues and Real Vices

How can we defend the claim that some qualities of character really are virtues and other vices, regardless of time and place? This is a very serious question, and so we must try to be clear about the answer. We will find it in the answer we have already given to the question "What could make a quality of character a virtue or a vice?" (see chapter 6, pp. 125–7 and p. 151 above). To be a virtue, the quality in question must contribute to *eudaimonia*, either that of the community (the common good) or of the individual person who possesses it, or both. To be a vice, the quality in question must be deleterious to (adversely affect) this *eudaimonia*; in other words, be the cause of misery, ill-being, and unhappiness, either communal (which affects everyone) or personal. It can be this, and only this, that makes a quality of character something that it is universally desirable or undesirable for everyone, oneself included, to possess – which must be the case if the quality of character in question genuinely is a virtue or a vice. Only then would everyone have a reason for cultivating and encouraging (or seeking to avoid, discourage, or get rid of) a particular quality of character in themselves and in others. *Without these values as its end or purpose, aretaic morality would lack any foundation in practical reason, in which case the only thing to do would be to forget about it altogether* (see chapter 4, p. 87 and chapter 5, p. 114). The question to ask, then, when we are wondering whether some quality of character really is a virtue or a vice, is whether its possession by everybody (its universal possession) is or would be a contribution to communal and individual well-being, communal and individual ill-being, or neither.

We have already dealt with honesty (trustworthiness), cruelty, kindness, generosity, and courage (chapter 6, pp. 121–2, 124–7). We saw that the first four (in the case of cruelty, its absence) could be seen to relate to social or communal well-being (the common good), from which everybody benefits. If we have succeeded in making out a case for each of these, then that is enough to establish that honesty, kindness and generosity are virtues, and that cruelty is a vice. Courage was somewhat different for we saw that it was of direct personal benefit to its possessor as well as to society in general (and hence indirectly to its possessor). Had we not been able to make out a case for the benefits or harms, social and personal, of these dispositions, then we would not have been able to support the claim the they were virtues or, in the case of cruelty, a vice. Any other quality of character purporting to be a virtue or a vice must be able to pass the same test (the scrutiny of practical reason). If it cannot pass the test, then its candidacy for being a virtue or a vice must be rejected or at least brought into question. (Go back to the list above and try out the test on all the ones that refer to specific qualities in a person, and are not, like "really nice person," "great guy," "swine" and "bitch," comments on a person's moral character as a whole.)

Bernard Williams Again

In discussing Bernard Williams's relativist views (chapter 2, pp. 25–7), it was said that Williams was surely right in saying that what he calls "thick" moral concepts, such as "liar," "brutal," and "bully" carry their moral meaning in themselves, that bullying is bad, or an evil in itself, and that it is redundant or unnecessary to say it. ("If we know what bullying *is*, we already know that it is bad" (chapter 2, p. 27).) And this is, indeed, how aretaic moral language functions. Williams also says that if we start asking such questions as "Is bullying really bad?" or better "Is there really such a thing as bullying?" we step outside our evaluative perspective, and no answers are forthcoming, there being no such thing as a universal moral truth. (The reason why "Is there really such a thing as bullying?" is better, from the Williams point of view, than "Is bullying really bad?" is that if "bully" and "bullying" really are "thick" moral concepts within our evaluative perspective, then bullying's being bad is built into our very concept of bullying, and so the question *cannot* be asked. We have therefore no choice except to ask "Is there really such a thing as bullying?" Either way, according to Williams, we get no answer.)

But this is quite different from what has just been said in this chapter. For we have said of something, designated by a "thick" concept (a virtue or vice word or phrase, such as "bully"), that if we want to *defend* it as being a virtue or a vice, we must consider its relation to *eudaimonia* or well-being – whether it is constructive or destructive of it. But then again – and this is consistent with Williams – we said (chapter 6, p. 124): "To say cruelty is bad is redundant, for cruelty itself is a negative moral value (something to be shunned, avoided, or prevented, and on moral grounds). Do you believe that there is such a thing as cruelty? If you do you are committed to the making of moral judgments." But, unlike Williams, we then went on to ask the question "But what makes cruelty a negative moral value?" and we proceeded to give an answer based on practical reason: that cruelty breeds cruelty, hatred, resentment, and adversarial conflict and that it is therefore a social evil. Whatever Williams says, asking this question and answering it in this way seems to be a perfectly legitimate procedure, and it is precisely what we have just been recommending should be done in connection with all would-be virtues and vices. Williams sees the "thick" concepts of a culture as being essentially part of the "evaluative perspective" of that culture, and not in any way justifiable, questionable, or even open to objective rational examination without destroying moral belief or conviction. By contrast, it is being claimed here that these thick concepts may either pass or fail to pass the scrutiny of universal practical reason, and that genuine virtues and vices are virtues and vices regardless of time or place.

Dubious Virtues and Vices

We must now consider some cases where there is doubt as to whether something really is a virtue or a vice. This means doubt as to whether it passes the test of being either conducive to or destructive of *eudaimonia* (whether it survives the scrutiny of practical reason). To take a couple of examples, suppose "chaste" and "firm" really are virtue words, which would mean that chastity and firmness really are virtues, that the statements "Chastity is good" and "Firmness is good" really are redundant, and that when we use the words "chaste" and "firm" we are necessarily making moral judgments. Then we can ask, "What makes chastity a positive moral value?" and "What makes firmness a positive moral value?," just as we asked "What makes cruelty a negative moral value?" But suppose we are unable to provide an answer. Suppose we cannot see how either one of them is or would be a contribution to well-being (*eudaimonia*), social or personal? Then we would be forced to reject the view that chastity and firmness are virtues, and that would mean one of two things: either we deny that "chaste" and "firm" are virtue words after all, or, if they are so understood, we would have to stop using them. They cannot be virtue words in *our* vocabulary.

Now, it can happen that what was once a virtue or a vice word ceases to be one, not because our vocabulary has changed and the word has dropped out of use to be replaced by another, but because the disposition in question is no longer regarded as a virtue or a vice. Thus we can give a definition of "chastity", for instance (and this is the one likely to be found in a dictionary) that is morally neutral, e.g. "sexual abstinence, virginity" (*The Concise Oxford Dictionary*, 8th edn, 1990), and we can say that chastity, *so defined*, is not a moral virtue. Why? Because it is not only not, as such, a contribution to *eudaimonia*, but may often very well be detrimental to it. It is not the case that everyone has reason for everyone, including themselves, to be sexually abstinent. This is not to say that a person might very well, without moral fault, choose, for personal or religious reasons, to be sexually abstinent. (It is not being claimed that sexual abstinence is a *vice*.)

We must conclude that if "chaste" (or "firm") is understood as a virtue word, the question we must ask is "Is there really such a thing as chastity?" And if the answer we give is "yes," then we are committed to the view that sexual abstinence and virginity are moral virtues. On the other hand, if it is no longer a virtue word, or we do not so understand it, we can ask whether chastity, simply defined as "sexual abstinence, virginity," is or is not a moral virtue by asking whether it is or is not a disposition worth everyone's having – as a contribution to the general well-being of society and the individuals in it. (You must remember that if a disposition of character is a moral virtue it is something worth everyone's having, and if it is a moral vice it is desirable than no one should have it.) If sexual abstinence and virginity are not moral virtues, then "chaste" and "chastity" *should not function as virtue words*, and if they *are* understood as virtue words, then we should stop using them. But that would be only a temporary need. For if sexual abstinence and virginity cease to be regarded as moral virtues, the words "chaste" and "chastity" will cease to be understood as virtue words. This has already happened with "humble" (humility was once supposed to be a virtue), and it has almost happened with "chaste" and "chastity", although it also seems that these words, except in a religious context (e.g. "vow of chastity") are passing out of common use.

The conclusion to be drawn from all this is that the question of what are virtues (good qualities of character) and what are vices (bad qualities of character) is not simply a matter of the "evaluative perspective" which one happens to inhabit, although that perspective does determine what words *function as* virtue words. Rather, the question has to do with whether the quality of character in question contributes to or is destructive of general happiness or well-being (*eudaimonia*). This is the test to which all would-be virtues and vices must be put. And remember, what it is for something to be a virtue or a vice is for it to be a quality of character that it is desirable *for* everybody *that* everybody – oneself included – should have or not have. And on what basis, other than conduciveness to, or prevention of destruction of, general well-being or *eudaimonia*, could this be so?

Two Important Virtues from Ancient Greece

An important virtue for the Greeks was *sophrosune*, translated into Latin as *temperantia*, and into English as *temperance*. Given the deterioration in meaning of the word "temperance" in English, the best translation we can give of *sophrosune* is *self-discipline*. The vice which is the opposite of this is *self-indulgence*, mainly in one's own pleasure, at the expense of losing one's mettle and hence the ability to do or accomplish other things that are of value, things that might require hard work or application (such as me writing this book or you trying to get the most you can out of reading it), things which, if one fails to do them, one is the loser. While self-discipline is mainly valuable to oneself, it is also often of value to others, but it is still not a *social* virtue even to the extent that courage is, courage being another virtue that is personally valuable to its possessor apart from its social benefits.

Another important Greek virtue was *phronesis*, translated into Latin as *prudentia* and into English as *prudence*. For Aristotle, this – the ability to reason well practically, or to work out the best means to good ends – was the *intellectual* virtue that made the possession of the moral virtues (virtues of character) possible. The Greek *phronesis* is now usually translated into English as *practical wisdom*. In English the word "prudence" developed a narrower meaning – being wise enough to look after your own long-range self-interest through careful planning and the avoidance of unnecessary risks – and this *is* generally regarded as a virtue, a quality of character to be admired, encouraged, and emulated, and its opposite, *imprudence* or *foolishness*, a quality of character to be despised and discouraged in others and prevented or avoided in oneself. Since prudence is, by definition, the ability to reason well enough to be able to know what choices will protect one's own best interests over time, together with the disposition to actually make those choices, it qualifies, by the criteria I hope have been established, as a moral virtue, even though it is exclusively concerned with oneself and not with the social or the common good. Philosophers often contrast the *moral* with the *merely prudential*, but when they do this it is obviously *deontic* morality that they have in mind. Of course, one is not *morally obliged* to look after one's own best interests over time, but one is foolish if one does not (within the restrictions imposed by other moral considerations). So there is at least one moral virtue that is directly and exclusively concerned with one's personal well-being.

The Virtues and Ethical Egoism

We have see that there is one moral virtue exclusively related to self-interest, namely prudence, and two that both directly serve self-interest but also serve the common good, namely self-discipline (temperance) and courage. But what of the virtues we have examined that do not directly serve self-interest, but *only* the common good, such as honesty, kindness, generosity? And what of the vices such as cruelty and the opposites of the virtues just mentioned, whose adverse effect is not (or not directly) on the possessor of the virtue, but on others or the community as a whole? (To these we could add many from the list that appears on pp. 152–3, fixed aspects of character designated by such words as "incorruptible," "thoughtful," "caring," "sincere," "fair-minded," "loyal," "considerate," "polite," "reponsible," "liar," "fraud," "thief," "bully," "brat," "rude," "vicious," etc.)

We must remember that if a certain quality of character genuinely is a virtue, then it is worth *my* possessing (my having it is a value for me) and therefore *I* have a reason for seeking to acquire it and preserve it *in myself*. A virtue is something that it is strong, noble, and admirable to possess. Similarly, if a certain quality of character genuinely is a vice, then it must be of value *to me* not to possess it, which gives me a reason not to allow it to develop, or to try to get rid of it *in myself*. But if the virtue is a virtue or the vice a vice, not because my possessing it has effects which directly benefit or harm me (as is the case with prudence and self-discipline), but because it has effects which benefit or harm others or the community as a whole, how can it be a value (positive or negative) for *me*? How can it give *me* a reason, if it is a virtue, for seeking to acquire or preserve it *in myself* or, if it is a vice, trying to avoid acquiring it or to get rid of it if it is there?

The answer we gave to this question in chapter 6 (pp. 125–8), and which we repeated in this chapter (p. 151), is that the possession of the virtues, and the absence of the vices, creates a social atmosphere in which everyone can thrive and flourish. Thus, by contributing to the common good, we contribute to the good of everyone, including ourselves. If people were to act strictly as individuals, each one pursuing his or her own personal interests exclusively, forgetting what I have been calling the social virtues and being solely concerned with himself or herself, the result would be an unhappy social atmosphere, full of adversarial competition, which in the long run is of no benefit to anyone. (This is largely the situation as it exists today.)

The question we must now ask is, are the reasons for seeking to acquire and preserve the social virtues in myself not in the end egoistic? Are the social virtues not, after all, values for me because they benefit me? And, if this is so, does this not amount to a form of ethical egoism? The answer to this, once more, is that (as was said in chapter 6, pp. 127–8), because of our social nature and our dependence on one another, both materially and emotionally, the good of the community or the common good is an essential ingredient in the good of each individual member. Therefore, the good of the community, and of others as members of it, is a value for every member of it, including me. But my reason for being a good member of the community, which is my reason for cultivating the social virtues in myself, is nevertheless not an egoistic reason. This is because I am not a wholly separate individual living in a world of many separate individuals, all required, in order to survive and flourish, to act exclusively in their own self-interest, but I am, rather, a social being, a member of a community whose social relations with other members are both real and important. I do not have reason to be a good member of the community, hence to possess the social virtues (and not to possess the social vices), because of the benefits this brings to me as a separate individual whose good is independent of the good of others. This *would be* an *egoistic* reason. Rather, I have a reason to be a good member of the community because of the benefits it brings to me and others, jointly and together, as members of one community with interests in common. While that is not an *altruistic* (self-denying) reason, it is not an egoistic reason either. (If you think this one through carefully you will realize that in today's one-world situation, the moral community is the human community generally, and that exclusively national, ethnic, or tribal interests, which lead unavoidably to adversarial competition and, at worst, wars and even genocide, are equivalent, on the global scale, to exclusively self-regarding and therefore egoistic interests.) It is a commonplace of our culture to suppose that a reason must be either egoistic or altruistic – a devastatingly destructive dichotomy. We have now seen that the reason we have to be persons of good character (prudence excepted) is neither.

Power and the *Macho* Virtues

Sometimes people are admired, not for being kind and generous, friendly and good-natured, gentle, courteous, compassionate, nurturing, honest, and the like (qualities that would pass our test for being genuine social virtues, contributing to a good social atmosphere for all). Instead, they are admired for being tough, "cool," independent, firm and unyielding, determined and able to get their way, able to inspire fear and dominate others, not allowing moral scruples to interfere with their power and influence, able, as the expression has it, to "kick butt." These are what I referred to earlier as the *macho* virtues. If one sees these qualities as virtues, then the traditional virtues just mentioned would be seen not as strengths of character but as weaknesses, their possessors as foolish and ineffectual, lacking the hard and tough qualities of character that they need to exploit other people or push them aside in order to make it big in the world.

This represents an outlook that some would wish to deny was a *moral* outlook at all, and they would describe these people as *immoral*, which they arguably are in deontic terms. For such people commonly scoff at the very idea of deontic morality, the idea that there are certain rules or principles that place limits on what we may or may not do in the pursuit of our aims and objectives, limits that must be imposed (lines we must not cross) for the sake of some higher moral good. (The subject of deontic morality and its foundation in practical reason is the subject of chapter 9.) But the fact that these *macho*, kick-butt qualities are admired simply as qualities of character, and hence seen as virtues, while the traditional social virtues are despised and regarded as weaknesses – thus in effect treated as vices – shows that this *macho*, go-for-it view is a genuine *aretaic* moral view.

Now it is quite clear that people who see things this way see the human world as essentially a set of individuals in competition with one another for power, influence, status, and wealth. The ones who are tough, smart, and unyielding make it to the top, which is what they deserve, their competitors being eliminated or placed in a powerless and inferior position, while others, contemptible for what is seen as their weakness, are simply exploited, which is what *they* deserve. If we want to look quickly for extreme examples, we could mention political leaders like Stalin, and Saddam Hussein (of Iraq), Mafia bosses, and big-time drug dealers. But we do not have to look hard for people committed to *macho* morality. Look in government or in the giant corporations. *Macho* morality, when it is brought out into the open, often has a lot of popular support. A number of years ago, G. Gordon Liddy (the mastermind of the famous Watergate conspiracy, aimed at ensuring the re-election of US Republican President Richard Nixon by playing dirty tricks on the opposing Democrats) traveled to university campuses and received a lot of money for making speeches advocating just the kind of go-for-it, kick-butt morality that I have been talking about here. At my university he received a standing ovation. A good friend of mine, not so long ago, heard his teenage daughter's then current boyfriend saying to her: "Why should I be honest when I can make more money being dishonest?" This friend of mine, who happened to be a professor of moral philosophy, strongly advised her to break with the guy, which she did.

Now if we were just a bunch of individuals in adversarial competition with each other, and making it big in terms of power, influence, and wealth and being admired for that, were the sole objectives worth pursuing, then something could be said for *macho* morality. Those of us who knew we couldn't make it big (at least right now) could ensure *something* for ourselves by serving the big guys in a servile and obsequious way, perhaps biding our time while waiting for the chance to topple our rivals and become big and powerful men or women ourselves. But look at the values we would have to sacrifice: friendship, good will, love and affection, good feeling, mutual aid and support, a sense of community and belonging, all things without which we are certainly worse off. Power, influence, domination, wealth, and being admired for these, no matter how attractive they may seem, or how much value they may actually have, cannot compensate for the loss of these other things, for in the end they leave a person friendless, alone and isolate, and that is a source of the deepest misery. The *macho* virtues can only be seen as virtues if they are seen as sources of happiness and well-being, but we have reason to believe that, in most cases, they are nothing of the kind. Human happiness, for most of us anyway, cannot be constituted by these things and these things alone, whatever thrills of admiration, self-congratulation, and the sheer exercise of power and domination they may bring, not to mention the misery of all those who are subject to their will.

But we must not forget, in the midst of all this, that we do need to look after ourselves. We cannot expect everybody in the world to possess the social virtues and not to have the social vices. We cannot expect everybody to be kind and friendly and generous and just. Some people may malign us or betray us, or order us about when they have no authority to do so. Or they may try to hurt us or attempt to walk all over us. We must be able, in such circumstances, to stand up for ourselves and what we believe in and not just give in, hide, or creep away. This obviously has a great deal to do with courage, but we also need the virtue of self-reliance to fall back on when we find ourselves alone, and we must be able and willing to defend ourselves when attacked and to assert ourselves against nasty competitors who are trying to do us in. These are genuine strengths or virtues of character, hence moral virtues, and their opposites are weaknesses of character, hence moral vices. These may resemble the *macho* virtues and vices in that they call for the strength to fight for oneself against adversaries, but they are needed only under adversity; they are not, like the *macho* virtues, simply a means of raising oneself above others in respect of power, influence, wealth, and the status which, for one's fellow *macho* moralists, goes with having "beat out" one's adversaries and competitors and thereby "made it big."

The Nobility of Happiness

One question remains, although the answer should be obvious, and that is "Why do so many of the traditional virtues and vices remain in place as virtues and vices in the common understanding?" The answer is that they do in fact pass our test: they do in fact contribute to the flourishing, thriving, well-being, or happiness (*eudaimonia*) of human beings seen as individuals living together in community, and that is why they are admirable or contemptible, strong or weak, noble or base, and for that reason desirable in themselves. Although we may, indeed, have lost sight of this, it was well known to the ancients up to the time of the Stoics (second century BC to third century AD) for whom moral goodness, understood in this way, was the most important ingredient in being happy (*eudaimon* [Greek] or *beatus* [Latin]). Happiness was seen as the noblest thing in the world and the ultimate ground for admiration and congratulation.

SUMMARY

1   Our vast vocabulary of terms used to judge a person's moral character shows how deeply aretaic morality is embedded in our ordinary ways of thinking and talking about people.

2   Our aretaic moral vocabulary changes over time, and virtue and vice words change their meaning, and this seems to suggest cultural relativism.

3   However, we have the test of practical reason to determine whether something is a genuine virtue or a genuine vice: namely, is it conducive to or destructive of *eudaimonia*, both personal and communal?

4   If an alleged virtue or vice does not pass this test, we have no alternative but to reject it as a genuine virtue or vice.

5   Self-discipline (what used to be called "temperance") is a virtue mainly useful to ourselves, although it is also of social value, though not to the same extent that courage is.

6   Prudence – the ability to reason well enough to be able to know what choices will best protect our own interest – is a virtue exclusively concerned with one's personal well-being.

7   The virtues that serve *only* the common good, and the vices that affect adversely *only* the common good, although they are of value for anyone and everyone to possess, are nevertheless not altruistic, since the common good is part of the good of each individual person. Thus, while the reasons for having these virtues and not having these vices are not egoistic, they are not altruistic either.

8   There is a set of alleged virtues, which we may call the *macho* virtues (being tough, "cool," independent, firm and unyielding, determined and able to get one's way, being able to inspire fear and dominate others, etc.) which belong to a certain aretaic moral outlook. These would be virtues if we were simply separate individuals in competition with one another for power, influence and wealth, and this were the only way of

seeing things. But we are also social beings for whom such things as friendship, good will, love and affection, good feeling, a sense of community, etc. are genuine values without which happiness (*eudaimonia*) is impossible, and *macho* morality requires the sacrifice of these.

9   Still, we cannot expect everyone else to possess the virtues, and we must be able to stand firm in the face of attempts to abuse or exploit us. This is a genuine strength or virtue of character.

10   The traditional virtues and vices (kindness, courage, etc.) remain in place in the common understanding because they do in fact contribute to the flourishing, thriving, well-being, or happiness (*eudaimonia*) of individuals in community.

11   The ancients believed that moral goodness, understood in this way, was the most important ingredient in being happy (*eudaimon* or *beatus*), and that happiness was the noblest thing in the world and the ultimate ground for admiration and congratulation. We seem to have lost sight of this.

QUESTIONS FOR THOUGHT

1   You think somebody is really a great guy. Why? (The answer you give will show at least some of the things you believe to be moral virtues.) Consider what makes these moral virtues (admirable qualities of character).

2   Do you want to be a *macho* man or a really tough lady? Why or why not?

3   "It is nobler to forgive small injuries than to seek to return them." Do you agree? Explain why or why not. What moral virtue or virtues are involved? What makes it (or them) a virtue (or virtues)?

4   Is wit a moral virtue, as Hume thought? (*A Treatise of Human Nature*, part III, section I, p. 590 in the Selby-Bigge edition). Explain why or why not.

9

The Avoidance of Wrongdoing (Deontic Morality)

Aretaic morality has essentially to do with the dispositions in respect of which a *person* is said to be of morally good or bad character, and in which that morally good or bad character is displayed. These dispositions are called virtues if they count toward a good moral character, vices if they count toward a bad one. The virtues are strengths of character, the vices weaknesses. Possessing a virtue is admirable; possessing a vice is contemptible or despicable. A person is said to be noble (to use the traditional language) to the extent to which he or she possesses virtuous dispositions; base or ignoble to the extent that he or she possesses vicious ones. Clearly this is universal and must be understood to apply to all human beings. The possession of a virtue is universally desirable (desirable in everyone – oneself included – from every point of view), the possession of a vice universally undesirable. To have a virtue, therefore, must be a positive value for the possessor, as well as for others, thus giving him or her reason to seek to have it. The possession of a vice must be a negative value for the possessor, not just for others, hence giving him or her reason to prevent acquiring it, or to try to get rid of it if he or she already has it.

It was argued in chapter 8 that in order to be a genuine virtue – one satisfying all these conditions – an aspect of character must be conducive to well-being, happiness, or *eudaimonia*, personal or social or both, while a true vice must be detrimental to it. There could be no other grounds, it was said, on which a supposed virtue or vice could be rationally defended as being an actual one. It was observed that most of the traditional virtues – e.g. honesty, courage, kindness, etc. – were able to pass this test.

While aretaic morality is essentially concerned with the character of persons as expressed or manifested in their conduct, *deontic morality is essentially concerned with the avoidance of wrongdoing*, whether by doing something that is morally wrong, or failing to do something that is morally required. It is therefore essentially concerned with *acts* as being of a certain kind, e.g. lying, causing harm to others, keeping promises, aiding the distressed when our aid is needed, not neglecting our responsibilities in the social roles we occupy (*duties* in the narrow sense). Certain of these are morally required to do (morally wrong not to do), or morally required not to do (morally wrong to do). If a person fails to do what he or she is morally required to do or does what he or she is morally required not to do, without a valid justification or excuse, he or she is guilty of a moral violation or transgression, of *moral wrongdoing*.

Deontic Morality: an Ethics of Limitation

The model for deontic morality is *law* and, like the law, deontic morality tells us that there are some things we must do, whether we like it or not, and other things we must not do, whether we like it or not, on pain of violation or transgression (felony or misdemeanor in the case of the law, moral wrongdoing in the case of deontic morality). The law leaves us free to do anything that it does not prohibit or forbid, anything that is not an instance of law-breaking; deontic morality leaves us free to do anything that is not forbidden by certain moral rules or principles, anything that does not constitute moral wrongdoing. To do what the law requires, we must never, by act or omission, do anything illegal, or to put the same thing in other words, we are only to do what is legal. To do what deontic morality requires, we must never, by act or omission, do anything that is morally wrong (illicit), or, to put the same thing in other words, we are only to do what is morally right (licit).

Moral philosophers, especially in the twentieth century, have often made the mistake (and many continue to make the mistake) of treating "morally right" as if it meant "morally obligatory" or "morally required." The actual meaning of "morally right," as the account above shows, is "morally licit," which is to say morally allowable or permissible – what may be done (or left undone) without being guilty of any wrongdoing, without any moral transgression. Thus, if I am wondering whether it is really right to have an extramarital love affair, I am not wondering if it is really morally obligatory – I am wondering if it is really morally permissible (not wrong).

The words "right" and "wrong," wherever they appear (right way/wrong way, right answer/wrong answer, right key/wrong key, right house/wrong house), are always strict contradictories; that is, if it's not right it's wrong and vice versa, with nothing in between. (It can't be neither right nor wrong; it must be one or the other.) "Not right" and "wrong" have the same meaning, as do "not wrong" and "right." This obviously applies to "morally right" and "morally wrong" as well as to "right" and "wrong" when they are used by themselves as moral terms (as in the example above). This means that if something is not morally wrong, it must be morally right, so "morally right" can only mean what "not wrong" means, i.e. "morally permissible," as the example shows.

Now, suppose we do what many twentieth-century philosophers have done and take "morally right" to mean not "morally permissible" but "morally required" or "morally obligatory." This would mean (because if something is not wrong it must be right) that if an act is not wrong, then it is morally obligatory.[1] But think what an absurdity this is! It would mean that if it is not morally wrong to go swimming on Sunday (which it obviously isn't), then it is morally obligatory. We would *have* to go swimming on Sunday, whether we liked it or not, on pain of moral transgression! The consequence of taking "morally right" to mean "morally obligatory" – remember that if something is not right it is wrong and vice versa – is that all acts would be either morally wrong or morally obligatory, with nothing in between! *Thus we would eliminate, by a verbal misdefinition, the whole realm of the morally permissible – the things we may or may not do at our pleasure without moral transgression either way – and without these, surely, life would not be worth living!* Yes, of course, all acts are either morally right or morally wrong (this follows from how the words "right" and "wrong" function), but "morally right" cannot mean "morally obligatory;" it must mean "morally permissible," which is obviously what "not wrong" means.

There are therefore not *two* deontic categories (right = obligatory, and wrong), but *three*: (1) morally required to do (obligatory); (2) morally required not to do (wrong); and (3) neither morally required to do nor morally required not to do (neither obligatory nor wrong), which is to say morally permissible to do or not do as one pleases.[2] (We shall call these, for short, the obligatory, the wrong, and the permissible, avoiding the word "right" where possible.) This accords with our understanding that deontic morality is modeled on law, which requires some acts and forbids others, leaving us free to do or not to do whatever is not illegal. In a perfectly parallel way, deontic morality requires some acts and forbids others, leaving us free to do or not do whatever is not immoral. We may therefore call deontic morality (or the deontic dimension or morality), an ethics of *limitation*, one that lays down certain lines that must not be crossed, but otherwise allows us to live our own lives and pursue our own projects.

In our discussion of "right" and "wrong" above, we overlooked one important phrase: "the right thing" or "the right thing to do." It might, when the rightness in question is *moral* rightness, look as if "right" in these phrases means "obligatory." And when we say that something is the morally right thing to do, or the only morally right thing to do, it is understood that anything else would be morally wrong, and that does make the choice morally obligatory. (We must do it if we are to avoid wrongdoing.) But let us look at the kind of context in which the phrase "the right thing" is actually used. It is only used when, in a particular situation, we have some difficulty in deciding what, all things considered, we ought to do. This need not be a problem about what we *morally* ought to do. We might, for instance, be wondering whether we should paper a certain wall or paint it, or whether we should buy a car in the showroom that takes our fancy now, or risk losing it by waiting for a month until the prices go down. We are wondering what is *the right thing to do*, which is equivalent to wondering just what we ought to do in this situation. To take a moral example, should we tell a close friend of ours that we saw her boyfriend with another woman, or should we just leave it alone and mind our own business? What, in the circumstances, is *the morally right thing*? One or the other of these choices would be morally wrong, yet we must either tell or not tell. One choice or the other – the one that is the right thing to do – must be morally obligatory, since we must avoid wrongdoing (either by telling or by not telling). Thus if something is *the morally right thing to do*, it *is* morally obligatory, for *anything else* would be morally wrong.

But notice that we speak of the right thing to do, whether or not we mean the *morally* right thing to do, only in the special case where there is a problem about deciding exactly what we should do. We could go wrong and we want to be sure we make the right choice. Now these problems of making the right choice do often arise in the course of living, but quite obviously not all our choices are problematic in this way. We do not need to consider, for every choice we make, whether or not it is the right thing to do (anything else being wrong). More often we simply decide what to do and go ahead and do it; there are no worries, whether or not of a moral kind – no suspicion and no reason for suspicion that what we are proposing to do might not be the right thing (might be wrong or a mistake). Life does not consist in trying to figure out, on every occasion of choice, what is *the right thing* to do, let alone the *morally* right thing to do. Nor need we say, for *every* choice we make, that our choice was or was not *the right* one.

We have seen that the use of the phrase "the right thing to do" implies that any other choice would be wrong. "Right," all by itself, however, does not imply any such thing. "Are you sure it's really morally right?" means "Are you positive it's not morally wrong?" and that means "Are you sure it's really morally permissible?" And if I decide that it is morally permissible, say, to have an extramarital affair – in other words that it is right in the sense that there is no moral objection to it – this does not mean that it is *the morally right thing to do*, for that would only be true if *not* doing it was morally wrong! If I always want to do what is morally right, this does not mean that I never want to do anything except what is morally required, but rather that I never want, whether by act or omission, to do anything that is morally wrong. In other words, I want to do or leave undone only what it is morally permissible to do or to leave undone.

Kant and Deontic Morality

The great German philosopher Immanuel Kant (1724–1804), whom we have already had occasion to mention is connection with Sartre (chapter 3, note 3), Hare (chapter 4, note 14), and the dominance of the deontic conception of morality in recent times (chapter 7, p. 137) is the man we might call the father of the exclusively deontic conception of morality. Kant has often been misinterpreted as saying or implying that we are only to do what we are morally obliged to do or what it is our moral duty to do, and that to do anything else is morally wrong. This would make anything that was not morally obligatory morally wrong, and vice versa, just as taking "morally right" ("not morally wrong") to mean "morally obligatory" does – the mistake we have just been talking about. But in fact Kant said nothing of the kind. What he actually said was that we were only to do what we would be willing (what it would not be contrary to reason to will) that all others do as well, whenever they are so motivated.

Unfortunately, Kant formulated this principle, which he called *the categorical imperative*, in a rather ambiguous way: "Act only according to that maxim which you can at the same time will that it should become a universal law."[3] This could be taken as meaning that you should only do what you can will that *everybody* do, but that is absurd, for it would mean one couldn't take up farming – what would happen if everybody did? – or flush the toilet at a certain time – if everybody did that, it would destroy the water system! On the other hand, it is perfectly possible to will that anyone take up farming *if that is what they wish to do*, or that everyone flush the toilet *when they need to*! It becomes plain, from what Kant says elsewhere, that what he means is that we are not to do anything that we would not be willing to have people do *whenever they wanted to*. In other words, we are only able to regard as *licit* for us what it is not contrary to reason to will to be licit for others. The universality in question is what Kant calls, in his essay *Perpetual Peace*, "universal lawfulness."[4]

But *even if* we take Kant to be saying that we are only to do what it is not contrary to reason to will that everybody actually do (whether they want to or not), the categorical imperative is still a principle that tells us what is or is not permissible. He would not be telling us that it is our moral *duty* to do whatever we would be willing to have everybody do; he would be telling us that we may *only* do what we would be willing to have everyboody do, that only what we would be willing to have everybody do is *morally permissible*, and that anything else, whether act or omission, is *morally wrong*.[5] The categorical imperative does not tell us what to do ("For every choice you make, do as the categorical imperative directs"), it tells us what *not* to do, whether by act or omission ("Never do what the categorical imperative forbids" or "Only do what the categorical imperative *allows*.")

In several places Kant makes it clear that he understands the categorical imperative as placing restrictions on what we may or may not do ("an absolute limit on our freedom"), not as prescribing what we must do on every occasion of choice.[6] If I am right in saying that what the categorical imperative really says is that we are only to do what we could rationally will that others do *whenever they want to*, or, in other words, that we are only free to do (or not do) what we could rationally will that everybody be free to do (or not do), then we have a principle that at least looks as if it might make some sense.

Notice that we are talking about two different difficulties here. First, is Kant saying that the categorical imperative dictates to us, on every occasion of choice, just exactly what we are to do, or is he saying that it places restrictions or limits on our doing or not doing as we please? Secondly, does Kant mean by the categorical imperative that we are only to do what we could rationally will that everybody do whether they want to or not, or does he mean that we are only to do what we could rationally will that everybody be *free* to do? I have opted for the latter interpretation in both cases, partly because we do not want Kant to appear a fool, and partly because these are the interpretations that best accord with what Kant actually wrote. And if the latter interpretation in the first case is the correct one, this makes it all the more likely that the latter interpretation in the second case is the correct one too. For if Kant is saying not that in all our choices we should do what the categorical imperative dictates (that, in other words, we are only *free* to do or omit what we are *morally obliged* to do or omit – the absurdity we have already rejected), but rather that the categorical imperative places limits on what we are otherwise free to do or not do as we please, he can hardly be saying that we are only free to do (or not to do) what we could rationally will that everybody do (or not do) whether they wanted to or not.

But how did this first misinterpretation ever get off the ground at all? The answer is simple. Kant is adamant in saying that the only *motive* that has moral worth is doing something, or not doing something, *because* the moral law (the categorical imperative) requires it. He calls this the motive of duty. This is perfectly consistent with our interpretation because the moral law would require an *act*, or make doing something a moral *duty*, when the categorical imperative dictates that not doing it is impermissible or wrong. Similarly, the moral law would require an *omission* (require *not* doing something) when the categorical imperative dictates that *doing* the thing is impermissible or wrong.

Only the motive of duty has moral worth, according to Kant, because all other motives stem from our natural desires, which are not the product of our rational will. Kant calls the will (the impulse to action) when we are motivated by our natural desires *heteronomous* (not determined by us but by nature, which is an external cause). When we will to do a thing because we recognize that it is morally required, however, the will is said to be *autonomous*; the motive comes from our own reason, and by acting with an autonomous will we transcend the order of nature. It is this and only this, Kant says, that gives us our distinctive worth as rational beings, and makes us worthy of respect. Kant calls this *the good will*, which he says is the only thing that has value in its own right. ("It would sparkle like a jewel with its own light.")[7]

Now this may be a strange view, and it is certainly peculiar to Kant, but Kant never says that we must never act on our natural desires, upon which we may and indeed must act, being creatures of flesh, provided the actions are licit, that is not contrary to the moral law. He only says that these actions have *no moral worth*, by which he means that we do not gain any moral credit from doing them. People have mistakenly taken this claim — that acts done from natural desire (from anything other than the pure moral motive) have no moral worth, or that only acts done from the motive of duty (recognition of the law as law) do have moral worth — to mean that we should *only* act out of the recognition of duty, and that it is always wrong to act so as to satisfy our natural desires. But this piece of foolishness is not something that Kant ever said. On Kant's view, we are perfectly at liberty to act in order to satisfy our natural desires, so long as those acts are licit, that is so long as they are not forbidden by the moral law (the categorical imperative). We just must not make the mistake of thinking that we get any moral credit for doing these things, even if they are done out of sheer beneficence. We only get moral credit if we act from the pure motive of duty, in total disregard of our inclinations ("the material of the faculty of desire.")[8]

Now we don't have to accept Kant's view about what does and does not reflect well on us morally — for one thing it would eliminate most of the traditional virtues as qualities of character commanding admiration — but we must not attribute to Kant moral doctrines that would make him appear utterly foolish. Kant's views are completely in accord with the account given here of deontic morality: that it is modeled on law, that it prescribes (requires) certain actions and omissions and proscribes (forbids) others, and that it otherwise leaves us free to do as we please without moral transgression.

The Grounds of Deontic Morality

We now know what deontic morality (or the deontic dimension of morality) is, and we know that Kant's understanding of it is the very same as our ordinary understanding of it, as already described (see above and chapter 7, pp. 136–7).

Deontic morality does not dictate to us, on every occasion of choice, what we are to do (what we morally ought to do), or what is *the right thing* to do (see above, pp. 167–9). Rather it tells us that there are certain things that we must not do because we are *morally* required not to do them, i.e. they are morally wrong, and certain other things that we must do because we are morally required to do them, i.e. they are morally obligatory. The questions we must now ask are: Are there any such things? If so, what are they? And why?

We already know, in advance, that if something is morally wrong, that it is a reason for everyone, including ourselves, not to do it, and if something is morally obligatory, then that is a reason for everyone, including ourselves, to do it. We know, furthermore, that something can only be a reason for someone's doing or not doing something, if there is something of value or worth to be gained, or not lost, by doing it or by not doing it. In the case of deontic morality, as in the case of aretaic morality, these must be distinctly moral values. In the case of aretaic morality, these moral values (positive and negative) turned out to be dispositions (strong or weak, noble or base, admirable or contemptible) that counted toward our being persons of morally good or of morally bad character, and these virtues and vices turned out to be (if they were real ones) either conducive to or destructive of well-being or happiness (*eudaimonia*), both social or communal (from which everyone gains or loses) or purely personal, or both. We must now ask why, if at all, we have reasons, distinctly moral reasons, for restricting our freedom to do or not to do as we please, as must be so if there is a valid deontic morality – one with a rational foundation (a foundation in practical reason). And there can only be such reasons if deontic moral values can be shown to be genuine values, providing reasons for all of us thus to restrict our freedom.

It is not as if we were bringing up this subject for the first time, for in chapter 6, when we were considering moral reasons and the values that make them reasons, we examined promise-keeping and fairness and what made them values (chapter 6, pp. 121–4). These are clearly deontic reasons and deontic values, for it is seen as *morally wrong* to break your promises, or to do anything that is unfair (without a valid justification or excuse). We also mentioned not cheating and not telling lies (traditionally and commonly seen as morally wrong acts) as things that could be treated in much the same way as promise-keeping. (We also noted the relation of promise-keeping, not cheating, and not telling lies to the virtue of honesty. We will have more to say about this in chapter 10 when we discuss the relationship between the aretaic and deontic dimensions of morality.) Besides, we have frequently mentioned causing hurt to others and aiding the distressed when our aid is needed, as things traditionally and commonly thought to be morally wrong (the first) or morally obligatory (the second), again unless there is a valid justification or excuse.

"You promised you wouldn't" was offered in chapter 6 (pp. 120–22) as a moral reason for not doing something, and we can now see that this is a *deontic* moral reason. And what sort of account did we give of *why* this is a reason, of what the value or values are that make it a reason? We saw, first of all, that it is not a reason directly related to my own immediately perceived interest, for it may be, or be seen to be, *to my advantage* to break a promise, or it may be seen simply to be inconvenient or a nuisance. And, of course, if I were never tempted, for reasons of advantage, or mere inconvenience, to break my promises, there would be no point in supposing that there is a moral rule or principle against promise-breaking to which I should bind myself – a line I should not cross (without a valid justification or excuse) whatever my inclinations may be. The reasons given were (1) that the person to whom the promise is made, and who is counting on us to do what we said we would do, is let down (which is bad for that person); (2) that any trust there may have been between us is destroyed; (3) that this is a contribution, however minor, to the general breakdown of trust, which is bad for everybody. We can add to this that *if there were no general rule* against breaking promises, the practice of making promises, which only has a point if they are generally kept, would simply disappear, to everyone's disadvantage.

Neither I nor anyone else can rationally will that everybody break their promises whenever they think it is to their advantage to do so, for (1) I could be the loser and I could not complain, and (2) this would contribute to a situation in which no one could trust anyone else, a bad social situation in which everyone would be left on his or her own without being able to count on anyone else for anything, which would, in turn, encourage adversarial conflict rather than mutual cooperation for the common good. I could, of course, rationally will that *everybody else* keep their promises, thus maintaining a general faith in the institution of making and keeping promises, while taking advantage of the situation by exempting myself in order to exploit others. What I cannot do is publicly claim that it is *morally permissible* for me to do this, for then I would be granting a licence to others to do the same, which would defeat my whole purpose, which is to have *them* keep their promises so as to create a situation that I can use for my own private advantage. It would be self-defeating to say that it is morally permissible for others to act as I propose to act. If trust in promise-keeping broke down altogether that would be to everyone's disadvantage including my own. In other words, I cannot *universalize* my belief that *I* am free to act in this way by willing that others be equally free or, in Kant's language, my maxim is in violation of the categorical imperative: I may only do what I would be willing that others do when they are so motivated.

But *why*, some of you might ask, should I have to be able to universalize what *I* am free to do? Why should I restrict myself in such a way that I only allow myself to do (or not do) what I would be willing that all others do (or not do) whenever they want to? It is true that I can only regard as *morally permissible* for me what is morally permissible for everybody, but why should I think in terms of moral permissibility at all? Why not just go ahead and exploit others in the pursuit of my own private advantage? Why make moral judgments at all? Why not simply be *amoral?* Kant's answer is that all people, as possible possessors of a good will (p. 171 above), are "objective ends," of worth in themselves, and therefore to be treated as such, i.e. respected. Therefore, I must behave toward them in the same way that I would have them behave toward me, i.e. I must treat them with the respect that is their due as rational beings like myself, and universalizing my permissions (obeying the categorical imperative), which exemplifies the good will, accomplishes just this.

Kant claims that theoretical reason or "pure reason" alone obliges us to accept the categorical imperative. He believes that there is no rational escape from it. (This, he thinks, is how pure reason becomes practical.) But theoretical reason alone does not forbid us, as individuals, from exploiting others to our own advantage if we can get away with it. (Kant must introduce the conception of "objective ends," worthy of respect, in order to produce a reason why we should not.) What theoretical reason does make certain is that, if we make sincere deontic moral judgments at all (saying that this is morally wrong, this morally obligatory, and this morally permissible), then we have no alternative but to judge the acts and omissions of others by the same standards by which we judge our own. If lying as such is morally wrong (unless there is a valid justification or excuse, one that everybody could accept), then it is morally wrong for everybody, including oneself. This is inescapable, because it is built into the very way that moral language, including deontic moral language, functions. (As has been said, again and again, moral judgments are inherently universal.)

We are thus able to produce the following undeniable principle:

If an act is of a kind such that there is a reason for everybody for having it generally proscribed (not done by anybody unless there is a valid justification or excuse) then no one is to do it, i.e. acts of that kind are morally wrong, and if an act is of a kind such that there is a reason for everybody for having it generally prescribed (not left undone by anybody unless there is a valid justification or excuse), then everyone is to do it, i.e. acts of that kind are morally obligatory.

Kant thought that such a principle, which, in effect, *defines* the morally wrong and the morally obligatory (and hence is true *a priori*), was sufficient to show that reason required the acceptance of the categorical imperative. (He may even have confused this principle with the categorical imperative.) But it is not sufficient, for we can always ask the question "Are there really any such reasons?" And it is possible to deny that there are. "I have a reason, from my own point of view," a person might say, "for not wanting something done by other people whenever they feel like it – things that would have an adverse effect on me – but I don't have sufficient reasons for not doing it myself if it is to my advantage. After all, it's no skin off *my* ass." By contrast, what the categorical imperative says is:

> If an act is of a kind such that there is a reason for everybody for not wanting people to do it whenever they feel like it, then acts of that kind are not to be done by anybody, i.e. they are morally wrong; and if an act is of a kind such that there is a reason for everybody for not wanting people to leave it undone whenever they don't feel like doing it, then acts of that kind are to be done by everybody, i.e. they are morally obligatory.

The differences between these two principles are very important, for if you accept this second principle, there really is no escape from deontic morality, for there *are* things that nobody could rationally want people to do whenever they felt like it, and other things that nobody could rationally want people to neglect to do whenever they felt like it. These are the things from which one would be likely to suffer oneself if people were to do certain of them, or not do certain others, whenever they pleased, and this includes lying, promise-breaking, hurting, neglecting the responsibilities attaching to one's social roles – all of which are things which one could not rationally will that people do if they happened to feel like it – and giving aid to the distressed when your aid is needed, which one could not rationally will that people not do if they happened not to feel like it. Why? Because *you* might be the victim. This second principle (the categorical imperative) reflects the sort of thing we say to children when we are trying to make them understand the moral reason why they shouldn't do something. "How would you like it if somebody did that to you?" we say, or "Put yourself in the other person's shoes" or "What would it be like if *everybody* did that whenever they felt like it?" with the implication "What makes you special?"

What the person committed to deontic morality says is that if an act or omission satisfies the "if" clauses of the second principle, then it satisfies the "if" clauses of the first, or if an act of a certain kind isn't something you could rationally will that everyone do or leave undone whenever he or she feels like it, then everyone, including yourself, has sufficient reason for not doing it or for doing it. That is, if there are things that you don't want others to do, or not do, whenever they happen to feel like doing them or not doing them, then either they shouldn't do them or they should do them, and that means that you shouldn't or should do them yourself. In other words, they are morally wrong or morally obligatory.

And why should such a view be accepted? Simply the recognition that you and everybody else are in the same boat. You are simply recognizing the reality of others, and the fact that they see things from their point of view the same way as you see things from yours. This is the *individualist* answer. If I come to this recognition and see its force, I can only accept that there is a moral rule against promise-breaking, etc. applicable to everybody, one from which I cannot claim a moral exemption for myself. I must judge myself by the same standards by which I judge others, and if I have a justifiable complaint against someone because he has broken his promise to me, he, *on exactly the same grounds*, would have a justifiable complaint against me if I were to break a promise I made to him. If I were to claim exemption for myself, because it is to my advantage to do so, I would have no moral grounds for criticizing anyone who broke his promise to me, for he could claim exemption for himself on the very same grounds. If I only accepted the first of the above principles (which, unlike the second, I am compelled to accept because it is true *a priori*) I could, of course, deny that anyone has reasons for restricting the pursuit of his own advantage, but this would mean, in Hobbes's words, "a war of all against all," which would be to the disadvantage of everyone. That is the *social* reason for accepting the truth of the second principle, which is the supreme governing principle of deontic morality. Things are better for everybody if nobody violates trust, etc., and if everybody is willing to give aid when their aid is required. It creates a social atmosphere from which anyone benefits, and this gives one an interest in holding one's own end up for the sake of the common good.

Deontic Morality: Egoism, Altruism, or Neither

The *individualist* reason for accepting the second of the two above principles is obviously not egoistic, for it involves treating others with the same respect as you would be treated yourself, for the reason that they are, as persons like yourself, on an equal footing with you. But it is also not *altruistic*. It ultimately involves no self-denial or self-sacrifice because being (deontically) moral – the avoidance of wrongdoing – becomes something of importance to you, something that really matters, something that, in the end, you prefer. Being (deontically) moral also contributes to your own sense of well-being as a trusted and trustable member of society, willing to accept your moral responsibilities, and avoiding what, if you accept the second principle, can only be seen as wrongdoing. Again, while this is not altruistic, it is not egoistic either, for the end is not your personal or private good, but being a participating member in a good community. The *social* reason for accepting the second principle, namely that it contributes to a social atmosphere in which individuals, including yourself, can thrive and flourish in mutual understanding, friendliness, cooperation, and good will is again not altruistic. It is true that you are one of the beneficiaries, but once more, because it aims at a social good and not a merely individual or personal or private good, it is not egoistic either. The good of the community is what is being aimed at, but the good of the community (the common good) is part of the good of every individual member. Once more *eudaimonia* (well-being), communal and individual, is seen as the supreme value upon which all other values providing reasons for choice depend.

SUMMARY

1   While aretaic morality is essentially concerned with the character of persons as expressed or manifested in their conduct, deontic morality is essentially concerned with the *avoidance of wrongdoing*, whether by doing something that is morally wrong, or failing to do something that is morally required.

2   The model for deontic morality is *law* and, like the law, deontic morality tells us that there are some things we must do, whether we like it or not, and other things we must not do, whether we like it or not, or be guilty of wrongdoing.

3   The law leaves us free to do anything that it does not prohibit or forbid. Deontic morality leaves us free to do anything that is not forbidden by certain moral rules or principles.

4   To do what deontic morality requires, we must never, by act or omission, do anything that is morally wrong (illicit), or, in other words, we are only to do what is morally right (licit).

5   "Morally right" has often been taken by philosophers to mean "morally obligatory" but this is a mistake. "Morally right" means "morally permissible." If we take "morally right" to mean "morally obligatory", then, because what is not right is wrong and vice versa, every act would be either morally obligatory or morally wrong. This would eliminate the whole realm of the morally permissible – what we may or may not do at our pleasure without transgression (wrongdoing) either way.

6   There are not two deontic categories (right = obligatory, and wrong), but three: (1) morally required to do (obligatory); (2) morally required not to do (wrong); and (3) neither morally required to do nor morally required not to do (permissible to do or not do as one pleases).

7   Deontic morality is therefore an *ethics of limitation*, one that lays down certain lines that must not be crossed, but otherwise allows us to live our own lives and pursue our own projects. (As far as deontic morality is concerned, we may do or not do whatever we like as long as it is not immoral.)

8   While "morally right" means "not morally wrong" or "permissible to do," if we say something is *the morally right thing to do*, then we do mean that it is obligatory, and that anything else would be morally wrong. However, we only use this phrase when we find ourselves in a moral dilemma, just as we only use the phrase "the right thing" in non-moral contexts when there is some serious difficulty about what choice to make. However, most choices are not problematic in this way. Life does not consist in trying to figure out, on every occasion of choice, what is *the right thing to do*, let alone what is *the morally right thing to do*.

9   Kant, contrary to some standard interpretations, *did* see deontic morality as an ethics of limitation. He did *not* say that we must only do what it is our duty to do, let alone that we should always act out of a sense of duty. Kant's categorical imperative does not dictate to us what we are to do on every occasion of choice; rather, it forbids us from doing or failing to do certain things.

10   What the categorical imperative forbids is the doing or not doing of anything that we could not will that everyone do or not do at their pleasure. This would obviously include most of the things that are typically regarded as morally wrong – all the things (such as lying, promise-breaking, causing harm, failing to aid the distressed, neglecting the responsibilities attached to social roles) that if everyone did do them at their pleasure (whenever they felt like it), we would all be likely to suffer.

11   The individualist reason for obeying the categorical imperative is *the recognition of the reality of other people*, and the realization that things are no different for them than they are for us.

12   The social reason for obeying the categorical imperative is that it helps to create an atmosphere in which people can live comfortably together, without worrying about being done in by others.

13   Therefore, everyone has a reason for general obedience to the categorical imperative which is the supreme governing principle of deontic morality.

14   Neither the individualist nor the social reason for obedience to the categorical imperative is egoistic, but neither is it altruistic. The individualist reason is *universalist*. The social reason is tied to the common good. Both are clearly tied to *eudaimonia*, both individual and social, although Kant would certainly deny this.

QUESTIONS FOR THOUGHT

1   It is certainly true that everything is either morally right or morally wrong, but it is not true that everything is either morally obligatory or morally wrong. Explain the importance of this.
2   A woman interviewed on the street on the question "Is it morally wrong to cheat on your taxes?" replied: "I didn't know morality had anything to do with taxes. I thought morality was about sex." How would you enlighten her?
3   Is there anything that you could not will that others do whenever they feel like it? Why couldn't you will it? What are the moral consequences of this?
4   Does anyone really profit from wrongdoing? Explain.

Recommended Reading

Chapter 7   Three Different Approaches to Ethics

For attempts to assimilate deontic morality to aretaic morality or to abolish deontic morality altogether, see the following:

G. E. M. Anscombe, "Modern moral philosophy," *Philosophy*, 33 (1958), pp. 1–19.

Philippa Foot, "When is a principle a moral principle?" *Proceedings of the Aristotelian Society*, suppl. vol. 28 (1954), pp. 95–110.

Philippa Foot, "Moral beliefs" (1958–9), reprinted in Philippa Foot, *Virtues and Vices* (Blackwell, Oxford, 1987), pp. 110–31.

P. T. Geach, "Good and evil," *Analysis*, 17 (1957), pp. 33–42.

For an answer to these three, see:

E. J. Bond, "Moral requirement and the need for deontic language," *Philosophy*, 41 (1966), pp. 233–49.

See also:

Philippa Foot, "Virtues and vices," in Philippa Foot, *Virtues and Vices* (Blackwell, Oxford, 1978), pp. 1–18. Foot deplores the prevalent exclusively deontic approach to ethics, argues for the superiority of a virtue approach, and considers some of the problems in connection with the virtues and vices.

For an attempt to assimilate *moral* virtues (as distinct from what the author calls *personal* virtues) to deontic morality, see:

Bernard Gert, *Morality* (Oxford University Press, New York and London, 1988), chs 8 and 9. An earlier version of this book was published under the title *The Moral Rules* (New York, Harper, 1967, 1970, 1973).

On supererogation, see:

J. O. Urmson, "Saints and heroes," in A. I. Melden (ed.), *Essays in Moral Philosophy* (University of Washington Press, Seattle, 1958), pp. 198–216.

Joel Feinberg, "Supererogation and rules" (1961), reprinted in Joel Feinberg, *Doing and Deserving* (Princeton University Press, Princeton, NJ, 1970).

David Heyd, *Supererogation* (Cambridge University Press, Cambridge, 1982).

Millard K. Schumaker, *Rights, Duties, and Supererogation.* Unpublished PhD thesis,

Queen's University at Kingston, 1970. A complete and thorough examination of the subject of supererogation. Though recommended for publication by the external examiner (Joel Feinberg), it was not published as a book because *at the time*, supererogation was regarded as too narrow a subject for book-length treatment. How things have changed! We now have full-length books on courage and lying, for instance, as well as supererogation (see recommended readings for chapters 8 and 9). Available on microfilm from the National Library of Canada.

For attempts to show that deontic morality (as rule-bound) is essentially *masculine*, while the "ethics of care" (a version of aretaic morality) is essentially *feminine* and superior, see the following:

Carol Gilligan, *In a Different Voice* (Harvard University Press, Cambridge, Mass., 1982).

Eva Kittay and Diana Meyers (eds), *Women and Moral Theory* (Roman and Littlefield, Totowa, NJ, 1987).

For a virtue approach seen as the fundamental aspect of morality see:

Alasdair MacIntyre, *After Virtue*, 2nd edn (Duckworth, London, 1985), chs 14 and 15.

Chapter 8   Goodness of Character (Aretaic Morality)

You couldn't do better than to start with:

Alasdair MacIntyre, "Virtue ethics," in Lawrence C. Becker (ed.), *Encyclopedia of Ethics* (Garland Publishing, New York and London, 1992), vol. II, pp. 1276–82.

Also:

Edmund L. Pincoffs, "Virtues", in Lawrence C. Becker (ed.), *Encyclopedia of Ethics* (Garland Publishing, New York and London, 1992), vol. II, pp. 1283–8.

Peter Geach, *The Virtues* (Cambridge University Press, Cambridge, 1977).

James D. Wallace, *Virtues and Vices* (Cornell University Press, Ithaca, NY, 1978).

Philippa Foot, "Virtues and vices," in Philippa Foot, *Virtues and Vices* (Blackwell, Oxford, 1978), pp. 1–18.

Douglas D. Walton, *Courage: A Philosophical Investigation* (University of California Press, Berkeley, Calif., 1986).

Chapter 9   The Avoidance of Wrongdoing (Deontic Morality)

See the references to Kant in the notes for this chapter. (This is the primary source but it is difficult.) See also:

Bernard Gert, *Morality* (Oxford University Press, New York and London, 1988). (Or see the earlier versions of this book published under the title *The Moral Rules*, Harper, New York, 1967, 1970, 1973). Gert clearly understands deontic morality as an ethics of *limitation*. He also sees deontic morality (the moral rules) as central to ethics, and everything else as peripheral, much of it related to the moral rules.

Sissela Bok, *Lying: Moral Choice in Public and Private Life* (Pantheon Books, New York, 1978).

Part IV
Tying Things Together

10

The Relations between Aretaic and Deontic Morality

We have seen that aretaic and deontic morality both exist in the common understanding, as expressed in the concepts of our moral language. We do admire people for certain attributes of character, such as courage and generosity, and we despise them for certain other attributes of character, such as laziness, greediness, and dishonesty. We also tend to suppose that, in living our own lives in the pursuit of our own projects, there are certain lines that must not be crossed, typically that we are not to kill, or hurt, or injure, or otherwise abuse or maltreat people, that we are not to lie or steal or cheat, nor to do anything that is unjust or unfair, that all these things are kinds of moral wrongdoing, as are failing to do certain things, such as aiding the distressed when our aid is needed. All these things, the not-doings or the doings, are seen as moral *requirements*, that is we either must not do them or we must do them, whatever our inclinations may be, that is whatever we may desire otherwise, unless we have an acceptable justification or excuse (one that could be consensually agreed upon). If we do what we are morally required not to do, or fail to do what we are morally required to do, we are guilty of wrongdoing. Things that we are neither morally required to do nor morally required not to do, we may or may not do as we please without wrongdoing or moral transgression either way. (This is the realm of the *morally permissible* and it constitutes a huge proportion of our actions, including most of those that make our life worth living.)

We have seen (chapter 7, pp. 139–45) that we cannot give an account of aretaic morality in terms of deontic morality or vice versa. Neither dimension is collapsible into the other. We have also seen (chapter 7, pp. 145–6) that we cannot dispense with either, that we need both, and that therefore *any adequate moral theory must take account of both*. We must now consider what the relationship is, if any, between these two different aspects or dimensions of morality, and how they fit together.

Honesty and the "Deontic Virtues"

A good place to begin is with the virtue of honesty, and the corresponding vice of dishonesty. You will remember that the subject of honesty came up in our discussion of "You promised you wouldn't" as a moral reason against doing something (chapter 6, pp. 121–2). We can say now, what we couldn't say then, that this is a *deontic* moral reason against doing something, since it implies that there is a moral rule or principle that forbids promise-breaking. And yet we saw, almost at once, that promise-keeping and promise-breaking were related to honesty, which is a moral virtue, and dishonesty, which is a moral vice, and these, since they are attributes of character, belong by definition to the aretaic dimension of morality. So we have, in the case of at least one virtue and its corresponding vice, an obvious connection between the aretaic and the deontic. We must now try to see exactly what that connection is.

Let us try to make things as simple as possible. Honesty, as we noted at the time, is connected with trustworthiness: an honest person can be trusted and a dishonest person cannot. With perhaps some oversimplification – here in the interest of the connection we are trying to get clear about – we can describe the virtue of honesty as the strong *disinclination*, understood as a fixed quality of character, to lie, steal, or cheat. That this is related to trustworthiness should be plain and obvious. And yes, you have seen the connection. Lying, stealing, and cheating (as we noted in the opening paragraph of this chapter) are all acts that are taken to be morally wrong; in other words, it is commonly understood that they are things that we are morally required not to do, that there are moral rules forbidding them. Yet honesty does not consist simply in not lying, stealing, or cheating, but in the settled disinclination to do any of these things. When an honest person is compelled to lie, steal, or cheat, he or she does so only with difficulty, and may feel very uncomfortable about it. Similarly, a person is not dishonest just because he or she occasionally violates one of these rules, especially if he or she has a bad conscience about it; a dishonest person is one who lies, steals, or cheats *easily*, who simply has no moral compunctions about it. If she or he doesn't lie, steal, or cheat, when it would be to her advantage, it is only to keep up appearances, or out of fear of being found out, not because she has a sincere conviction that these things are morally wrong, as the honest person does. But being honest is more than having a sincere conviction that lying, stealing, and cheating are morally wrong, for a person may have that conviction without having the strong disinclination to do them which is the mark of honesty. Such a person may in fact never, or hardly ever, do any of these things without a valid justification or excuse, but he may have to *struggle* against his inclinations to lie, steal, or cheat when it is to his advantage to do so and he thinks he can get away with it. Thus we cannot say he is *dishonest*, but the virtue of honesty is lacking in him until he no longer has any inclination to lie, steal, or cheat, until the *disinclination* to do so is part of his settled character.

The fact of the matter is, if lying, stealing, and cheating are *morally wrong* (unless there is a valid justification or excuse) – and this is a matter of deontic morality – then we are morally required not to do any of these things whether we possess the virtue of honesty or not. As Kant rightly noted, we must, if something is morally wrong, be able to restrain ourselves from doing it simply by recognizing that this is so, regardless of any contrary inclinations we may have. If this were not true, if we were unable to restrain ourselves from doing (by act or omission) what is morally wrong simply on the understanding that it *is* morally wrong, deontic morality could have no point. *It could not be practical.* It would be a vain and empty notion. If deontic morality is not just a fake, then we must be able to act on what Kant saw as the pure moral motive: the recognition that an act or an abstention, if it is of a certain kind, is morally wrong, or, to say the same thing in another way, that not doing one thing or doing another is a moral obligation or a moral duty. (Just how deontic morality – which he saw as determined by pure reason – *could* be practical, was a problem that preoccupied Kant.)

Thus we can see that simply refraining from lying, stealing, or cheating, in the belief or conviction that these things are morally wrong, while it means that we are not dishonest, is not the same thing as having the virtue of honesty (being an honest person), which requires that the *temptation* to lie, steal or cheat for our own advantage either does not exist or has been overcome. Still we can call honesty (if we wish) a *deontic* virtue, for it can be analysed as the fixed disposition to avoid certain acts which are traditionally thought to violate moral rules, and moral rules, of course, belong to deontic morality. Similarly, dishonesty, which involves lying, stealing, and cheating without compunction when it is to your advantage and you think you can get away with it, could be called a deontic vice.

There are a few other deontic virtues and vices, analyzable in the same way as honesty and dishonesty, some of them more or less identical to honesty or dishonesty and others very closely related to it. These qualities are named by such words as (from our list in chapter 8): "incorruptible," "straight," "fair-minded," "trustworthy," "polite," "considerate," "responsible," "fraud," "liar," "thief," "rude," "shifty," "devious," "sly," "deceitful," "treacherous," "crooked," "disrespectul," "ungrateful." I will leave it to you to figure out just what moral rule or rules a person having one of these characteristics shows a strong disinclination to violate, or what moral rule or rules a person having one of these characteristic disobeys without compunction if he wants (or doesn't want) to do it and he thinks he can get away with it.

Other Virtues and Vices

Most of the virtues and vices, however, are not analyzable in the way we analyzed honesty and dishonesty, i.e. as a strong disinclination to violate certain rules or principles, or the disposition to violate them without compunction, which justified us in calling them (I hope not too confusingly), deontic virtues and vices. Try doing it with courage, or self-discipline to start (and their opposites, cowardice and self-indulgence); then try kindness or generosity. Then see how you make out with some of the others on the list.

Let us consider kindness, for instance. Is kindness the strong disinclination to violate a moral rule forbidding unkindness? Or is it the powerful inclination to obey a moral rule requiring kindness? No, for while there is a traditional moral rule or principle forbidding us to cause hurt or harm to others unless there is some valid justification or excuse, there is no moral rule or principle *requiring* kind acts of *forbidding* unkind ones. An act of kindness (a kind act) or, for that matter, an act of generosity (a generous one) may very well be supererogatory, that is we are under no obligation to do it and no one can demand it of us as a right (see chapter 7, p. 141). Secondly, kindness can sometimes be inappropriate, or in excess. Should we be kind to criminals, for instance, and let them go? Finally, we cannot *decide* to *be* kind, even on some particular occasion, any more than we can decide to *be* honest. The most we can do, if we don't happen to be kind or honest, is to act as the kind or honest person would.[1] Consider Hamlet speaking to his mother (chapter 7, p. 142). A genuinely kind act can only come from a kind heart, from someone who possesses the virtue of kindness.

Kindness was chosen for a detailed examination because of all the virtues and vices we named as *not* being capable of an analysis in terms of a strong disinclination to obey a moral rule (or rules), or having a disposition to disobey it easily (without compunction), kindness and unkindness looked most likely to be capable of such an analysis. It is more obvious in the case of courage and cowardice, generosity and stinginess, self-discipline and self-indulgence, that no such analysis can be given of them, nor can such an analysis be given of most of the virtues and vices describable in the terms on our list, including "good-hearted," "good-natured," "nasty," "dedicated," "caring," "warm," "enterprising," "loyal," "arrogant," "vain," "conceited," etc., etc. These virtues and vices bear no relation to the deontic, and this, of course, is one of the reasons why aretaic morality cannot be understood in deontic terms (cf. chapter 7, pp. 139–44). But, as we have just seen, even the deontic virtues and vices, as we have agreed to call them, such as honesty and fair-mindedness, do not simply consist – for the virtues – in regularly obeying or not violating a moral rule or rules, or – for the vices – being unable not to violate them. If we are convinced that a rule is really binding, we can obey it, even on a regular basis, through pure determination and strength of will; and through weakness of will we can regularly violate a rule that we accept as binding, even if this entails suffering from a bad conscience. (That is why we can be said to be responsible for our acts or failures to act.) The virtues and vices, however, must be settled dispositions of character, part of what we are or have become. Because we actually *possess* the virtue (say, of honesty), there are no contrary inclinations and therefore no effort of will is required not to violate a rule. We do not have to struggle against the temptation to do so for no such temptation exists.

Kant *v.* Aristotle

Suppose, like Kant, we take the deontic dimension – requirement (duty, obligation), wrongness (obligation not to do), and permissibility (licitness) – to be the whole of morality, ignoring most of the traditional virtues and vices. Suppose we then try to consider this in aretaic terms. What we come up with is a single virtue – moral rectitude, i.e. always doing what is morally right, or, to say the same thing in another way, never doing, either by act or omission, anything that is morally wrong. What this means is never violating any moral rule or principle,[2] i.e. any rule or principle requiring or forbidding (requiring the omission of) a certain kind of act (e.g. promise-keeping, lying), and justified by some form of what Kant called the categorical imperative (see, for example, the version of the categorical imperative offered in chapter 9, pp. 175–6).

But is it strictly appropriate to call rectitude a virtue if we define it in this way? If it really were a moral virtue, in the sense in which we have been talking about moral virtues, it would have to constitute a settled disposition, in this case, never to do, either by act or omission, anything that is morally wrong (anything that violates the categorical imperative). But what, then, of acting from what Kant called the pure moral motive, or the motive of duty – acting (or abstaining from action) out of the sheer recognition that the moral law requires it – which he said was the only motive that had moral worth? This is the only motive that commands admiration, according to Kant, because it alone exemplifies what he calls the good will, all other motives coming from our morally worthless natural desires. According to Kant, we only act from the pure moral motive if what we do or abstain from doing is done or not done *in spite of* any inclinations we have, all inclinations coming from "the faculty of desire." Yet we only have a moral virtue, as Aristotle understands it, and in the account that has been given here, if we are *strongly inclined* to act (or abstain from action) in ways that manifest it, because that is the kind of person we are or have become. This, you will remember, is what we said above about the virtue of honesty, and about the deontic virtues in general, and what could rectitude as a *virtue* be but the sum of all the deontic virtues? We can, by sheer force of will, resist the temptation to lie, steal, or cheat, but we do not possess the virtue of honesty until the temptation no longer exists.

What, then, are we to say about the alleged virtue of rectitude? If it is simply the sum of all the deontic virtues, including honesty, then we would have to give the same account of it that we gave of honesty: we can, through moral strength and determination, never do, either by act or omission, what we recognize to be morally wrong, in spite of any contrary inclinations we may have. But we do not possess the *moral virtue* of rectitude unless or until there are no contrary inclinations, until we *desire*, because that is the kind of person we are or have become, only to do what is morally right (not morally wrong). Kant, however, would see the determination to act (or not act) as the moral law requires, in total disregard of our inclinations – something which may require strength of will – as the only thing that merits moral praise, the only thing that reflects well upon us morally. The virtues, as we understand them, since the actions that manifest them flow from desire, would be nothing for which we could take any moral credit, and that would include honesty and the other deontic virtues. Rectitude, considered as the sum of all the deontic virtues, would obviously have to go on this list. We started with the suggestion that we might try to treat Kant aretaically by interpreting him as saying that there is but one moral virtue, namely rectitude, but we have now seen that this is impossible, given what we understand a moral virtue to be. For this would exclude the pure moral motive – restraining our actions (or inactions) for the sake of the moral law – which Kant saw as the aspect that raised human beings, as rational creatures, above the rest of the natural world.

Let us try to put this in ordinary, common-sense terms. For what does a person deserve moral praise? For what does a person gain moral Brownie points? You might very well say, given that you believe there is such a thing as moral right and wrong, that you earn credit by mastering your inclinations, so enabling you to do what you morally must do and nothing that you morally must not do; in other words, enable you never to do anything, by act or omission, that is morally wrong. Why, after all, should you gain any credit for what flows naturally from your character as it is or has become, without any need, or any further need for self-mastery? Do you gain any moral credit for something you would do anyway because that is the kind of person you are and can't help being? This is a perfectly natural view to take, especially in our culture, but it is absolutely counter-aretaic. It is therefore in conflict with our equally natural aretaic views, for we really do admire people for being honest, generous, kind, courageous, dedicated, prudent, self-disciplined, etc., etc., for possessing these virtues as part of their character, part of the kind of person they are, or have become, with no (or no more) struggle or effort of will involved.

So you must ask yourself which reflects more credit on you: to actually *be* honest, i.e. to have a strong disinclination to lie, steal, or cheat, or to have enough strength of will to overcome your temptations to do so? The answer of Aristotle and his successors is loud and clear. One's aim in life should be to try to become a person of good character, where goodness, because one's desires are right and one's reasoning sound, flows effortlessly. If you lack a virtue you must emulate those who have it in the hope that you will eventually acquire it yourself. For this you will need moral strength or force of will (*engkrateia*), by which you may eventually succeed in acquiring the virtue, but this is a far lesser thing than actually possessing it. Unless or until you do possess it, you may also fail, through weakness of will (*akrasia*), to act as the virtuous person would. The contrast with Kant could not be more stark. Which side do you take?

The solution to this dilemma, where the deontic virtues are concerned, seems to be, yes, it is better to *be* honest than merely to act honestly (refrain by an effort of will from lying, cheating, and stealing), but it is nevertheless better, if you need it, to have the moral strength (the strength of will to resist temptation) than to lack it, to be morally weak.[3] (Remember, if deontic morality is to be practical, a person must be able to avoid wrongdoing simply on the understanding that an act or omission would be morally wrong, see p. 187 above.) You are most praiseworthy if you actually are honest (possess the virtue of honesty), but you also earn credit for having the strength of will to resist your temptations.

Is Rectitude Enough?

But let us leave aside, for now, the issue of what earns us moral credit, and simply consider rectitude, defined as always doing right in the sense of never doing, by act or omission, anything that is morally wrong. Remember that rectitude, so defined, is the sole concern of deontic morality, regardless of whether it can be understood as a virtue in the Aristotelian sense. We have already noted that if morality simply consists in rectitude and nothing more, most of the traditional moral virtues and vices − all those that cannot be analyzed in deontic terms as a strong disinclination to violate a moral rule or rules (virtues), or doing so easily, without compunction (vices) − will simply have been eliminated. That would include such important virtues and vices as kindness and unkindness, generosity and stinginess, courage and cowardice, self-discipline and self-indulgence, prudence and foolishness. Surely we can only conclude that rectitude, however it is construed, is not enough.

The character Scrooge, in Charles Dickens's *A Christmas Carol* (1843), before his encounter with Marley's ghost and the Spirits of Christmas Past, Christmas Present and Christmas Yet to Come, was the very model of rectitude, doing nothing to which he was not entitled by moral right, and discharging all his moral obligations. Yet he had a heart of stone. There was not a trace of kindness or generosity. The encounter with Marley's ghost and the Spirits changed him, making him realize that being kind and generous was not only better for Bob Cratchit and his family, *but also for his own happiness and well-being*. Should these virtues and their corresponding vices (unkindness and stinginess) count for nothing morally, or are they an important part of what it is to be of morally good and praiseworthy character? It is plain that perfect rectitude is compatible with a complete and uncaring cold-heartedness, to say nothing of cowardice, foolishness, self-indulgence, and all the other non-deontic vices. Does being morally good, then, consist only in never violating the rules or principles of morality, in never doing anything that is morally wrong? Are the non-deontic virtues of no moral importance? I believe you will have no trouble providing the answer.

Kant and Aristotle Reconciled

Let us return now to the question of which is better, actually to possess the virtues and so be of good moral character, or to have the strength of will (moral strength) always to act as a person who possessed the virtues would act, even if you have to fight with contrary inclinations? This would apply not only to the deontic virtues, such as honesty, but to all the virtues; one can, with difficulty, act in a particular situation as a courgeous person would act, without actually possessing the virtue of courage as a settled disposition of character. A person could refrain from lying to you for one or the other of the following reasons: (1) because she or he likes you, does not want to make you a victim of her dishonesty nor damage a close and valued relationship, or (2) in order to obey the stern command of duty, although she has no *feelings* about the matter at all. Which motive would you prefer? Which would make her the better person? Again, I may return a favor freely, in a spirit of friendliness and good will, or I may return it grudgingly, only because I believe not to do so would be morally wrong. Which would be more agreeable to you if you were the person to whom the favor was being returned? And which of these motives would make me the better, more praiseworthy person? Again, which kind of motive makes for better social relations and a happy life in general for all parties? My vote would go to the former in both cases. How about yours? Would you be willing to throw away the virtues of character and settle for sheer rectitude and, in the case of the non-deontic virtues, mere imitation or "assumption" of the virtues, to use Hamlet's word when addressing his mother? (see chapter 7, p. 142).

The answer seems clear that, where moral rules and principles are concerned, it is better to possess the relevant virtues than simply to obey the stern command of duty or, where rules or principles are not involved, better to possess the virtues than simply to act, with difficulty, *as if* one possessed them. Furthermore, it is clear that if one possessed all the deontic virtues in full measure, which would mean one possessed the deontic *virtue* of rectitude, then one would, without effort or struggle against contrary inclinations, never be guilty, whether by act or omission, of any moral wrongdoing. Nevertheless, no person ever does or ever could possess all the deontic virtues, or the single virtue of rectitude – which is all of them rolled into one – in perfect measure. Therefore, one must still be able to do what one is morally required to do, and not do what one is morally required not to do, simply because one recognizes that such a moral requirement does exist, that there is a moral rule or principle requiring you either to do something or not to do something, regardless of your inclinations. It is better to possess the virtues, including the deontic ones. Yet deontic morality, understood simply as a set of principles that must be followed regardless of one's inclinations otherwise, must stay in place as a fall-back or fail-safe device, for it will be needed when the relevant virtue is either not there or is temporarily on vacation, as can indeed happen!

SUMMARY

1   Aretaic and deontic morality both exist in the common understanding, as expressed in the concepts of our moral language (e.g. "morally wrong," "courageous").

2   We cannot give an account of aretaic morality in terms of deontic morality or vice versa. Nor can we simply dispense with either one.

3   The virtue of honesty is the strong *disinclination*, understood as a fixed quality of character, to lie, steal, or cheat.

4   Lying, stealing, and cheating are all typically thought to be morally wrong. We may therefore call honesty a "deontic virtue."

5   However, honesty does not simply *consist* in not lying, cheating, or stealing, for there are rules forbidding us to lie, steal, or cheat whether we possess the virtue (the settled disinclination) or not.

6   Honesty is more than the *conviction* that lying, stealing, and cheating are morally wrong, because one can have that conviction and act accordingly without possessing the virtue (the settled disinclination).

7   As Kant noted, we must be able to refrain from lying, stealing, and cheating simply from the recognition that these things are wrong, even

if we are severely tempted. (If the recognition of moral wrongness could not motivate us, moral rules or principles could have no practical use.) However, the possessor of the virtue is not tempted.

8   There are other deontic virtues associated with such words as "incorruptible," "straight," "fair-minded," etc.

9   Dishonesty is the disposition to lie, steal, or cheat without compunction. (One may occasionally, without justification or excuse, violate a moral rule, but this does not make one dishonest. One is not dishonest unless this becomes a habitual tendency, with little or no conscience.)

10   Most of the virtues and vices, however, are not analyzable in this way; that is, they cannot be construed as strong disinclinations to disobey some moral rule or principle, or as the disposition to disobey it without compunction. Kindness is a clear example of such a virtue, as are the virtues associated with such terms as "warm," "enterprising," "arrogant," "vain," "brave," etc.

11   If we try to construe deontic morality in aretaic terms, we come up with the single virtue of *rectitude*, which would consist in always doing what is morally right (never doing what is morally wrong). But rectitude is not strictly a virtue if we define it in this way, for we might by sheer strength of will in the face of temptation never do anything morally wrong. We would not possess the *virtue* of rectitude unless there were no contrary temptations, in which case *strength of will* would not be needed. This would exclude Kant's *pure* moral motive.

12   You might think that you gain no moral credit for what flows effortlessly from your character, but only from strength of will in the face of temptation. But we do admire such things as kindness, generosity, etc. There is therefore a conflict here.

13   Where the deontic virtues, such as honesty, are concerned, it is better to possess the virtue, but if you lack it, it is better to be morally strong in the face of temptation than to be morally weak and give in to it.

14   Rectitude is not enough. You can possess perfect rectitude (be *righteous* in the Biblical sense) and yet be quite a nasty person. The other virtues are necessary for goodness of character.

15   It is better to possess the virtues than simply, from strength of will, not to do any wrong (by act or omission), but deontic morality must stay in place as a fall-back device when the relevant virtues are not present.

QUESTIONS FOR THOUGHT

1   Which reflects better on you morally, being able by strength of will to resist the temptation to lie, steal, or cheat, or to possess the virtue of

honesty, which means you are not tempted to do any of these things? Do you side with Kant or Aristotle?

2   Is there a virtue of rectitude? Explain why or why not.

3   It has been claimed that politeness is a deontic virtue, while loyalty is not. Spell this out in detail and see if you agree.

4   How, if at all, is the virtue of courage (and the corresponding vice of cowardice) related to doing what you are morally required to do?

11
Justice and Rights

No moral theory is complete without an examination of justice and rights, and that will be our task in this chapter. The subject is taken up *here* because of its direct relation to what is said in chapter 12, as you will see. When the subject of supererogation – doing *more than* is morally required – came up earlier, it was pointed out that we are only under a moral obligation or requirement to do something for somebody, or not to do something to somebody, if they have a *moral right* to demand it of us (chapter 7, p. 141), and that, if doing it or not doing it is supererogatory, that means they do *not* have a moral right to demand it of us (chapter 10, p. 188). It can now be stated bluntly that it can only be true that I have a moral obligation toward you (either to do or not do something that will affect you), if you have a *moral right* to demand it of me, and it can only be true that you have a moral right to demand something of me (to do or not to do something), if I am morally required (am under a moral obligation to you) to do it or not to do it for you or to you. (This is built into our very understanding of moral language, which means that it is true *a priori*.) If I do have a moral obligation toward you, either to do or not to do something, which means that you have a moral right to demand it of me, and I fail to honor that obligation (fail to do, either by action or inaction, what is morally required of me toward you), then you have been *wronged*, you have a justified complaint against me, a complaint justified *on moral grounds*, and you may be morally entitled to seek redress or reparation, perhaps to punish me or to demand that I be punished (pay a penalty), perhaps to demand that I make amends, or both.

Violation of Moral Rights: Some Concrete Examples

Let us take some concrete examples. Suppose you borrow a hundred dollars from me and promise to pay me back on Monday. Monday comes and, after hearing nothing from you, I ask for the hundred dollars, which I am morally entitled to do both because you owe it to me and because you promised to pay it back today. You tell me you can't be bothered – it's inconvenient – and I'll just have to wait. I'm mad at you, yes, but more than that I'm morally indignant, because you have done me a wrong. (And someone else could be morally indignant on my behalf.) I loaned you that hundred dollars on trust and you have violated that trust. (How do I know I'll ever get the money back?) I'll certainly have nothing more to do with you until you either explain or apologize and give me back what you owe me, maybe with interest! If I cut you off and never do anything for you again that will be your punishment, and it will be just, for it is what you deserve. If you return the money, explain yourself to my satisfaction, sincerely apologize, and then do me a favor, you will have made amends, and justice will have been served. I would have no resort to the law in a case like this unless there was a written contract, but if there was a written contract, and I took you to a small claims court and received satisfaction, justice would again have been served.

To take another example, suppose that, in anger, I hit you and knock you down, seriously injuring you. My anger *may* have been justified, but I was certainly not justified in causing you such harm. I have done wrong – I have violated the moral rule against hurting or harming people without an accept-able justification or excuse – but I have also *wronged you*, for you had a *moral right* not to be treated that way, especially since you didn't deserve such treatment. Again you feel not just anger but *righteous* anger because you have been done a wrong, and again you would be morally justified in calling for punishment or reparation or both. Here you might very well have resort to the law. If you report the incident I may be charged with criminal assault, or you may file a civil suit for aggravated assault. Or I may try to make amends by paying your medical bills and looking after some of your responsibilities until you recover, and you may accept this in reparation for the wrong that has been done you. Certainly you have a right to some form of redress or other, and I have an obligation to make it up to you if I can. If I do not, or cannot, you may be satisfied if I am punished by the law. Justice would seem to require one thing or the other. It would be unjust if I got off scot free, that is unless you decided to forgive me, but I cannot demand forgiveness as a moral right. A person who is wronged can always rightfully demand reparation or punishment and sometimes perhaps both. No one is *morally required* to forgive a wrong that is done them. To forgive is always an act of supererogation.

Another example. Suppose I quite consciously give you a low mark on your philosophy assignment, not because you haven't done well, but because I dislike you personally, or I have a grudge against you, or because you are of a certain race or sex or age or religion or sexual orientation. I sincerely believe your assignment is worth an "A," but I give you a "C" because you are black, or Jewish, or old and ugly, or a woman, or a homosexual, or you have offended me personally in some way. To begin with, you have been wronged because I have treated you unfairly. I have not given you the mark that, in my sincere judgment, you have earned and you deserve, based on the standards by which I judge white, non-Jewish males whom I don't dislike or have a grudge against.[1] If you have solid evidence for this, you have a right to demand redress or punishment or both. I certainly deserve, at best, a reprimand and a warning, and you should be given the mark you earned and are therefore entitled to, together with the assurance – even if it means firing me – that it will not happen again.

Examples of the violation of *rights*, which means doing some individual or some group a *wrong* – treating them in a way they do not *deserve* to be treated, or not treating them in a way to which they are *entitled* (have a right) to be treated – which is *unjust*, can be multiplied endlessly. Just to give one very important and very common example, a person may be convicted of a crime of which he or she is not guilty because the police or the prosecuting attorneys have fabricated evidence of guilt, or concealed evidence of innocence, in order to get a conviction. Nor can there be any doubt that we are dealing with moral truth and hence moral reality in these matters. Just place yourself in the position of the victim. Would *you* not claim you had been wronged, that you had been done an injustice? And would you not claim on another person's behalf that this was true of him or her? No one can doubt that there is such a thing as injustice, and to say that doing what is unjust is morally wrong is redundant. "Unjust" is a full, thick moral concept (chapter 2, pp. 25–7), bearing its own – in this case deontic – moral weight. Therefore, no one can doubt that there are some things that are – really are – morally wrong.

Rights, Wrongs, Deserts, Entitlements, and Justice

It is time now to generalize. If you have a *right* to something from me, then you can demand of me that I not violate that right, and if I do violate it I have done you a *wrong*. This can be a positive right, as for instance a child's right to parental or other adult care, or my right to claim from you what you owe me, or my right to demand of you that you not lie to me, and that you keep the promise you made to me, or my right to fair treatment from those in authority. (These are sometimes called *demand* rights or *claim* rights.) Some positive or claim rights are based on what I have *earned* or *merited*. Thus, if I earn my pay or my marks or my credit-rating or my standing, I am wronged if I am not given it, for I am not only entitled to it, I *deserve* it. And if I have won the competition fair and square, I *deserve* the acknowledgment of this fact together with the award, or the prize, or the honor, or the job, or whatever it was for which I was competing, and I am wronged if I do not receive it.

There are also negative, or *permissive* rights, which can all be put together (generalized) as my right, as an adult, to live my life as I see fit, within the limits of deontic morality and the law (provided it is just). (This is often called the right to liberty.) If I have a right to do something, in this sense, then you and everyone else, including the government, have the moral obligation to stand aside and allow me to exercise that right. (For a ruler or a government or an overbearing parent to violate this right by coercion or attempted coercion is what is called *tyranny*.)

It has been said (above), that if I have done some person or persons a wrong, then that person, or those people, or other people, or the state on his or her or their behalf, may demand punishment, either as a substitute for reparation, or in addition to it. If the wrong done is serious enough, then we may say that the *punishment* is earned or deserved. Whether it is reparation or punishment or both,[2] the person who has committed the offence, has been deprived of a right or rights, the right not to try to make amends, i.e. make it up to the person or persons he or she has wronged (the permissive right not to be required to do something he or she may not want to do), the permissive right to liberty (if he or she is put in jail) or, as some would have it, the claim or demand right not to be hurt or harmed (in the case of capital or corporal punishment). (A child may be punished by depriving him or her of some pleasure which she or he would otherwise be allowed.) If the infringement on freedom or the punishment is *not* deserved, either because it is too harsh, or because the person is innocent, then a wrong has been done to that person, and *she* has a right to redress, or to demand punishment, or both.

Finally, on the subject of desert, if someone has *not* merited or deserved an award or a prize or an honor she or he has received, an injustice has been done. We are entitled to what we have earned or merited and hence deserve, in the way of awards and honors and the like, and we can claim these things as a right. But we are not entitled to awards and honors which we have not earned or merited, and hence do not deserve.

Let us try to summarize the relations between these different ideas, all centering around the ideas of justice and rights. I have a moral right to something if I can demand or require of some other or others that he or she or they do the thing for me, or sometimes not do it to me as, for example, cause me injury or treat me unfairly (claim rights), or not interfere with or try to obstruct or prevent my doing a thing or not doing it as I please (permissive rights). My right has been violated if my claim is ignored or over-ridden (claim rights), or if my liberty to do or not do as I please (within the restrictions imposed by deontic morality or the law, if it is just) has been interfered with (permissive rights). In either case, I have been done a wrong, and the party who has wronged me has committed an injustice. One kind of claim right is my right to what I have earned or merited, and which I therefore deserve. If I don't receive the reward for what I deserve, then my right has been violated; I have been wronged and an injustice has been done. And if I receive a reward which I have not earned or merited, I do not deserve it and again an injustice has been done, an injustice that is quite independent of the injustice that may have been done to another person who did earn or merit this particular reward. Finally, if my right is violated, I, or others on my behalf (including the state) may seek redress from or punishment for the offending party, a punishment that may be justified. But if an innocent party is punished, or a guilty one is punished too severely, then again an injustice has been done. Injustice (doing some person or person a wrong) consists in the violation of rights; justice is respect for and protection of those same rights. We have now seen how all these ideas are interconnected.

The preceding paragraph showed only the interconnectedness of certain *ideas* that exist in the common understanding. Except for the examples given in parentheses, it said nothing about what actually is just or unjust, or about what moral rights we actually have. But if you want to know this, all you need do is return to the "concrete examples" given in the last section, which are *undoubted* examples of the violation of rights. And one could give many more. Suppose there are five hungry children who I am responsible for feeding, and what I have is a pie, which I divide into four pieces, leaving one child out, for no reason except that it's easier to divide a pie into four pieces than it is to divide it into five. The child left out is not allergic to pumpkin, is not sick, likes pumpkin pie, has not violated any rules and so is not being punished, and has had as little to eat as and is as hungry as the others. I am clearly guilty of an injustice, and the child is quite right if she thinks she has been unfairly treated and it is natural for her to feel *righteously indignant*. If the other four children were given a piece of the pie, so should she have been, even if the others, out of kindness, a sense of fairness, and a willingness to share, each give her a little piece of their own. She has not only been left hungry, at least by me, but her right to fair treatment by the person in charge has been violated. Could there really be any doubt about this? Wouldn't any observer agree? One can sometimes argue or be in doubt about whether something is unjust or not, but there are also many clear and undeniable cases of injustice, as I hope this and the other examples show. I'm sure you can think of many others for yourself. And don't overlook the significance of this, which is very great, given the interconnectedness of ideas summarized in the paragraph above. For if there is such a thing as injustice – and we know there is – then there are rights, for injustice consists in the violation of rights.

The next thing to notice is that justice and rights, and the things related to them – wrongs done to people (injustices), entitlement, desert, reparation, redress, and punishment – all belong squarely in the domain of deontic morality. It is part of our understanding of what a moral right is that there is a *moral requirement* not to violate it and that to do so is *morally wrong*. Not all moral obligations can be treated under the heading of the obligation not to violate rights.[3] If I deliberately cause you hurt or harm, for instance, I may be violating your right not to be so treated, but that is not the only thing that is wrong about it. The fact that I caused you hurt or harm without an acceptable justification or excuse is wrong in itself, because I have made you suffer, and making people suffer is one of the things (because I might be the victim myself) I cannot will that people do whenever they happen to feel like it. It is something which, if I recognize the reality of others, and that they are in a position no different from my own, I can only will never be done (without an acceptable justification or excuse) by anybody, including myself. In other words, I can only see it to be morally wrong (see chapter 9, pp. 173–6). Thus I did something morally wrong, in the example above, simply by letting the fifth child go hungry, but *in addition*, I violated two of her *rights*: the right of a child to parental or other adult care, and the right to fair treatment from those in authority. We cannot, of course, because of the universal nature of moral language, claim moral rights for ourselves that we are not prepared to grant to others. The sincere use of the language of rights and justice in my utterances or in my thoughts, like the sincere use of the language of moral obligation or requirement, implies my belief in a universal moral reality. And what we wish to regard as the violation of a right must, like everything else that is morally wrong, be, simply for what it is, something that we could not rationally will that people do whenever they feel like it, since we, or our group, could be the victims. Respect for rights (justice) is necessary to prevent evils (bad things) from happening to individuals or groups, and it serves all of them equally.

Rights and the Separateness of Persons and Groups

It was said in chapter 10 (p. 193) that, because human nature is frail and non-perfectible, and we cannot expect everyone, or perhaps even anyone, to possess all the moral virtues in full measure, we need deontic morality as a moral safety-net when the relevant virtue is lacking or is temporarily on holiday (as sometimes happens, especially in times of stress). For whether or not, for example, we possess the virtue of honesty, we still must not lie, steal, or cheat (unless we have a justification or excuse that others could accept) and we must have the strength of will to be able to restrain ourselves when we are tempted to do one of these things. We have now seen that justice, rights, and everything that goes along with them, belong squarely in the domain of deontic morality. Clearly, these are legalistic concepts, for if a right is violated, a wrong is done to some person or persons, and wronging people is something that we are *morally required* not to do. Further, if we do violate a right we are *morally required* to make reparation if we can, and we may *justly* be reprimanded and sometimes *justly* punished. If deontic morality as a whole is a moral safety-net, or fall-back device, as has been claimed, we would then expect that justice and rights and everything associated with them, since they belong to deontic morality, would be part of that safety-net or fall-back device. We must now see whether and why this is really so.

If I have a claim right, then that claim *morally must* be granted by the relevant person or persons. If I have a permissive right, then others *morally must* stand aside and allow me to exercise it at my pleasure. Rights then, are always rights *against* some person or persons, or a state (including our own), *requiring* him or her or them to do a certain thing for us or not to do a certain thing against us, regardless of any contrary motives or inclinations they may have. Now, under ideal conditions, there would be no need to have to invoke the pure moral motive – doing something because you recognize that it is a thing you are morally required to do, or not doing something because you recognize that it is a thing you are morally required not to do – for the possession of the moral virtues in full measure, including what I have called the deontic virtues (e.g. honesty), would ensure that no one would be *inclined*, whether by action or inaction, to do anything that we would regard as morally wrong. People would not be *inclined* to do anything, either by action or inaction, that was contrary to communal well-being (the common good), and this means that they would not be inclined to do anything that we would regard as the violation of a right, for it is contrary to communal well-being that anyone should be unjustly treated. However, such an ideal is obviously not attainable, and we need justice and respect for rights because opposition and conflict do exist in the world, and even under the best possible conditions will continue to exist to some degree.

Every individual has his or her own interests, and the same is true of every group (blacks, Jews, Muslims, Canadians, francophones, Puerto Ricans, employees, women, gays), and when these interests are under threat they must be protected. That is what rights are for. But notice, interests are only in conflict when they are under threat, or when they are perceived as being under threat, from another individual or group; in other words, when there is adversarial competition or the fear of it. What this means is that it is necessary, or perceived as necessary, for each individual to protect his or her interests against the incursion of others, and the same for each group. Now this would not be possible if each individual did not have his or her own private or personal interests, and if each group did not have its own group interests, and that is undeniably true. Both individuals and groups are undeniably separate and different. Nevertheless, there is a *common human interest* in individuals and groups being decent to one another and respecting one another, and it would be better for every individual and every group if fear and adversarial competition could be eliminated. It is only because these things can never be completely eliminated, that universal solidarity can never be achieved, that we need the protection of rights, which, as has already been said (p. 202 above), are always rights *against*. Rights are always adversarial, and provide *deontic moral grounds* for preventing actions or inactions that are contrary to the interests of the person or group whose rights they are. They are needed because such a danger will always continue to exist. This does not mean, of course, that universal solidarity, however unachievable, is not the ideal, for the closer we can get to it the better the interests of all individuals and all groups are served.

In conclusion, we need rights because of the unavoidable separateness of individual persons and the factual separateness of groups and political entitities such as nation-states, each of which has separate interests that may be or be seen to be in conflict with, or under threat from, other competing individuals, groups, or political entities. Rights, being rights of individuals against other individuals, groups against other groups, the government against the governed (the right to punish law-breakers and to prevent sedition), the governed against the government (to prevent the abuse of power), are inherently adversarial. They are necessary because the ideal, which is universal solidarity, good will, and concern for the common good, where the possibility of conflict has been totally eliminated – a state of affairs from which everyone benefits – though it is still to be aimed at, can never be completely achieved. If such a state of affairs did exist, and could be maintained, there would be no need for the protection of rights.

How Important is Justice?

Let us bring things closer to home, I mean literally to home – and the family. Let us suppose there is a husband, a wife, both employed outside the home, and four children all of school age, able-bodied, and old enough to help out with the domestic chores. Justice would seem to require that these chores be divided up in an equitable way. It would be unjust if one person did all the work and nobody else did any. Unless that one person volunteered to do all the work and was unhappy with any other arrangement, this would be sheer exploitation and a cause of justified resentment. It would be unjust, except in special circumstances, if even one member of the family contributed nothing at all, taking what was given him and otherwise devoting himself to his own pleasure. Given that these are chores which must be done but which no one particularly enjoys doing – they would rather be doing something else – justice would seem to require that everyone do their fair share. Now this can develop into a situation which is fundamentally adversarial, with everyone insisting that they do no more than their fair share so that they can have time to do what they want to do, squabbling over whether they have done their fair share or not, or whether perhaps they haven't done more than their fair share while that other person has not been contributing enough. Perhaps this is really true; perhaps that other person has not been contributing enough, and deserves to be reprimanded. In any case this is an unhappy, or at least less than an ideal situation. It is also a situation based on the insistence upon justice. Everyone is trying to do as little as possible and, in any case, no more than his or her fair share, and feeling resentment toward others if they are doing less. Everyone is *insisting on his or her rights*.

Now let us imagine a happier situation. Everyone is aware that there are chores to be done and sets out voluntarily to help out. The work is accomplished smoothly and efficiently, without any squabbling, leaving everyone time to enjoy their leisure when the work is done. Their sense of fairness, rather than breeding resentment at others doing less than themselves, is an incentive to get the work done in a cooperative and friendly manner. No one is trying to do as little as possible. No one is or feels exploited. There is no heavy concern with justice and rights. Insistence on justice and rights only comes in when there is adversarial conflict, where any one person would exploit any one of the others if they could get away with it by letting them do the work, and measures must be imposed to ensure equity and keep the peace.

But notice that this friendly, cooperative approach must be general. Kindness must not be mistaken for weakness. If just one person tries to take advantage of the willingness of someone else to do the work, resentment and hostility will follow. The person who has, out of good will, volunteered to do something, will find more and more tasks unloaded on her and will, with justification, feel resentment. The attitude of willing and friendly cooperation must be shared. Otherwise the whole thing will fall apart, and questions of justice and rights will once more take precedence over everything else. The conclusion? Yes, insistence on justice and rights may be necessary to prevent exploitation, but friendly and willing cooperation makes this insistence unnecessary. The less questions of justice and rights have to be raised, or even thought about, the better off the family is.

What has been said here about the family can be extended to all the institutions of society, and in a quite general way to people living together and sharing the same planet. That is where the moral virtues come in, including kindness, generosity, and good will.[4] Of course, justice is important, for injustice − the violation of rights − is an evil that cannot be tolerated. But friendliness, cooperation, and good feeling, to the extent that they prevail, eliminate resentment, contention, and the need for constant attention to justice and rights. Thus they are, because of their greater contribution to the common good, and hence to everyone's individual good, much more to be admired. The more egoism (or, in the world at large, its equivalent for groups) prevails, the more attention must be paid to justice and rights. The more people are aware of the importance of the common good (and it is to this that the social moral virtues relate), and happily contribute to it in association with others, the less potential conflict of interest there is, with correspondingly less need to be concerned with justice and rights.

SUMMARY

1   A has a *moral right* to something from B only where B is morally required (under a moral obligation) to provide it for him, and where B *is* morally required to provide something for A, then A has a moral right to that provision. (This is true *a priori* since it is built into our moral language.)

2   If B fails to honor A's right to something from his/her/it, then A has been *wronged*, has a justified complaint against B, and is entitled to demand reparation and possibly punishment.

3   One may forgive a wrong done, but no one is *morally required* to forgive a wrong. To forgive is always an act of supererogation.

4   To do someone a wrong is to treat him/her in a way he/she does not *deserve*, and is therefore *unjust*, as for instance when I give you a low mark because I don't like you.

5   "Unjust" is a concept that bears its own deontic moral weight. Since there are acts which are unquestionably unjust, there are some acts that are unquestionably morally wrong.

6   There are positive rights, e.g. a child's right to parental or other adult care. These are called *demand* rights and sometimes *claim* rights, and they are often based on what I have *earned* or *merited*, e.g. a student's right to a fair mark or grade, or my right to the named reward in a competition that I have won fair and square.

7   There are also negative or *permissive* rights, which can all be put together as my right, as an adult, to live my life as I see fit, within the limits of deontic morality and the law (provided it is just). This

means that you and everyone else, including the government, are under an obligation to stand aside and not interfere with my exercise of these rights. These rights may collectively be called the right to *liberty*.

8   If a wrong done is serious enough, then punishment may be *deserved*. But whether the penalty is reparation or punishment or both, the offender has forfeited a right or rights. If the reparation is excessive or the punishment too harsh, or the accused person is innocent, then *she* has been wronged and can rightfully demand reparation or punishment of the offending party or both.

9   If I receive a reward I have not earned or merited or otherwise come by honestly, I do not deserve it, and again an injustice has been done, quite independent of the injustice that may have been done to someone else who did merit or deserve it.

10   Thus the ideas of rights, justice, and desert are all interconnected.

11   There is a *moral requirement* not to violate a right, and the violation of a right is *morally wrong*. Therefore, justice and rights belong squarely in the domain of deontic morality.

12   The sincere use of the language of rights and justice, like the sincere use of the language of moral obligation or requirement implies belief in a universal and objective moral reality.

13   Rights are always rights *against* some person or persons, or the state, requiring him or her or them or it to do a certain thing for us or not to do a certain thing against us.

14   Rights are always adversarial and provide *deontic moral grounds* for prohibiting actions or inactions that are contrary to the legitimate interests of the person or group whose rights they are.

15   We need rights because of the unavoidable separateness of individual persons and the factual separateness of groups (collectivities) and political entities such as nation-states, each of which has separate interests that may be or may be seen to be in conflict with, or under threat from, other competing individuals, groups, or political entities.

16   The more friendliness, cooperation, and good feeling (fostered by the moral virtues) exist, the less need there is to concern oneself with justice and rights.

QUESTIONS FOR THOUGHT

1   Do you have a right to do whatever you please? Why or why not?

2   If someone has violated a right, he or she may *deserve* punishment. Would it be unjust, then, if he or she was *not* punished? Explain.

3   Rights are always rights *against*. Why is it important to recognize this fact?

4   Kindness should not be mistaken for weakness for, if it is, you will simply be exploited and taken advantage of. How does this relate to the question of justice and rights and to the desirability of possessing the moral virtues?

12
The Best Life for All

In part I of this book, we exposed the flaws in several doctrines – all of them common and influential – that, if we accepted them, would require us to deny the possibility of there being a morality that is valid for all humanity (a universal morality), or a morality that involves sometimes caring about, and acting for the sake of, something other than our own, narrow, individual self-interest. The possibility of a universal morality is ruled out by cultural relativism, subjective relativism, meta-ethical subjectivism, and non-cognitivism. The possibility of a morality not based on narrow, individual self-interest is ruled out by psychological egoism. The disbelief that a universal, non-egoistic morality could exist may justifiably be called *moral skepticism*, for everyone who understands and sincerely uses such words as "kind" and "kindness," "generous" and "generosity," "honest" and "honesty," or who understands that there are some things that *are* morally wrong (not just believed to be so) and others that are morally obligatory, is appealing to such a universal and non-egoistic morality, and if it does not exist, he or she is deluded.

But on what basis could we claim that such a morality, the reality of which is implied in all our sincere moral judgments, does exist? We saw that, unless there are *reasons* for our being kind and generous and honest, a morality according to which states of character such as kindness, generosity, and honesty are honorable and admirable could have no foundation. And unless there are reasons for limiting, by *ruling out* certain kinds of actions and omissions, our freedom to do or not do as we please, a morality according to which certain limiting rules or principles are necessary guides to conduct could have no foundation. We further saw that practical reasons – and these, because morality is a practical matter concerned with character and conduct, are the only kind of reasons that could provide a grounding for it – only exist where there is something of value to be gained by the kind of character or conduct in question (see chapter 5). We also saw that the ultimate source of all value was *eudaimonia*, which is to say thriving, flourishing, happiness, or well-being, and, since we are social creatures, this can only mean the happiness or well-being of individuals living in community. If morality could not be shown to be grounded in *that*, it could have no foundation in practical reason at all, and we could simply forget about it. However, we were able to show that there is such a thing as moral value, and that it *is* grounded in *eudaimonia*. This gave us the foundation for an acceptable moral theory (see chapter 6). The succeeding chapters attempted to spell out the details of that theory, taking account of both the aretaic and deontic dimensions of morality, their relationship to each other, and how each is grounded in communal and individual well-being (*eudaimonia*).

The Central Problem for Ethics

Morality, we have said, both aretaic and deontic, is a value for all humanity, because it *profits* us, because it is a contribution, a necessary contribution, to our thriving, flourishing, happiness, or well-being (*eudaimonia*). But why morality? And why does a fully justified morality take the form it does? The answer is as follows. We are, each of us, separate and distinct individuals, each with his or her own unique individual nature, and each with his or her own individual happiness or misery, his or her own self-fulfillment or the lack of it. Yet we live together in communities and societies, being part and parcel of such institutions as the family, ethnic associations, clubs, teams, corporations, other business enterprises, unions, professional associations, political parties, committees, schools, colleges and universities, groups of various kinds (including a simple circle of friends), cities, towns, villages, states, and finally the community of all human beings, the world community.

While we all must live our individual lives, we are social creatures by nature, and in all such associations or groupings we have shared objectives and live in relationships of mutual dependence, even if we are powerful and at the top. What others do is bound to affect me, and what I do is bound to affect others. My life situation, and therefore my happiness and well-being, is bound to be affected by my relationships with others (my social relationships), either within or outside an institutional context, just as the well-being of at least some others is bound to be affected by their relationship with me: father/daughter, teacher/student, doctor/patient, lawyer/client, employer/employee, political authority/citizen, colleague/colleague, work associate/work associate, friend/friend, lover/lover, just to take some obvious examples. While everybody has to live his or her own life, and her own happiness or the lack of it is personal to her, nobody is, or only a very, *very* few people are, able and happy to go it entirely alone.

The question then becomes: is each individual to pursue his or her private and personal interests exclusively (after all his well-being or the lack of it is *his own*), taking others into account only when it benefits him or, given that his social relations are an ever-present part of his own life, should he consider as well the interests of others in their own right, and not simply with regard to his personal profit? If we opt for the first choice, this means we see society as a set of individuals each pursuing his or her own profit without any real concern for others and fundamentally in competition with them. Such *individualism* could lead to hard ethical egoism – go for as much as you can get and let the devil take the hindmost – which is plainly not only competitive but adversarial. Or, if cooperation exists, this would be on a tit-for-tat basis: I will give you something if and only if you give me something, or I will put myself out for you only if you put yourself out for me. This is the basis of contractarian ethics (chapter 1, p. 16), which is still fundamentally egoistic as well as individualist. *Exchange* becomes the basis of human relationships, and the only ethics possible is an ethics of rights and justice.

We might try to ask the same question about groups: should a group, as an association of individuals with a common or collective interest, take into account the common interest of its own members only, or should it take into account as well the common or collective interest of other groups in their own right, and not simply for how its own members may be affected? But, asked about groups, the question has a strange ring. Groups or associations *exist* to foster their own members' common interest; indeed, as groups or associations they seem to have no other purpose. How, then, could it be part of their business to concern themselves with the common interest of other groups, except in so far as their own interests are affected? Furthermore, groups often have an adversarial relationship with other groups, for the members are characteristically banded together to protect or expand their own common interest *in opposition to* other groups which they see as threatening them, or as rivals for wealth or power or honor or privilege. At the very least, members of other groups are *excluded*. That the interests of groups are distinct belongs to the very conception of a group, and they *may be* in competition, often adversarial competition. Think of labour *v.* management, blacks *v.* whites, women *v.* men, Jews *v.* Arabs in the Middle East, Democrats *v.* Republicans, conservatives *v.* liberals, Protestants *v.* Catholics in Northern Ireland, Serbs *v.* Croats in the former Yugoslavia, nation *v.* nation, alliance *v.* alliance. (Isn't it the business of a nation, or an association of nations such as the European Community, to advance and protect the collective interests of its citizens to the exclusion of all others?)

There are two important points to notice here. (1) Members of groups of the kind we have been talking about *do* have a *common* or shared interest, as distinct from their purely personal or private interests, and it is this common interest which holds them together and gives them their identity. (2) Groups are often opposed to one another and in competition with one another, and sometimes they are in adversarial conflict. The first point is important because it shows that there *is* such a thing as a common interest, something which benefits all of the members of a group equally. This alone is enough to kill purely egoistic individualism, for each member of a group, *as* a member of that group, is, or usually is, concerned with the common interest of the group, and not exclusively with purely personal and private interests, and if he is not and he is found out, he will be reprimanded and perhaps ostracized (cut out). This shows that a person *need* not think of himself or herself *only* as a separate individual, but he can also see himself as member of a group with a common interest that he wishes to advance and protect for the good equally of all the members. Further, it is true that, while each member of the group benefits from the promotion of this common interest, she is not acting exclusively for herself in acting for its sake. As to the second point, where there is common defence, opposition, competition, rivalry, or adversarial conflict, this amounts to egoistic individualism on a larger scale. Distinct groups in competition or conflict with each other are analogous to separate individuals in competition or conflict with each other, each concerned with nothing but the pursuit of his or her own perceived interest to the exclusion of anything else.

The problem which morality is supposed to solve – and this is the central problem for ethics – is *how to reconcile the unavoidable separateness of persons* (for everyone's happiness or well-being or the absence of it is after all his or her own) *with their inherently social nature*, their dependence on other people, and the fact that they live together in and share a common world.

Some Attempted Solutions

Every moral outlook and every moral theory is an attempt to solve this problem. Hard or tough egoistic individualism (a form of ethical egoism) says you should go ahead and exploit other people as much as you can for your own advantage. Notice that what is being said is that *everyone* should live this way, that it is *admirable* to do so, and that anyone who doesn't is a fool. Because it is offered as universal and said to be the best way to live, it is recognizable as a *moral* position. If *you* see morality as necessarily involving respect or concern for others, you can call this "the morality of immorality." Of course, if everyone adopted this view, everyone would be in perpetual adversarial conflict with everyone else, and the devil *would* take the hindmost. ("Nice guys finish last.") A happy situation?

To avoid this state of affairs while remaining an egoistic individualist, you can take the contractarian or Hobbesian view. It would be better for everybody, me included, if there were an agreement (perhaps unspoken) among all of us to limit our freedom in such a way that we do not live in perpetual fear of one another. This way each of us will be better able to get on with his or her own projects. Anyone who does not abide by this agreement will be punished or ostracized. I don't give a damn about the rest of you and you don't give a damn about me, but it would be better for me and you too if we agree to hold off a bit. But you'd better keep your side of the bargain or you've had it, Buddy.

This is a considerably better situation. Justice and rights have been instituted, but there is still no real concern for others and the common good except in so far as it affects *me*. (You will remember from chapter 11 that rights are essentially rights *against*, hence essentially adversarial, and that justice consists in respect for rights. Here they are rights that everyone has against anyone who would do anything to him or her that would be in violation of the contract.) Each of us has an interest in maintaining the contract, and so this is a shared or common interest, but the common interest *as such* is not the concern of anyone. We are still only concerned with our individual selves. The best deal for me would be one where I could exploit anyone I liked for my own advantage. (An all-powerful tyrant, like Hitler, a Mafia boss or a drug king? How often have they fallen?) But since I am unlikely to succeed forever in having power over others to use them as I please and since I do not want to live my life in perpetual fear, I had better be a party to the agreement.

This is admittedly second best for me, but it is the best that I can hope for, and far better than winding up as one of the exploited. The trouble with this view – if it is a trouble – is that if I have reason to believe I can violate the agreement and get away with it, there is no reason why I shouldn't do just that. Why not go for it? I'd be a fool if I didn't. Justice schmustice. (If there is concern for justice only in so far as it profits *me*, there is no concern for justice itself.)

An individualist but non-egoistic solution is the Kantian one. No one is to do or fail to do anything of a kind such that she could not rationally will that others do it whenever they feel like it, or fail to do it whenever they don't feel like doing it (the categorical imperative) (see chapter 9, pp. 173–6). Lying is wrong, right? Why? Just place yourself in the position of the victim, remembering the fact that if people were to start lying whenever they felt like it, you or someone you care about could be a liar's victim. And if lying to get out of difficulties, or to promote your own advantage at the expense of someone else, became a general practice, then no one would be believed if there was the merest suspicion that she or he was lying, and there would be a general breakdown of trust, something that would severely affect you. You cannot rationally will, therefore, that people lie whenever they are so inclined. Since you cannot will that everybody tell lies whenever they want to, you must, if you accept the moral force of the categorical imperative, agree that nobody, including yourself, should tell lies, or in other words that lying is morally wrong. Otherwise you are making an exception in your own favor, which is just what the categorical imperative prohibits.

Now this applies clearly to lying in order to get out of difficulties, or for your own advantage at the expense of others (one or the other of these being the standard motive for lying), but to the claim that lying is morally wrong I have added the non-Kantian proviso "without an acceptable justification or excuse," by which is meant a justification or excuse that is itself consistent with the categorical imperative and therefore one that everyone could accept. Should we tell the attempted rapist the truth when he asks which way his would-be victim went? The answer here is clearly "no." There is a genuine justification for lying here, to which all who accept the categorical imperative in the form presented here would agree. No one could rationally will that people tell the truth in these circumstances whenever they happen to feel like it. For, after all, you or your wife or your girlfriend or your sister or your mother or your daughter or a close friend could be a rapist's victim.

But to get back to the main point. You cannot will that everybody tell lies in order to get out of difficulties or to gain advantage at the expense of others (which are the standard motives for lying). According to the categorical imperative, you must therefore accept that nobody should do it, including yourself; in other words, that it is morally wrong. If you do not accept this and go on lying for the standard reasons, thus making an exception in your own case, *you are not recognizing the reality of others*, who are in exactly the same position that you are in. (Note, too, that you cannot claim a *moral right* to lie whenever you want to, for if it is a right, then everyone has it, even when you would be the victim, and you would have no right to protest. You must declare yourself *amoral*, though perhaps only in your private thoughts. You cannot advocate that everyone be amoral since you would suffer from that; indeed, you want them to be what they call "moral" so that you can better exploit them. And by seeing yourself as amoral you are not exempted from morality except in your own eyes, for we who accept that lying is morally wrong will declare you to be *immoral*.) That in making an exception in your own favor you are failing to acknowledge the reality of others is the *individualist* reason for accepting the categorical imperative, as was said in chapter 9 (p. 176). On this account, we are seen simply as individuals who happen to live together and who should acknowledge and respect one another; we are not conceived as a community having a common or shared good.

We have seen (chapter 9, pp. 176–7) that the individualist reason, valid as it may be, is not the only reason for accepting the categorical imperative and the principles of deontic morality. There is a *communal* reason as well, for as was said, to the extent that people restrict their freedom, as the categorical imperative would require, by not doing things that they could not have others do at their pleasure (lying, hurting, injuring, cheating, breaking promises, treating unfairly, etc.), and by not failing to do things they could not have others neglect at their pleasure (e.g. warn people of dangers, summon or render aid when required, do what is expected of them in their social roles, etc.), they help to create or maintain a social atmosphere in which everyone can thrive and flourish in mutual understanding, friendliness, cooperation, and good will, which is a better state of affairs altogether than one in which these things are lacking, since it permits each individual to live a richer, happier, and more fulfilling life. And, once more, the communal reason for acting as the categorical imperative would require, while not *altruistic*, is not egoistic either (as the contractarian reason for being moral is) for in restricting my freedom for this social reason, my thoughts and concerns are not directed to myself, but to the common good for its own sake, something which the solidarity of groups has shown us to be possible (see above).

The *individualist* reason for restricting one's freedom in accordance with the categorical imperative, while it is clearly not egoistic, is not altruistic or selfless either (although it is certainly unselfish in the sense of being other-regarding; see chapter 1, p. 8). Essentially, it comes to recognizing the reality of others by not making exceptions in my own favor where things that I could not have *them* do or fail to do whenever they feel like it are concerned. That is, I acknowledge myself as *one among many*, and I recognize that so far as these non-universalizable things are concerned, everyone must see it just as I do myself. It differs from the communal reason in that the value is not to be sought as something from which I benefit at all, even indirectly (even if I do so benefit). Rather I am thinking of *everyone equally*, in respect of his or her common humanity. We may therefore call such a reason *universalist*, and this Kantian view a form of *ethical universalism*.

None of the attempted solutions to our problem just considered take into account the traditional virtues, such as courage, kindness, and generosity. Where these solutions are not egoistic, they are deontic, or, in the case of the contractarian solution, both. Except for what I have called hard ethical egoism, where "look after no. 1" is the sole moral principle and being smart at doing so the sole moral virtue, the moral concern is exclusively with duty, obligation (positive or negative), rights, and justice. This is in keeping with the typically modern concern (since Kant) with questions of right and wrong (deontic morality) as the only moral questions.

Universalist Consequentialism (including Utilitarianism): an Unacceptable Solution

John Stuart Mill, whose influence has been very great, is one of the moderns who has seen morality exclusively in deontic terms. Thus, in his widely read *Utilitarianism*, he says, very early on, that if we succeed in discovering the *summum bonum* (the ultimate or final good), we will thereby have discovered the foundation of morality, by which he understands deontic morality, or moral requirement (obligation). The *summum bonum* is soon declared to be the greatest happiness of the greatest number. From this he infers that it is morally obligatory that all our actions be directed toward the greatest happiness of the greatest number.[1]

Looking at J. S. Mill means that the time has come to redeem the promise, made in chapter 7, to take up in detail what I called the third approach to morality, there said to be a mistake. This third approach sees morality as providing a complete, cradle-to-grave guide to conduct, requiring us, on every occasion of choice, to determine what it is we morally ought to do, or what is *the morally right thing* to do, an understanding of morality, conceived in exclusively deontic terms, that is clearly implied in Mill's assumption. We have discovered a supreme or ultimate or final good and, Mill assumes without argument, we are morally required to direct all our actions toward its attainment. This third approach need not take exactly this form. There is no need to suppose that there is one thing, such as the greatest happiness of the greatest number, which is the *summum bonum*. We can simply say that we are morally required to direct our actions to the good of everyone equally, counting ourselves only as one among many. Thus everyone is morally obliged, in all his actions, to try to advance the good, *whatever that may be*, of everyone indifferently, with no special favor to himself. Mill saw his or her own happiness as everyone's personal good, but he was a hedonist (chapter 6, p. 119) for whom happiness was simply pleasure and the absence of pain. Latter-day or neutral (as distinct from hedonistic) utilitarians, often understand a person's good as the satisfaction of his or her desires. (Mill would have regarded the two as identical.)

Utilitarianism is a form of what has come to be called *consequentialism* because it is the view that we are morally obliged in all our actions to try to produce *the best consequences on the whole*, by which is understood the greatest possible good for all persons indifferently or disinterestedly considered. Well, the first and most devastating objection is that it is false to what moral obligation or moral requirement is in our ordinary understanding. For, as we have noted at length (chapter 7, pp. 138, 146; chapter 8, p. 150; chapter 9, pp. 166–7), the model or paradigm for deontic morality is law, and deontic moral considerations (rules, principles) forbid us to do some things and forbid us not to do others, just as the law forbids some actions and some failures to act. And just as the law leaves us free to do or not do anything that is legal, or not contrary to the law, deontic morality leaves us free to do or not do, as we please, anything that is morally permissible or *licit*, i.e. anything that is neither morally required nor morally forbidden.

Consequentialism, as it has been defined here, because it *requires us always to do the morally right thing*, namely promote the greatest good of everyone indifferently (i.e. with favor to no one including oneself), would make a thing morally wrong if it is not morally obligatory and morally obligatory if it is not morally wrong. Thus it would rule out the whole realm of the *morally permissible*, the things we may do or not do as we please without moral transgression, which, as we have said (chapter 9, p. 167), are most of the things that make life worth living. Saying that we are obliged, in all our choices, to do *the morally right thing* has exactly the same effect as taking "morally right" and "morally wrong" to be contradictories (which they are), while defining "morally right" as "morally obligatory"), something of which consequentialists, but not only consequentialists are often guilty (see chapter 9, pp. 166–7).

Of course, we must always do what is morally right because if it is not morally right it is morally wrong, but here "right" means "permissible" not "obligatory." There can be any number of things that are morally right in this sense (i.e. not morally wrong), such as choosing jam rather than marmalade to put on your toast if there is a plentiful supply of both! It is nonsense to suppose that you must decide which of the two is *the morally right thing* (which, for the consequentialist is the choice that would bring the greatest good to everyone indifferently), or to wonder whether choosing the jam or choosing the marmalade isn't perhaps morally wrong (that is provided they're both yours, and you haven't made any promises, or there is some other genuine moral reason against choosing one or the other).

Here is another difficulty, perhaps not for Mill's version of utilitarianism, but for the modern consequentialism that sees each and every one of us as being under a perpetual obligation to produce the greatest possible good for everyone indifferently, with favor to no one, including ourselves. Mill said or implied that we were under a perpetual obligation to produce the greatest happiness for the greatest number, with favor to none, so Mill could be read as allowing that it is the right thing to do to choose the marmalade, if that is what we would prefer, since choosing it would add to our happiness and choosing the jam would both make us less happy and not make anyone else any happier, that is given that there is not some other more happiness-spreading thing that we should be doing instead of putting spread on our toast. But if everyone, at every instant, is morally required to do what will produce the maximum amount of desire-satisfaction for everyone indifferently, with favor to none, as many consequentialists would have it (although most of them are prepared to allow that a case can sometimes be made for a justified exception), then people can never act just for themselves, but must always act for everyone indifferently. But that is surely absurd! This is supposed to be a universal morality, applicable to everyone, but just imagine the situation in which everyone is acting, or is trying to act, for the good of everyone indifferently! What a mess! Now one *could* try to say that in acting for oneself one *is* acting for the good of everyone indifferently. If everyone is acting for themselves, it might be suggested, then the good of everyone is served. (Just add them up!) But what would be the point, then, of saying that we should act for the greatest good of everyone indifferently, with favor to none?

The fact of the matter is that we must all lead our own lives in pursuit of our own projects. We cannot, nor should we, be constantly attending to the good of everyone indifferently. We would just be a bunch of busybodies and we would not accomplish any of our own personal objectives (unless somebody else, also acting for the good of everyone indifferently, managed it for us)! Many of our moral obligations consist simply in leaving people alone to do their own thing, without interference, something to which both they and we have a moral right, provided there is no moral transgression, and we do transgress morally when we prevent or try to prevent another person from exercising his or her moral right. Deontic morality is an ethics of *limitation*, for which the model is law, and to treat it as an ethics of *general prescription*, as consequentialists do, is simply a huge mistake. We should note, however, that, like the individualist justification of the categorical imperative, consequentialism, although it does require thinking of every other person equally with ourselves, does not require altruism in the sense of complete selflessness. We are not to act *only* for other people; we can take ourselves into account as long as everyone else is given equal consideration. Consequentialism of the kind we have been considering is a species of *universalism* (see p. 214 above). Unlike the Kantian kind, however, which simply limits our freedom, it requires us to act positively, all the time, for everyone's good equally. Both Kantian morality (based on the categorical imperative), understood individualistically (chapter 9, p. 176 and pp. 213–14 above), and the univeralist consequentialism we are here considering, have, as their end, the good of everyone equally, with favor to no one, but the second of these two is always *requiring* us to do something, and thus there is nothing it simply *allows* us to do in the pursuit of our own ends. Since without such moral permissibility no one can achieve his or her own personal ends through living his or her own life, consequentialism of this kind is clearly a misguided universalism.

If utilitarianism has any viable function at all, it is in the political sphere, where it really is the business of legislators, political executives, the judiciary, and officers of the law, to make, administer, enforce, and render judgment in accordance with laws which are for the good of every law-abiding citizen or subject indifferently, showing favor to none. This really is their business, even if the realities of power mean that they rarely can and perhaps never do, in fact, act with such complete disinterest.

Finally, we should note that consequentialism of the kind we have been considering (which includes utilitarianism of any kind) is essentially individualistic. There is no reference to the common good but only to the sum or aggregate of individual goods. Again, as with the individualist justification of the categorical imperative, people are conceived simply as individuals who happen to occupy and share the same world and have an effect on one another. Shared or communal goods are just not in the picture at all. But because, as we have argued in this book (chapter 6, pp. 127–8), these shared or communal goods, which constitute good social conditions under which to live, are an important part of the good or well-being of each individual person, individualist consequentialism (always acting for the good of all persons indifferently with favor to none) would not do, even if it did not have its other glaring faults, as a full account of the moral picture.

Communitarianism, Collectivism, and Communalism

All the attempted solutions examined so far in this chapter to what I have called the central problem for ethics, namely how we are to reconcile the unavoidable separateness of persons with their inherently social nature, have been essentially *individualistic*. These include hard ethical egoism, contractarianism, Kantianism (the individualist justification of the categorical imperative as the supreme principle of morality), and universalist consequentialism, which includes all forms of utilitarianism. It should also be noted that all these theories, with the exception of hard ethical egoism, interpret morality in exclusively deontic terms. While wisdom in the sense of prudence, understood as being wily, clever, or smart at looking after your own interest while outwitting others, finds a place in hard ethical egoism, and a place for justice understood as a virtue of character might possibly be found in the contractarian view, there is no place for such traditional virtues as kindness, generosity, friendliness, and courage, which can only be interpreted aretaically, in any of these theories. Individualism and an exclusively deontic understanding of morality, which we have seen to be inadequate (chapters 7 and 10), appear to go hand in hand. This should come as no surprise, since if the deontic story is the whole story of morality, there could be but one virtue, namely rectitude (which might include justice and honesty), and this (only doing what is morally right or never doing what is morally wrong) is typically understood in individualistic terms, although we have found a communal justification for it as well (chapter 9, pp. 176–7; p. 214 above).

What is strikingly absent from these individualistic theories is any conception of the common good. This is not simply the personal or private good of each and every individual, or the good special to each group or collectivity, but the good of the community as a whole, a good which is shared by all its members. The common good is something which is *in itself* a value for every member of the community *as* a member of the community, and something, therefore, which he or she has a reason for helping to create or to preserve. Furthermore, we cannot create or preserve the common good without attention to the virtues other than those that can be understood in deontic terms (under the general heading of rectitude). Individualist theories recognize that our social relationships are important to us, that we must somehow deal with the fact that we share the world with others, but individuals are still seen as essentially isolate and self-contained, each one locked within his or her private world, a separate ego fundamentally unattached, though each finds himself or herself (itself? – is the ego gendered?) in relationships with others in which she is affected by them and they are affected by her. These theories all ignore the common good. But, as we have seen, there really is a *common* good, something in which we all do or could or should participate, and which benefits us not just as separate individuals but as *belonging to*, or being *a part of* the community of which we are members. This is a good which is an essential part of each individual's well-being, and a good in the absence of which something is seriously lacking in any individual life. Therefore, these theories cannot give a complete and adequate account of what it is to be a person in the world.

About our separateness there can be no doubt, but if this were the whole story we could not – since we can't get away from each other – help but be essentially in endless competition with one another for superiority, either seeking to exploit or dominate others for our own benefit, or elbowing them out of the way so that we can get on with our business. That so many people see what it is to be a person in this way explains why contractarianism, with its heavy emphasis on justice and the rights of individuals, a theory according to which morality exists to prevent what Hobbes called a war of all against all, is so popular a view. This is a sad state of affairs.

In reaction to the extreme individualism of modern moral theory, a new kind of ethics has recently emerged called *communitarianism*. According to this theory we are not separate, self-enclosed egos, or what communitarians are likely to call "unattached selves," but rather our social relations, which exist within a particular society with its particular institutions, are an essential part of each of us as individuals. Rather than being unattached selves, each one an island unto himself, each of us is enmeshed within the historically located community or society to which we belong, with all its existing institutions, and this is part of our very being. This would mean that the common good, or at least the common good for our community or communities, *would be* part of the good of each individual member, and thus there would be a reason for everyone, *as enmeshed* in his or her community, to concern himself or herself with *its* good, the common good, and not merely her good as an isolate self.

Now it has been repeatedly said in this book that the good of the community or communities to which a person belongs is an essential part of his or her own good as an individual. It has also been said that morality (both aretaic and deontic) not only serves and protects this good, but is an essential part of it, of what I have called (after the ancient Greeks) communal *eudaimonia*. The trouble with communitarianism, at least in the form it most commonly takes, is that it does not scrutinize or call into question *existing* institutions and *existing* social relations. The common good, according to this communitarian view, must be found within the existing institutions and social relations of a particular culture. The difficulty with this is that existing institutions and social relations, including relationships of power, may in fact be *damaging* to anything that can be described as the common good. This is especially true in a society such as ours, where individualism (or the same thing at the group level), with its attendant rivalry and competition, seems to be officially established.

Before we can talk sensibly about the common good, then, we must have some idea of what a good society or a good community is, and that must be one that *encourages* cooperation, friendliness, and good will (which implies mutual support). These must all exist in anything we could call a good community, for where they do not exist there is and can be no devotion to the common good. That is because everyone is thrown back upon himself or herself as an isolate individual struggling to exist with others, or upon his or her group, struggling to affirm its right against other groups. This means a heavy emphasis on justice and rights which, as we have seen (chapter 11, pp. 202–3), need emphasis only in an adversarial or potentially adversarial situation. Furthermore, this heavy emphasis on justice and rights at the expense of the common good is just what the communitarians want to get away from. Before we can talk about the common good, then, *we must have some idea of what a good society or community is and what its institutions will be like*; not just any existing society with any set of institutions and any relations of power and status will do, as communitarians often seem to imply.

Let us first consider the virtues and their relationship to the good community. It has been argued here that the social and partly social moral virtues, such as honesty, kindness, generosity, and courage, are virtues (hence something we all have reason for everyone including ourselves to possess), precisely because of their relationship to the common good (chapter 6, pp. 123–4, 127–8; chapter 8, pp. 154–5, 159–60), and that deontic morality can best be seen as a fall-back or fail-safe device that also serves the common good (chapter 10, p. 193). *A good society, then, must at least be one in which these virtues are encouraged and in which the fall-back device is safely in place and socially sealed.* (This would be a good starting place for political theory, but that is not the business of this book.) Because the communitarians do not question existing institutions, claiming that the common good can be served within the framework of *any* existing society or culture, their view seems to reduce in the end to a species of cultural relativism.

In reaction to the individualism of so many ethical theories, it is also possible to turn to *collectivism*, its polar opposite. According to this view, we should devote ourselves entirely to common or collective interests – often identified with the state viewed as the collectivity of the people – forgetting everything that is personal except the bare necessities. We are never to think only of ourselves but always of the common or social good. (Lenin is reported to have said that in the new communist society of the Soviet Union there was no room for a personal life.) But this, too, is no solution because it is out of accord with human nature. It ignores the separateness of persons and their need to live their own lives in pursuit of their own projects. But we do not need to choose between individualism and collectivism. If the common good, because it constitutes the social conditions under which individuals can *be themselves* as participating members of a good society and live rich and fulfilling lives, is *a part of the good of each individual*, then the conflict between individualism and collectivism is overcome. The desirable features of both are included, while the undesirable features are eliminated.

The view expounded in this book – which may be called *communalism* in order to distinguish it not only from any form of individualism, but from both communitarianism and collectivism – is that no, we are not isolated and self-contained individuals (although we are separate), and yes, our attachments and our mutual dependency are genuine and real, a part of human nature. Two key points, as follows, are emphasized in this communalist view. (1) We must attend to the common good, which is a necessary part of each person's individual good. This means that we should encourage both the virtues and the fall-back device of deontic morality because of the necessary role they play in establishing and maintaining that common good. (2) If this means some change or adjustment to our existing institutions, whether as a consequence of, or as a necessary means to, the flourishing of the virtues, then so be it. In the meantime we must do whatever we can, within the limits imposed by existing social conditions, to be good and to encourage goodness in others. But with these two emphases (commitment, through both aretaic and deontic morality, to the common good, and the importance, in this connection, of adjustments to existing social institutions in order to bring about the good community), communalism offers a solution to what has been called the central problem for ethics: how to reconcile the separateness of persons with their inherently social nature.

It is important not to forget that most of the traditional virtues – the ones that endure and are recognized across time and place – and deontic morality, as justified by the categorical imperative, seem to be genuinely defensible as contributing to the common good, which we have agreed is a necessary ingredient in the thriving, flourishing, well-being, or happiness (*eudaimonia*) of individuals living together in society. This would seem to indicate that the common good *is* seen in the popular understanding, as that understanding is manifested in our moral language, as a value of the very greatest importance. It gives us reason to believe that the good society is one in which this morality, both aretaic and deontic, is firmly rooted. Does this mean that the good society will look just the same in all respects wherever and whenever it is found? The answer is "no," for there are many aspects of culture – matters of custom and tradition – that have nothing to do with morality as such. We could start with language, music and dance, games and festivals, domestic arrangements, and dress. Perfect virtue and perfect rectitude, even if they are not obtainable, are compatible with as much cultural variety as one could ever wish for.

Internal and External Value

I spoke of the need for adjustment to our existing social institutions, in order for moral goodness – a necessary part of the good community – to thrive. Highly relevant to this is the distinction between values internal to practices and values external to them.[2] (Exactly what this means will be explained in what follows.)

In order to make clear what I am getting at, I am going to begin this section by speaking directly to you about my own experience as a student, teacher, and researcher within the institution of the university. I have been teaching philosophy in a university for a very long time, and I will tell you what I have found. In my university, as in most universities in North America, we have what is called the "course-grade" or "course-credit" system. Students enrol in a course in which they are given work to do, which is marked or graded, and perhaps required to write an examination, on which a mark or grade is also given. A calculation is then made and the student is given a final mark or grade on the course. This mark is recorded, to appear forever on a student's transcript, and determines, together with his or her marks (grades) in other courses, first of all whether he or she will graduate, and second the class of degree she is given. To earn that degree is very important because it profoundly affects two aspects of the student's future life: his or her social status and the kind of employment with its attached salary that will be available. (I know of one intelligent, experienced, and competent pilot who was unable to obtain a job with a major airline because he did not have a university or college degree. He was told that the wives of the other pilots – being an airline pilot was at the time an exclusively male occupation – would not be willing to associate with anyone who did not have a BA.)

This state of affairs encourages many students – not all, but perhaps a majority – to be exclusively concerned with marks or grades. If they learn anything, that is in their effort to earn an "A" or a "B," and unless the course is part of a professional or training program, such as medicine or engineering, they will soon forget – since they had no real interest in it – most of what they learned. What actually goes on in the classroom, or in doing required reading or assignments, gets lost in the struggle to "do well in the course;" that is, to get a high mark or grade. It is, after all, for many students, only something they have to go through to earn that mark or grade. It has no value in itself. That is why so many students are on the look-out for "bird courses;" that, is courses in which it is easy to get a high mark.

And now for the faculty. They are encouraged by the way the institution actually functions to concern themselves mainly with rank, status, tenure (job security), and salary. Yes, they are supposed to be good teachers and good researchers in their special fields, but much of the work that is published is produced under pressure from the administration, in order to earn status or prestige for the institution, and if an academic does not publish, he or she may not be promoted, or given tenure, or receive much of a salary increase. Similarly, there is pressure (and competition) to be popular with students, for that too may count toward promotion (rank), tenure, and salary. And both this and one's publication record determine one's status in the eyes of the administration and to some extent with jealous colleagues. Any *inherent* value of one's work, whether teaching or research, tends to get lost in the shuffle. Now I am not *blaming* students or faculty for taking part in this rat race, which tends to downgrade any inherent value in their work. They are under heavy social and institutional pressure to do so. I am only deploring this state of affairs.

Unfortunately, the situation that exists in the university extends to our society as a whole. Corporations and other commercial enterprises are in business to make money. If they *happen* to manufacture a good product or provide a good service, that is only in the interest of commercial success. Employers try to get as much work out of their employees as they can, while giving them as little monetary reward as possible. Unions have done something to remedy this, but workers too often try to do as little as possible for the highest financial reward they can get. As well, nearly every person, collectivity and institution tries to milk the government for as much as he or she or it possibly can, in the way of subsidies or hand-outs or tax-dodges, while the government tries to screw as much money as it can get away with out of them. Politicians and political parties are mainly concerned not with good government, but with being elected or re-elected (in a democracy), or otherwise gaining power and staying in power. And there is more. Everywhere there is a mad scramble for wealth, power, and status, a scramble which is encouraged by the institutions of our society such as they are.

We may now directly consider the distinction referred to at the beginning of this section. It goes back at least as far as Plato, but I have borrowed the terminology from Alasdair MacIntyre.[3] It is the distinction between values *internal* to practices and values *external* to them. Now a practice is any established form of learned human activity, requiring skill and technique, which has its own unique end, purpose, or value. The ancient Greeks had a word for this, *techné*, which is usually translated as "art, skill, or craft." To take a favorite example of Plato's, medicine is a *techné*, or, to use our terminology, a practice. Its unique purpose is the healing of the sick and injured and the prevention of disease. Farming is also a practice, as is boat-building and all specialized manufacture. Mathematics and philosophy are practices, as is teaching. So also are painting, sculpture, playing the piano, conducting an orchestra, acting, juggling, and writing fiction. While dribbling is not a practice since, though it is a skill, it has no end of its own, basketball is. Likewise chess. And another important example for Plato – government or ruling. You can think of many others for yourself.

We can notice some differences here. Games are practices, although they have no end unique to themselves beyond the game itself and its special pleasure, which is partly a function of the degree of skill attained and displayed. The end or aim of the fine arts of music, drama, dance, painting, and literature are the production of things having the kind of aesthetic value peculiar to that particular art form, but that is too difficult and complex a topic to go into here. Entertainment may also be the end or part of the end in certain cases; for example, music, theatre, juggling. The end peculiar to farming is the production of food. The end of government or ruling is internal peace and security, protection from enemies, and other things of benefit to all the citizens or subjects equally. In all cases there is pleasure to be taken in being a good practitioner, in developing and exercising skill at whatever the practice is. It is also part of the business of practitioners to advance the practice itself, to better serve its special ends.

All the ends, purposes, or values mentioned in the paragraph above are ends *internal* to the practices in question. They can be achieved only through devotion to the practice itself, through being a good practitioner. One achieves them by aiming at *excellence in the practice itself*, for which, of course, one must have a special talent. Ends or values *external* to the practices are ends or values, such as income (wealth), recognition (applause, honor, status, fame, rank), power, and influence, that can be obtained by using them as means. These external values are not unique to a particular practice, but rather any occupation, whether it is a practice or not (drug dealing?), can be the means to obtaining them, at least in some degree.

Now we can imagine two different states of affairs. In the first case, people are developing and exercising their special talents in the practices that constitute their occupations, aiming always at excellence in the production of the values internal to those practices, including good products and services, and also improvements in the practices themselves. These people receive the internal rewards of (1) the satisfaction of knowing that one is learning well or has succeeded in becoming a good practitioner, and (2) the pleasure taken in exercising one's developed skills and talents. They also receive the external awards of income and recognition according to their due. But what they are striving for is always excellence in the practice in which they are engaged, aiming always at the values internal to that practice.

In the second case people are aiming at and competing for the external values of wealth, fame, status, and power and they are using their occupations as a means to this end. (I once heard a teacher in England, who was forced to moonlight as a janitor to obtain an income large enough to support himself and his family, say on the radio that he did not enter the teaching profession for the income, but rather for the status. Entering the teaching profession because it had social value and one had a special talent or aptitude for it, or even because one liked it, were simply excluded as possible motives.) Their aim is not to produce an excellent product or service, or to do anything well, other than making money or gaining status or power. They will do anything they can to gain this wealth or status or power, and if this happens to involve providing a good product or service, or learning something well, that is a mere incidental effect. It is at best a pure necessity, never an end in itself.

Can there be any doubt as to which of these two states of affairs is the better? The second has two consequences: (1) the value of the product or service will suffer since internal values have either been forgotten altogether or have become, at best, a means to the achievement of external goods; and (2) there will be a competitive struggle for power, position, and wealth, which is a severe threat to the virtues and an encouragement to playing dirty tricks on one's competitors, or deliberately harming them, which is morally wrong. The common good has been lost sight of altogether. Where the first state of affairs exists, there is competition, yes, but only for excellence. When everyone is striving only for excellence, the common good, to which everyone contributes who can, is very much to the fore, the virtues thrive, and there is little motive for doing what is morally wrong. We can see, then, what is wrong with our society: it far more closely resembles the second state of affairs than the first, and the situation has been deteriorating over the past century, especially over the past 30 years.

Let us return, briefly, to the classroom. Under the first state of affairs, students will be studying and teachers will be teaching for the sake of the *internal* value of whatever is going on in the course. The teacher's main aim will be to teach as well as possible and the students' main aim will be to learn as well as possible, assuming, of course, that whatever is being taught is worth learning. But if it isn't worth learning that will presumably be discovered and the course abolished. (There will be no need to keep it going for the sake of external values. Of course, one hopes that there will be another course which the teacher can give which does have value!) Marks or grades will be earned by the students according to their due, and the teacher will be promoted, given tenure, and given a good salary increase in recognition of her degree of excellence both as teacher and as a researcher in her own area. Or, if she isn't any good, she won't receive any of these rewards, and perhaps she should look for another profession. But the only way she can advance herself is by concentrating on her work, not by rushing into print as often as possible, pushing herself heavily, entering into any shady deals, or attempting to undercut her colleagues.

What we must conclude from all this is that if the virtues are to flourish, and they go hand in hand with concern for the common good, we should aim at a society that resembles the first state of affairs rather than the second. If we find ourselves in the second kind of society, although we may have to push ourselves competitively in order to survive, we must do what we can to preserve the pursuit of internal goods and the virtues that go with them, and we must not compromise our moral integrity by playing power games or engaging in dirty tricks. In order to bring this off, we may have to be *in* some institution that encourages the pursuit of external rather than internal values, but, as far as we can avoid it, not *of* it, even if this is the game that is played. But we must not forget that since good breeds good (just as evil breeds evil), change in or adjustment to our existing institutions is a real possibility over time, provided enough people commit themselves to the pursuit of internal values.

Materialism and Related Matters

You often hear materialism decried. Our society is too materialistic, it is said. We should be attending more to spiritual values. What exactly is "materialism" and how is it a real threat to the morally good life? We must consider this last question before stating our overall conclusions. We certainly need food, warmth, and shelter in order to survive, and these are all material things, but no one can call us to task for seeking them! And there are other material things that we do not strictly need – we could live without them – but which nevertheless enhance our lives: a comfortable and aesthetically pleasing place to live, labor-saving devices such as hot and cold running water and, in our technically advanced culture, electric stoves (cookers), refrigerators, washing machines and vacuum cleaners. Also cars, telephones, radios, television sets, VCRs, sound systems, camcorders, computers. And there are other things that are not strictly material, but are nevertheless things that money can buy, such as books, magazines, live theatre, recorded music, and various entertainments. All of these things can enhance our lives, and surely no one can be faulted for wanting these things and buying them if he or she can afford it. Since materialism is supposed to be bad, this is not materialism.

What, then, is materialism in the bad sense? The answer, or part of the answer, is *greed*, or what the Greeks called *pleonexia*, grabbing as much as you can for yourself, at the expense of other people if necessary – which is a *moral vice*. There is no point in buying or owning something if it does not, for what it is, add something to one's life. There is no point, for instance, in accumulating as much as you can in the way of material goods just for the sake of accumulating them. There is also no point in scrapping a perfectly good and usable piece of equipment for the latest model unless it constitutes a significant improvement. There is again no point in buying or owning something just to keep up with the neighbors, or to have more than they have, an entirely useless competition for status that is nothing but a waste of resources. Finally, there is no point in accumulating money or riches for its own sake, far beyond anything one could possibly spend. (To do this is to be a miser, and that is a fault of character.)

The second part of the answer to the question "What is materialism in the bad sense?" is that it is putting all one's eggs in one basket, the material basket, understood as being all one needs for the good life. But one cannot even enjoy one's toys or gadgets, or even the most luxurious surroundings, if one is lonely or depressed, or under severe stress, perhaps in the pursuit of still more material wealth. Love, friendship, companionship, and good social relations generally (for which the virtues are needed) are necessary ingredients of the good life. Accumulation of yet more money or more material goods (a second mansion, a second luxury car, a second yacht, television in every room), can never compensate for the absence of these other goods. *If we regard possession of wealth and material goods as the only, or even the most important value (apart from what we need in order to survive), we are making a serious mistake about what makes for a happy life.* This, along with greed, constitutes materialism in the bad sense.

Materialism in the bad sense, like the competitive quest for power and status, is a kind of spiritual sickness – unfortunately one that is contagious. On the other hand, doing good work in one's occupation or practice as a contribution to the common good, and that includes raising food, which is as material as you can get, is both self-fulfilling and uplifting to the soul, and what could be more spiritual than that? Thus the apparent opposition between spirit and matter is overcome.

Conclusion

In Parts II, III, and IV of this book, a solution has been attempted to what I have called the central problem for ethics: how to reconcile the separateness of persons with their inherently social nature. A moral theory has been developed, at least in outline, which I have called *communalism*. It has been argued that:

1 There is a morality valid for all humanity (a universal and objective morality grounded in practical reason).
2 The ultimate source of all value, including moral value, is *eudaimonia* (thriving, flourishing, well-being, happiness), both communal and personal, the former being necessary for the latter.
3 The aretaic and the deontic are separate but necessary constituents of a single morality.
4 The theory of communalism, by showing the tie between moral goodness and the common good, said to be a necessary ingredient of the happiness of each individual, *does* reconcile the separateness of persons with their inherently social nature.
5 Being morally good is neither egoistic nor altruistic; moral goodness overcomes that unfortunate dichotomy.

If we wanted now to give a general answer to the question of what is morally good and what is morally bad, it would be something like this: what is morally good is whatever it is in conduct and character that brings people together in amity and good will, while allowing them to live fulfilling and self-directed individual lives; what is morally evil is whatever it is in conduct and character that divides people and sets them against one another, while hindering them from living rich and fulfilling self-directed individual lives. If this is so, and it has been argued throughout that it is, moral goodness does not require selflessness, self-denial, or self-sacrifice. Because the *common* good is an essential ingredient of the good of each and every individual, making it desirable that we act for *its* sake, the supposed opposition between egoism and altruism has been overcome. Our overall conclusion is that the morally good life, properly understood, is the best life for each and all.

SUMMARY

1   The problem which morality is supposed to solve, which is the central problem for ethics, is how to reconcile the unavoidable separateness of persons with their inherently social nature and circumstances.
2   Every moral outlook and every moral theory is an attempt to solve this problem.
3   Hard or tough egoistic individualism says you should exploit other people as much as you can for your own advantage. But if everyone adopted this view (and as a moral view it must be universalizable), everyone would be in perpetual adversarial conflict with everyone else. Not a happy situation.
4   The Hobbesian contractarian view, which is also egoistic, says it is too dangerous to try for the best we could have for ourselves, which would be to dominate and exploit everybody. Therefore, we should settle for second best and agree with others to limit our conduct in such a way that we do not live in perpetual fear of one another. This is a much better situation. Justice and rights have entered the picture, but we are still exclusively concerned with our own individual selves. There is no concern for the common good in its own right. The trouble with this view is that if I have reason to believe I can violate the contract and get away with it, there is *no* reason why I should not do just that. If there is concern for justice only in so far as it profits *me*, there is no concern for justice itself.
5   The Kantian view is non-egoistic but still individualist. I must not do what I cannot will that others do whenever they feel like it. I must be aware of the reality of others. But people are still conceived as a collection of individuals and not as a community. This view is not altruistic but *universalist*.
6   But there is also a *communal* reason for obeying the categorical imperative, for it helps to create the kind of social atmosphere in which people can live richer and more fulfilling lives. In other words, it is a contribution to the common good.
7   Consequentialist utilitarianism is not the solution because it sees deontic morality as *a complete and general guide to conduct*, an ethics of *general prescription*, when in fact we know that deontic morality is an ethics of *limitation* based on the idea of law. Consequentialist utilitarianism is once more not altruistic but universalist. It is also

individualistic, seeing only an aggregate of persons rather than a community.

8 Communitarianism sees the individual not as alone, unattached, and isolate, but sees his or her social relations and membership in the community as an essential part of himself or herself. This is a step in the right direction, but unfortunately communitarians see the individual's good as partly constituted by *existing* institutions and social relations whatever they may be. The question of what constitutes a *good* community is not asked. Communitarianism then seems to be a kind of cultural relativism in disguise.

9 Collectivism is the view that personal interests should be sacrificed to the general good, generally seen as represented by the state. But this ignores the separateness of persons and their need to lead their own lives. It is out of accord with human nature.

10 If the common good, for which morality exists, is a necessary part of the good life for each individual, the opposition between individualism and collectivism is overcome.

11 The view advocated in this book is that, yes, our social relations are real, and part of ourselves, but that *good* social relations require a community in which both the virtues and deontic morality are encouraged and supported. Moral goodness is necessary for, and partly constitutes, the good community.

12 If values external to practices are pursued to the detriment of values internal to practices, the result is adversarial competition and a loss of important goods. External values should be the reward of internal values and should not be pursued independently of them. If internal values are pursued for their own sake, not only will more things of real value be produced, but this will tend to encourage the virtues and discourage bad character and moral wrongdoing.

13 There is nothing wrong with material goods if they enhance our lives. Materialism in the bad sense is (a) greed, which is a *moral vice*; and (b) thinking of material goods as the only value in life. Good work in producing valuable goods and services is fulfilling to the spirit, no matter how material these goods and services may be. Thus the opposition between the material and the spiritual is overcome.

13 A moral theory has been developed in this book which we may call *communalism* (a) to indicate that it is not individualistic; and (b) to distinguish it from communitarianism and collectivism. It has been argued (1) that there is a morality valid for all humanity (a universal and objective morality grounded in practical reason); (2) that the ultimate source of all value, including moral value, is *eudaimonia* (thriving, flourishing, well-being, happiness), both communal and personal (the

former being necessary for the latter); (3) that the aretaic and the deontic are separate but necessary constituents of a single morality; (4) that the theory of communalism, by showing the tie between moral goodness and the common good, *does* reconcile the separateness of persons with their inherently social nature; and (5) that being morally good is neither egoistic nor altruistic, but overcomes this opposition altogether.

14 The most general answer we can give to the question of what is morally good and what is morally evil is this. What is morally good is whatever it is in conduct and character that brings people together in amity and good will, while allowing them to live fulfilling and self-directed individual lives; and what is morally evil is whatever it is in conduct and character that divides people and sets them against one another, while hindering them from living rich and fulfilling self-directed individual lives.

15 This means that morality does not require any real selflessness, self-sacrifice, or self-denial. The opposition between egoism and altruism has been overcome. The morally good life is the best life for each and all.

QUESTIONS FOR THOUGHT

1 If you are reading this book because it is a text in a college or university course, which is more important, that you learn something from reading it (though you don't have to agree), or that reading it carefully will get you a high mark in the course? Are these two aims incompatible? Explain.

2 Good social conditions are necessary for individual happiness (*eudaimonia*). The world is in bad shape. Is there any hope of improvement? What is the best way for you to live in the world such as it is?

3 No one can be happy (possess *eudaimonia*) unless they can identify with some group that is less than the whole human race. Is this true? If it were true what would be the consequences for morality?

4 It has been claimed that the moral life is the best life for each and all. Have you been persuaded? Give an account of why or why not.

Recommended Reading

Chapter 10   The Relations between Aretaic and Deontic Morality

Bernard Gert, *Morality: a New Justification of the Moral Rules* (Oxford University Press, New York and London, 1988), chs 8 and 9. Gert distinguishes between moral *rules* and moral *ideals*, and also between *moral* virtues and *personal* virtures, the first directly and the second indirectly related to the moral rules.

Chapter 11   Justice and Rights

An immense amount of writing in this area. The following are important:
Ronald Dworkin, *Taking Rights Seriously* (Harvard University Press, Cambridge, Mass., 1977).
John Rawls, *A Theory of Justice* (Harvard University Press, Cambridge, Mass., 1971).
Judith Jarvis Thomson, *The Realm of Rights* (Harvard University Press, Cambridge, Mass., 1990).
Joel Feinberg, *Rights, Justice and the Bounds of Liberty* (Princeton University Press, Princeton, NJ, 1980).
Jeremy Waldron (ed.), *Theories of Rights* (Oxford University Press, Oxford, 1984).

Chapter 12   The Best Life for All

Consequentialism:
J. S. Mill, *Utilitarianism* (1861). Many current editions.
James Griffin, *Well-being* (Oxford University Press, Oxford, 1986). Defence of a limited utilitarian consequentialism.
Samuel Scheffler, *The Rejection of Consequentialism* (Clarendon Press, Oxford, 1982). A limited defence of consequentialism.
Communitarianism:

Michael Sandel, *Liberalism and the Limits of Justice* (Cambridge University Press, Cambridge, 1982).

Michael Waltzer, *Spheres of Justice* (Basic Books, New York, 1983).

Will Kymlicka, *Liberalism, Community, and Culture* (Clarendon Press, Oxford, 1989). A liberal critique of communitariansim.

The good life:

Thomas Nagel, *The View from Nowhere* (Oxford University Press, New York and Oxford, 1986), ch. 10 ("Living right and living well"). According to Nagel, we must act as as morality requires, but this will involve some sacrifice of self-interest.

David Gauthier, *Morals by Agreement* (Clarendon Press, Oxford, 1986). The moral life is not the best life we could have for ourselves, but it is the best we can get.

Jonathan Lear, "Moral objectivity," in S. C. Brown (ed.), *Objectivity and Cultural Divergence* (Cambridge University Press, Cambridge, 1984), pp. 135–70. A view very similar to the one presented in this book.

E. J. Bond, "Theories of the good," in Lawrence C. Becker (ed.), *Encyclopedia of Ethics* (Garland Publishing, New York, 1992), vol. I, pp. 408–12.

E. J. Bond, "Morality and community," in Wayne Sumner, Donald Callen and Thomas Attig (eds), *Values and Moral Standing*, Bowling Green Studies in Applied Philosophy, vol. VIII (The Applied Philosophy Program, Bowling Green State University, Bowling Green, Ohio, 1986), pp. 57–67. The moral life is the best life for all.

Notes

Chapter 1   Psychological Egoism

1   Pure malice, if there is such a thing, or acting simply with the aim of harming others, although not self-regarding, would obviously not be called unselfish. But for it not to be self-regarding this *would* have to be *pure* malice, malignity, or ill will (malevolence). It could not be something done for revenge, the thrill of power, sadistic pleasure, or for the sake of any benefit or satisfaction to oneself.

2   How an act may be unselfish yet not involve any self-denial or self-sacrifice is the subject of the final paragraph of this chapter. It is further examined and explained in chapters 6, 8, 9, and 12, when we are doing substantive theoretical ethics proper. It is of central importance in the overall view of moral goodness presented here. For the moment just consider simple acts of kindness, friendliness, or courtesy, that are motivated only by good will.

3   This is the view of the sophist Thrasymachus in Plato's *Republic* (book I) and of the character Polus in his *Gorgias*, and it has been a commonly held view ever since. Plato (427–347 BC), an Athenian and the founder of the world's first school of higher learning (the Academy), was the first of the truly great philosophers and one of the most influential of all time. As we have it from Plato, a sophist was someone who, claiming to be wise, taught virtue to young men for a fee.

4   Something discovered through observation or investigation is said to be known *a posteriori*.

5   See his *Leviathan* (1651), part I, chs 13–16; part II, chs 17–22.

Chapter 2   Cultural Relativism

1   William Graham Sumner, *Folkways: a Study of the Sociological Importance of Usages, Manners, Customs*, Mores, *and Morals* (Ginn and Company, Boston and New York, 1907); Ruth Benedict, *Patterns of Culture* (Routledge, London, 1935); Edward Westermarck, *Ethical Relativity* (Harcourt, New York, 1932); Margaret Mead, *Growing up in Samoa* (Cape, London, 1929).

2   See Plato's dialogue of that name.

3   In logic, such an argument is called an *enthymeme*.

4   "Yeshua" is the Hebrew form of the name "Jesus." According to the Bible story (St Luke, ch. 2, v. 42–7), Jesus, at the age of 12, was treated by the rabbis ("doctors") in the Temple at Jerusalem as one of themselves when, after Passover, he stayed behind to discuss religious issues with them. ("Rabbi") in Hebrew means "teacher," as does "doctor" in Latin. It is also one sense of the word "doctor" in seventeenth-century English, the language of the King James Bible.

5   St John, ch. 8, v. 8.

6   Bernard Williams, *Ethics and the Limits of Philosophy* (Harvard University Press, Cambridge, Mass., 1985), pp. 126–70.

7   As Williams uses these terms, "thick" concepts such a "liar" and "brutal" are "world-guided" in a way that "thin" concepts, such as "ought," "right," "wrong," "good," "evil," are not. Thus we can, by common agreement, settle the question (from within our evaluative perspective) whether someone is a bully or a liar by taking note of what he or she does. We can observe someone being a bully, but we cannot observe, in the same sense, the moral wrongness of an act, or the goodness of a person's character.

8   Williams, *Ethics and the Limits of Philosophy*, pp. 148, 167.

9   In fairness, it should be pointed out that Williams denies being a cultural relativist (*Ethics and the Limits of Philosophy*, p. 25). But, by cultural relativism, Williams understands the "When in Rome" or "Do the done thing" doctrine, which would require us to adopt different perspectives at will, and this we cannot do if we have an evaluative perspective of our own deriving from our own culture. But, as we have seen, the "Do the done thing" doctrine is not a form of relativism at all, but something transcultural, hence universal or "absolute," something that Williams has failed to see. His view, by contrast, is a true relativism.

10   The full discussion appears in chapter 6.

11   Alasdair MacIntyre, *After Virtue*, 2nd edn (Duckworth, London, 1985); *Whose Justice? Which Rationality?* (Duckworth, London, 1988).

12   MacIntyre, *Whose Justice?*, p. 2.

13   MacIntyre, *After Virtue*, pp. 6–7.

14   MacIntyre himself introduces the expression "right to life" into one of his two anti-abortion arguments (*After Virtue*, p. 7). How then can he go on to claim, as he does (p. 8), that the dispute between those who favor and those who oppose abortion is based on the "pro" party invoking "premises which invoke rights," while the "anti" party invokes "those which invoke universalizability"?

15   Sabina Lovibond, *Realism and Imagination in Ethics* (Blackwell, Oxford, 1983), p. 42.

16   Ibid., p. 82.

17   The German word *sittlich* literally translates as "customary."

18   Lovibond, *Realism and Imagination in Ethics*, p. 151.

19   Ibid., p. 164.

20   "A world in which that condition obtained would be one where 'reality' in the positive sense (i.e., . . . fixed by the content . . . of the consensual world view) had

come to coalesce with 'reality' in the critical sense (i.e., that which is fixed by the content of the totality of propositions that I hold true)" (Lovibond, *Realism and Imagination in Ethics*, p. 164).

21   See note 9 above.

22   For the reasons why so many people think simple cultural relativism must be true, see the following section.

Chapter 3   Subjective Relativism

1   J.-P. Sartre, "Existentialism is a humanism," trans. P. Mairet, in *Existentialism from Dostoevsky to Sartre*, ed. W. Kaufmann (Meridian Books, New York, 1957), pp. 307–8. *Mauvaise foi* literally translates as "bad faith", but Mairet (like Kaufmann) prefers "self-deception" as coming closer, for anglophone readers, to what Sartre is getting at, namely failure to recognize one's own freedom or to accept responsibility for one's actions, for what one makes oneself by one's choices.

2   Sartre, "Existentialism is a humanism," p. 292.

3   Sartre's debt in this respect, even in the language he uses, to the German philosopher Immanuel Kant (1724–1804), is obvious. Kant's views will be treated in detail in chapter 9.

4   Sartre, "Existentialism is a humanism," p. 292 *ad fin.*

5   They had been reading the German philosopher Friedrich Nietzsche (1844–1900), no doubt his *Thus Spake Zarathustra* (1883), where the doctrine of the superman (*Übermensch*) is introduced. The *Oxford Reference Dictionary* (1986) has a rather neat summary of the views expressed there: "The principle features of his doctrine are contempt for Christianity with its compassion for the weak, and exaltation of the 'will to dominate' and of the 'superman', unscrupulous and pitiless, superior to ordinary morality, who tramples on the feeble and will replace the Christian ideal. He divided mankind into a small dominant 'master–class' and a large dominated 'herd'. . . ." However Nietzsche, while he would have regarded universalizability with contempt, would no more have condoned the actions of Leopold and Loeb in killing for pleasure a boy the regarded as their inferior than Sartre would have condoned the action of the woman who drowned her baby. Still, the dangers of such teachings as those of Nietzsche and Sartre should be obvious.

6   Sartre, "Existentialism is a humanism," p. 292.

Chapter 4   Subjectivism and Non-cognitivism

1   Some readers may find a contradiction in the following: If a judgment, e.g. of the form "*x* is morally wrong," which uses moral language, is, if said or thought sincerely, a true description of a person's feelings or attitudes of favor or disfavor, their likes and dislikes, as the subjectivists claim, how can it not be a truth claim

to some inner or private moral reality, as the subjective relativists claim? We seem to be saying, at the same time, both that there is and that there is not a personal moral reality. Doesn't subjectivism, if this contradiction is to be avoided, immediately turn into subjective relativism, which *does* claim that there is an inner or private moral reality? All that can be said here is that meta-ethical subjectivists *do* claim that a judgment of the form "*x* is morally wrong" means, not "I *morally* disapprove of *x*," but simply "I disapprove of *x*," or "I am personally against *x*," or "I dislike *x*," or "I hate *x*," or "I regard *x* with disfavor," so for them there is no contradiction. Emotivists, too, while denying that moral judgments, being mere exclamations of approval or disapproval, can be true or false of anything at all, do not say that they are exclamations expressing *moral* approval or disapproval, but amount essentially to something like "Up with *x*!" or "Down with *y*!" Both try to, as it were, take the *moral* out of moral judgments, to explain the moral in terms of something else. This undoubtedly cannot be done, but that is part of the criticism that will follow in this chapter.

2   Most self-styled Satanists, however monstrous their acts may be, are probably rebelling against externally imposed morality, especially morality imposed by religion, which they see as repressive, and they add a little mock-religion (religion against religion) for a wicked thrill and as a kick in the pants to "goodness." They delight in asserting themselves by being "wicked" as judged by conventional or religious standards. They find it exciting to break the rules, to do the forbidden. Because they see the morality around them as being either purely conventional or dependent on a discredited religious authority, they see all morality as being false and deeply hypocritical. They do not believe that anything is really wrong. (If they have a morality it is the morality of anti-morality.) This kind of Satanism is essentially rebellion against authority. The irony is in that doing exactly what conventional or religious morality sees as evil, they are unknowingly accepting the conventional or religious view of the matter – a view which tends to be repressive and puritanical. "I don't wanna be good," they say; "I wanna be evil. It's a hell of a lot more exciting." But that is simply inverse puritanism. This kind of rebellion against moral authority does not always go so far as to involve Satanic rituals or bizarre anti-goodness clothing, body paint, tattoos, hair styles, etc.; popular culture is just loaded with it. Thus the words "wicked" and "bad" have commonly come to mean something like "fantastically wonderful" in popular speech. They mean, for many people, what "really good" once meant, but that expression is seen by these people as one now only used by the dull and the square.

3   Cognitivist anti-realism will be taken up again at the conclusion of our examination of emotivism (p. 78 below), and once more in chapter 5 (pp. 101–3).

4   C. K. Ogden and I. A. Richards, *The Meaning of Meaning*, 8th edn (Routledge and Kegan Paul, London, 1946), p. 125. (This paragraph, usually attributed to Richards, is unchanged from the first edition of 1923.)

5   The view that ethical sentences are translatable into statements that might be verified by value-neutral observation (empirically verifiable statements) is often called *naturalism* (more of this later).

6   W. H. F. Barnes, "A suggestion about value," *Analysis*, 1 (1933–34), pp. 45–6.

7   See especially A. J. Ayer, *Language, Truth and Logic*, 1st edn (Victor Gollancz, London, 1936), 2nd edn (Victor Gollancz, London, 1946), ch. 6 and Introduction to the 2nd edn, pp. 20–2; also the early papers of C. L. Stevenson: "The emotive meaning of ethical terms" (1937), "Persuasive definitions" (1938). "Meaning: descriptive and emotive" (1948), and "The emotive conception of ethics and its cognitive implications" (1950), collected in C. L. Stevenson, *Facts and Values* (Yale University Press, New Haven and London, 1963), and the book in which Stevenson expanded on his theory in great detail: C. L. Stevenson, *Ethics and Language* Yale University Press, New Haven, 1944). The emotive theory of ethics was not seriously challenged from within the avant-garde until the publication in 1949 of Stuart Hampshire's paper, "Fallacies in moral philosophy," collected in *Contemporary Ethical Theory*, ed. Joseph Margolis (Random House, New York, 1966), pp. 157–76.

8   C. L. Stevenson, "The emotive meaning of ethical terms," *Mind, n.s.* 46 (1937), pp. 14–31.

9   Stuart Hampshire, "Fallacies in moral philosophy," *Mind, n.s.* 58 (1949), reprinted in *Contemporary Ethical Theory*, ed. J. Margolis (Random House, New York, 1966), p. 160.

10   Ibid., p. 171.

11   Ibid., p. 173.

12   R. M. Hare, *The Language of Morals* (Oxford University Press, Oxford, 1952).

13   Ibid., p. 69 (my italic).

14   In his 1950 paper "The emotive conception of ethics and its cognitive implications" (see note 7 above), Stevenson attempts to meet the challenge of Hampshire by tackling the issue of personal decision. The answer he comes up with is that in what we call "deliberation" (considering reasons for and against a certain course of action or trying to determine, all things considered, what we ought to do), all we are really doing is setting before our minds the different aspects and consequences of the course or courses of action we are considering, discovering for each whether our attitude is pro (approval) or con (disapproval), and awaiting the psychological process which will deliver a pro rating for some course of action as a whole and so produce the necessary motivation to follow it through. While each individual pro rating can be *called* a reason for, and each individual con rating can be *called* a reason against, no actual reasoning is involved. Hampshire and Hare, however, both believe there is such a thing as genuine practical reasoning, and both speak of reasons for, in the sense of justifications of, or grounding for, practical decisions, even if what is a reason for me need not be a reason for you.

15   Hare, *The Language of Morals*, p. 70.

16   We should also notice that both Hare and Sartre acknowledge their indebtedness to Kant (see note 3, chapter 3). Kant's views will be considered in detail in chapter 9.

17   For Stevenson's attempt to make up for this neglect, see note 14 above.

18   E. J. Bond, "The justification of moral judgments," in *Ethics and Justification*, ed. D. Odegard (Academic Printing and Publishing, Edmonton, Canada, 1988), pp. 56–7.

Chapter 5   Practical Reason and Value

1   J. L. Mackie, *Ethics: Inventing Right and Wrong* (Penguin Books, Harmondsworth, 1977), pp. 35, 48–9.

2   G. E. Moore, *Principia Ethica* (Cambridge University Press, Cambridge, 1903, many reprintings), pp. 5–17. A property, in philosophical parlance, is that which is denoted or designated by an adjective, e.g. "white," "pleasant," "sharp" (and supposedly) "good." Thus a thing is said to possess the property of being white or sharp or pleasant or (supposedly) good. A *natural* property, as Moore understands it, is any property to be found in the natural, observable world (such as the first three above). A *non-natural* property would be one that is not to be found there.

3   You may still be wondering why the question "Is *x* good?," where *x* is a natural property, is always open, or always makes sense, or always can sensibly be asked. After all, you may think, we have *defined* "good" as, e.g., "conducive to happiness" and therefore the question "Is being conducive to happiness really good?" is no more open than the question "Is a duckling a baby duck?" where "duckling" is defined as "baby duck." But *we* did not define "duckling" as "baby duck," rather "baby duck" is the *correct* definition of "duckling" as that word is used in ordinary speech. Now we may, of course, define a term, for our own purposes, in any way we like. Thus we can say, for instance, that henceforth by "good" *I* shall mean "conducive to happiness," whatever anyone else means and understands by the word. This is what is called a *stipulated* definition. But the definition of "duckling" is not stipulated; it is a report of how the word is used and understood in ordinary speech, or what is called a *reported* definition. Now Moore is not denying that a person can stipulate that by "good" he shall henceforth mean "conducive to happiness;" what he is denying is that this can be a correct account of how the word "good" is used in ordinary speech. And in ordinary speech, using the word "good" as it is ordinarily used, we can always sensibly ask, of any natural property, whether it is really good. Therefore "conducive to happiness" (or a word designating any other natural property such as "pleasant") cannot be the correct definition of the word "good" as it is used in ordinary speech. Or, in other words, it cannot be the correct *reported* definition. The real reason for this is not, as Moore thought, that good (the supposed property designated by the word "good") is a non-natural property, but rather that "good" is an evaluative term (a term used, and only used, in making value judgments), while the offered definitions ("pleasant", "conducive to happiness") are non-evaluative or value-neutral (need not be construed as value judgments). Notice that nothing Moore says forbids us from saying that whatever is conducive to happiness (or is pleasant, or loving, or whatever) is good, as long as this is understood as a value *judgment*, and is not to be taken as true by definition (reported), or as an identity statement (being conducive to happiness and being good are the very same thing).

4   David Hume, *A Treatise of Human Nature*, book III (1740), part I, s. 1. In the edition by L. A. Selby-Bigge (Oxford University Press, Oxford, 1888, many reprintings), the crucial remark about "is" and "ought" appears on pp. 469–70.

5   Truth is really a very simple thing. What does it mean to say that the statement "Today is Tuesday" is true? It simply means that today *really is* Tuesday. (If in doubt, check your calendar, or ask somebody.) Similarly, the statement "You ought to see the play" is true if indeed you *really ought* to see the play. (If in doubt, run through your reasons for and against once more, or ask a friend for advice.) Furthermore, if today *really is* Tuesday, then it's a fact that today is Tuesday, and if you *really ought* to see the play, then it's a *fact* that you ought to see the play (where "fact" is understood in the sense of "anything that is true").

Chapter 6   Moral Value

1   There is even a sense in which what a particular individual likes or dislikes, or what he or she finds pleasant or unpleasant (hedonic value), is objective even if it is personal. This kind of value is objective in the sense that one must *discover*, in the course of living, what one likes or dislikes or what one finds enjoyable or disagreeable, and one cannot discover, after all, what is not there to be discovered. These personal hedonic values are not a function of – cannot be created by – will, choice, or desire. Thus you can will or desire to like golf or jazz or beer or homosexual or heterosexual sex until you are blue in the face, but this will not make you like it. Nor can you simply choose to like it. You will find, in the end, after all sampling, struggling, thought, advice, encouragement, peer pressure, and therapies, that you either like it or you don't, and there is nothing you can do about it one way or the other. If you happen constitutionally to prefer blondes, that is just the way it is; it is *there* for you. This is not to deny that there is such a thing as an acquired taste, but not every taste can be acquired (and some, e.g. smoking, are not to be acquired or indulged for the reason that they are harmful to oneself or others).

2   The only kind of value that is not a value *for* some person or persons would be so-called *intrinsic* value, or the value that a thing is alleged to have *in itself*, which is a highly obscure notion. (The two major candidates for this have been life and beauty.) Thus G. E. Moore:

> Let us imagine one world exceedingly beautiful. Imagine it as beautiful as you can; put into it whatever on this earth you most admire – mountains, rivers, the sea; trees and sunsets, stars and moon. Imagine these all combined in the most exquisite proportions, so that no one thing jars against another, but each contributes to increase the beauty of the whole. And then imagine the ugliest world you can possibly conceive. Imagine it simply one heap of filth, containing everything that is most disgusting to us, for whatever reason, and the whole, as far as may be, without one redeeming feature . . . The only thing we are not entitled to imagine is that any human being ever has or ever, by any possibility, *can* live in either, can ever see and enjoy the beauty of the one or hate the foulness of the other. Well, even so, supposing them quite apart from any possible contemplation

by human beings; still, is it irrational to hold that it is better that the beautiful world should exist, than the one which is ugly? . . . I admit, of course, that our beautiful world would be better still, if there were human beings in it to contemplate and enjoy its beauty. But that admission makes nothing against my point. If it be once admitted that the beautiful world is *in itself* better than the ugly, then it follows, that however many beings may enjoy it, and however much better their enjoyment may be than it is itself, yet its mere existence adds *something* to the goodness of the whole. . . . (*Principia Ethica*, pp. 83–5)

If there is no one, or no conscious being, sufficiently like us to appreciate the beauty of the one or the ugliness of the other, what difference could it possibly make which world exists? The only reason Moore could think it does matter is because we can imagine what it would be like to live in or to look upon these two worlds, and naturally we would choose the first, since it would have positive value *for us*, rather than the second, which would have negative value. If there really were no human beings (or other living creatures enough like us) in the universe, to live in or observe these worlds, it could not possibly make any difference which one existed (unless, possibly, they were observed by God). Now there is such a thing as *instrumental* value, which is the value a thing has not because it is desirable in itself, but because it is a means to something else that *is* desirable in itself. (Thus we clean house because a clean house is something good to have; we do not clean house for its own sake.) And it is sometimes thought that the term "intrinsic value" must be introduced to contrast with "instrumental value." But if "intrinsic value" means the value that a thing supposedly possesses *in itself*, regardless of whether it matters or could matter to anybody, this is a mistake. Far better to use the terms "valuable as a means" and "valuable as an end." By the latter we mean something that is worth while having, getting, or doing for its own sake, not something that is valuable *in itself*. The only plausible candidate for intrinsic value is conscious life itself, or (possibly) existence itself. For isn't it objectively better, we might plausibly say, regardless of what it means to you or me, that conscious life exists rather than it does not, or that there is a world (a universe) rather than nothing at all? And what about my life? Or yours? Do they not have intrinsic value? True, it may be better from my (or your) point of view to exist and have a life rather than not exist at all, but it is difficult to say that my existence, or yours, however meritorious you or I may be, has *intrinsic* value.

3   This word is borrowed by philosophers writing in English from the French *valoriser*, a term adapted recently by French philosophers to signify this absurdity. In French, the word meant simply to develop the economy (of a region) or to enhance the value of a product by improving it. This belongs entirely to economics and there is nothing absurd about it – it can be done. In English, the dictionary meaning of the word "valorize" (*Concise Oxford Dictionary*, 8th edn) is somewhat different, though still in the realm of economics: "raise or fix the price of (a commodity etc.) by artificial means, esp. by government action". This again is something that can be done by choice; valuing is not. We value something if

and only if we actually believe it to be truly valuable. This shows how the very creation of a word (or in this case creating a new sense for an old word) can encapsulate a false and insidious belief, here the belief that you can make something valuable by an act of will. It shows how a false belief based on confusion of thought can be embedded and preserved in language!

4   There is another sense of the verb "to value" which is much commoner in ordinary speech. We find it in such expressions as "I really value friendship" or "I value friendship highly," which means the same as "Friendship is really important to me," or "Friendship really matters to me." The use of the word "highly" here shows that this kind of valuing admits of degrees. Thus it can be used in an explicitly comparative way, as in "I value love and friendship over material wealth." This, by the way, is where the expression "place a value on" has its real sense. For "I value friendship highly" can equally well be put as "I place a high value on friendship." Notice that this kind of valuing *presupposes* that the thing in question *has* value. It is a question of just how much this particular good matters to me, implicity or explicitly, compared to other good or desirable things. But, once more, this is not something we can *choose*; we *find* or we *recognize* that we value a certain good highly, or higher than some other good (see also note 1 above).

5   I say "not telling lies" in preference to "always telling the truth" because the latter can be misinterpreted as "Blab all," but, of course, there is a difference between always telling the truth in the sense of never telling lies, and *telling everything* (what in law is called "the whole truth"). There is pretty plainly no moral reason for telling all, and telling all is not a moral value. In fact it's often better, sometimes morally better, to keep your mouth shut.

Chapter 7   *Three Different Approaches to Ethics*

1   The deontic approach has been so common since the time of Kant (late eighteenth and early nineteenth centuries), that the very word "morality" is now often assumed to refer only to questions of moral right and wrong, moral obligation and duty, moral permissibility and impermissibility. Bernard Williams, aware of this, goes so far as to reserve the terms "moral" and "morality" for deontic morality, which, in the final chapter of his *Ethics and the Limits of Philosophy* (Harvard University Press, Cambridge, Mass., 1985), he calls a "subsystem of the ethical." You may be used to thinking of morality in exclusively deontic terms, and thus find it odd to find such things as courage or laziness described as *moral* qualities. But that is how they have been understood in the aretaic tradition from ancient times until the present day, and I (like many others) use the terms "moral" and "morality" in the broad sense that includes what I have called the aretaic dimension of morality.

2   That these are recognizably *moral* laws can be shown by giving a few examples:

Thou shalt not kill (Exodus 20: 12)
Thou shalt not bear false witness against thy neighbour (Exodus 20: 16)

Ye shall not steal, neither deal falsely, neither lie to one another (Leviticus 19: 11)
Thou shalt not defraud thy neighbour . . . (Leviticus 19: 13)
Thou shalt not go up and down as a talebearer among the people . . . (Leviticus
   19: 16)
3 We should also notice that a moral code consists of a set of *independent* rules
   or principles, prohibiting some acts and requiring others. There is no attempt,
   and no need seen, to ground the rules in some all-embracing value, such as
   the *eudaimonia* that, in chapters 5 and 6, we claimed to be the ultimate
   rational grounding for all action and choice. And we cannot expect every valid
   moral rule or principle to be self-justifying; we *need* a moral theory which will
   enable us to show when a moral rule or principle is valid or justified, when it is
   not, and why.
4 The only distinction I make between a moral rule and a moral principle is that the
   rule takes an imperative form, as in a moral code, while the principle takes an
   indicative form. Thus "Do not steal!" expresses a moral rule, and if it is a valid
   or acceptable moral rule, the corresponding principle "You morally ought not to
   steal" or "Stealing is morally wrong" is justified and true.
5 These are what we may call social responsibilities or *duties* in the strict sense.

Chapter 8   Goodness of Character (Aretaic Morality)

1 "Bad girl" can also mean something like "girl or woman who is sexually willing,"
   and when so used it has an air of wicked excitement about it. This is an example
   of the inverse puritanism talked about in chapter 4, note 1.
2 Even in the first quarter of the twentieth century, the list would have been quite
   different. Thus for "bad man" the 3rd edition of *Roget's Thesaurus* (Longmans,
   Green and Co., London, 1925) gives (among others) the following words: "rascal,
   scoundrel, villain, miscreant, caitiff, wretch, reptile, viper, serpent, cockatrice,
   basilisk, urchin, tiger, monster, devil incarnate, demon in human shape, Nana
   Sahib, hell-hound, hell-cat, rake hell, scamp, scapegrace, rip, runagate, ne'er-do-
   well, reprobate, loose fish, sad dog, black sheep, castaway, recreant, prodigal,
   blackguard, cullion, mean wretch, varlet, kern, *âme-de-boue*, cur, dog, hound, and
   scum of the earth."
3 It is interesting to note that in the nineteenth and early twentieth centuries
   the only words for ascribing badness to a woman's character as a whole had to
   do with sexual looseness. Thus the 3rd edition (1925) of *Roget's Thesaurus* (see
   note 1 above) gives only "bad woman," "jade," "Jezebel," "adultress," and then
   refers you to the section on sexual looseness where you get "whore," "fallen
   woman," etc. Apparently the whole character of a woman, as a woman, could be
   condemned simply on these grounds! Chastity, it seems, was regarded as so
   important that it put everything else in the shade. There are a very few
   ungendered terms – "reptile," "viper," "serpent" (all to do with snakes!) – which
   could be applied to both men and women, but otherwise being of bad moral
   character altogether, except for female unchastity, seemed to belong exclusively to
   males!

4   The meaning of many traditional virtue and vice words, including "temperance" (traditionally meaning self-discipline), "continence" (traditionally meaning strength of will to do what one thinks is best regardless of any contrary inclinations), and even "virtue" and "vice" themselves, deteriorated completely in the Victorian era. Thus, "temperance" came to mean total abstinence from alcoholic beverages, "continence" came to mean not wetting your bed, "virtue" came to mean female chastity, and "vice" came to mean such things (mainly, if not exclusively, for males) as excessive masturbation ("the solitary vice"), drinking, gambling, and whoring. The result of this puritan deterioration of our moral vocabulary – which shows the obsessive preoccupations of the Victorian age – is that we have lost the use of these words more or less completely unless we make a conscious effort to restore them.

5   The famous English philosopher, Bertrand Russell (1872–1970), defending the emotivist version of non-cognitivism, is reported to have offered the following "declension" to prove his point: "I am firm. You are stubborn. He is pig-headed." What we are supposed to see is that all these words have the same *descriptive* meaning but different *emotive* meanings. (C. L. Stevenson had claimed, in his "Persuasive definitions" [1938] – see chapter 4, note 7 – that what we are calling virtue and vice words had both a "conceptual" meaning *and* an emotive meaning. [A "persuasive" definition was one that changed or altered the "conceptual" (i.e. descriptive) meaning while leaving the emotive meaning intact. An important recent example is "date rape," which of course is not rape, for rape involves physical forcing or coercion, but rather a boy or a man's, without using physical coercion, talking a girl or a woman of his acquaintance into having sex with him after she has said "no." Still the negative feelings and attitudes associated with the word "rape" are intended to remain. Stevenson would say the *emotive meaning* of the word "rape" is intended to remain.]) "Firm" may be, in some quarters, a virtue word and hence laudatory, while "stubborn" and "pig-headed" are clearly vice words, hence condemnatory, but do "firm," "stubborn" and "pig-headed" really describe the very same disposition only with a different emotional edge, as Russell implicitly claims? If so, we could not ask the question 'Am I (is he) being firm or merely pig-headed?" But of course we can ask the question. I leave you to draw the conclusion for yourself. Whatever we say about Russell's "declension," however, it should show us the danger in regarding firmness as a virtue, or, indeed, of using the word "firm" (in this sense) at all.

Chapter 9   The Avoidance of Wrongdoing (Deontic Morality)

1   This mistake may be partly due to the misinterpretation of Kant (see the next section).

2   For those who have studied traditional logic, "obligatory" and "wrong" (unlike "right" and "wrong") are not contradictories but contraries, i.e. while they cannot both be true, they can both be false. The contradictory of "obligatory" (i.e. "not obligatory") is "permissible not to do;" the contradictory of "wrong" (i.e. "not wrong") is "permissible to do." A thing can be not wrong and also not

obligatory, i.e. permissible to do and also permissible not to do. On this strictly logical account, "obligatory" implies "permissible to do" ("not wrong"), and "wrong" implies "permissible not to do" ("not obligatory"). "Right," as excluding only "wrong," would mean "either obligatory or permissible." (In logical jargon, we say that "permissible to do" is the *subalternate* of "obligatory" and "permissible not to do" is the *subalternate* of " wrong", while "permissible to do" and "permissible not to do" are *subcontraries*.)

3   Immanuel Kant, *Foundations of the metaphysics of Morals* (1785), in Immanuel Kant, *Critique of Practical Judgment and other Writings in Moral Philosophy*, trans. and ed. Lewis White Beck (University of Chicago Press, Chicago, 1949), p. 80 (Prussian Academy Edition of Kant's Complete Works in German, vol. IV, p. 401). The word "maxim" is glossed in a footnote as "subjective principle of acting." The German words in the title that Beck translates as "foundations of" are "*Grundlegung zur*," which literally translates as "ground-laying for the." The complete title is often given in English as "Groundwork for the Metaphysics of Morals," which is closer to what Kant means and, in my opinion, preferable to Beck's English title.

4   Immanuel Kant, *Perpetual Peace: a Philosophical Sketch* (1795–6) in Kant, *Critique of Practical Judgment*, ed. Beck, p. 345 (Prussian Academy Edition, vol. VIII, p. 386).

5   If omitting (failing) to do something is morally wrong, then doing that thing is an obligation or a duty; if *doing* something is morally wrong, then *not* doing it is morally required. Both of these things, in Kant's terms, are required by the categorical imperative. Other acts and omissions are licit or permissible, that is they are allowed by the categorical imperative (do not contravene it).

6   See the following passages from Kant's works:

> This principle of humanity and of every rational creature as an end in itself [the categorical imperative] is the supreme limiting condition on freedom of the actions of each man. (*Foundations of the Metaphysics of Morals*, in Beck, p. 89; Prussian Academy Edition, vol. IV, pp. 430–1)
>
> Rational nature is distinguished from others in that it proposes an end to itself . . . [T]he end here is not conceived as one to be effected but as an independent end and thus merely negative. It *is that which must never be acted against* . . . [my italics]. *Foundations*, in Beck, p. 94; Prussian Academy Edition, vol. IV, p. 437)
>
> That in the use of means to every end I should *restrict* my maxim to the condition of its universal validity as a law for every subject is tantamount to saying that the subject of ends, i.e. the rational being itself, must be made the basis of all maxims of actions and thus be treated never as a mere means but as *the supreme limiting condition in the use of all means*, i.e., as an end at the same time [my italics]. *Foundations*, in Beck, p. 95; Prussian Academy Edition, vol. IV, p. 438)
>
> On this concept of freedom, which is positive (from a practical point of view), are founded unconditional practical laws, which are called *moral*

[author's emphasis] . . . According to these categorical imperatives, certain actions are allowed or not allowed, that is, are morally possible or impossible. (*The Metaphysics of Morals* (1797), in Immanuel Kant, *The Metaphysical Elements of Justice* (*The Metaphysics of Morals*, Part I), trans. John Ladd (The Library of Liberal Arts, Bobbs-Merrill, Indianapolis, New York, and Kansas City, 1965), p. 22; Prussian Academy Edition, vol. VI, p. 221) The book entitled *The Metaphysics of Morals* (1797) is not to be confused with the earlier *Foundations of the Metaphysics of Morals* (1785).

An action is *allowed* (*licitum*) if it is not opposed to obligation, and this freedom that is not limited by any opposing imperative is called license [Ger. *Befugnis*] (*facultas moralis*). Hence it is obvious what is meant by unallowed (*illicitum*) [author's emphasis]. (*The Metaphysics of Morals*, in Ladd, p. 22; Prussian Academy Edition, vol. VI, p. 222) (I have altered Ladd's translation of "*Befugnis*".)

7   Kant, *Foundations*, in Beck, p. 56; Prussian Academy Edition, vol. IV, p. 394.
8   Kant, *Critique of Practical Reason*, in Beck, p. 132; Prussian Academy Edition, vol. V, pp. 21–2.

Chapter 10   The Relations between Aretaic and Deontic Morality

1   This is how we would have to treat the example (chapter 6, p. 123) of returning a favor as an act of kindness.
2   See chapter 7, note 4. Rectitude, so defined, is not a virtue that would have been recognized by Aristotle, for he did not construe any aspect of morality in deontic terms.
3   This moral strength and moral weakness were what were originally signified by the English words "continence" and "incontinence," ultimately derived (via the Latin) from the Greek *engkrateia* and *akrasia* (cf. chapter 8, note 4).

Chapter 11   Justice and Rights

1   I say "black," "Jew," "woman," "homosexual" because I happen to be a white, non-Jewish, heterosexual male. If I were a black, Jewish lesbian I would have to change that to "man," "white," "Muslim," "heterosexual." Injustice (unjust discrimination) based on racial, religious, sexual, or any other generic hatred or dislike, remains injustice, wherever it comes from, no matter what group happens to be dominant or in the majority. In our culture, there is misandry (hatred of men) as well as misogyny (hatred of women), homosexism (heterophobia) as well as heterosexism (homophobia), and anti-white racism as well as racism directed against non-whites. Injustice may also be based on ethnic hatreds, and this obviously belongs in the same basket as any other form of unfair discrimination.
2   Punishment can be seen as a form of redress (if not reparation). Thus the parents

of the murder victims in the O. J. Simpson case (1995), after Simpson was acquitted, and because they still believed him guilty, brought a civil suit of "unlawful death" against him. This could have been simply a desire for revenge, but that is unlikely. More likely, they saw this as *compensation* for the death of their son and daughter. Somehow, if he was guilty, Simpson *owed* it to them (the dead son and daughter) to pay some penalty. Then the parents could be more at ease.

3   This is perhaps the time to bring up the much-debated question of whether non-human animals – henceforth beasts – have rights. If the account that has been given here of rights and justice is correct, the answer would seem to be obviously "No." One can certainly *hurt* a beast but can one do a beast a *wrong*? Can I make a promise to a beast or lie to it? Can a beast claim a right? (If so, it must acknowledge the same right in others. Other beasts? Other animals? Other *persons* (!)?) Can a beast feel righteous indignation? Can a beast demand reparation or punishment? Can a beast own property? Can a beast lie or cheat or steal; and, if it does, am I entitled to demand redress? Or am I entitled to demand redress if the beast injures me? Can I sue the beast for damages? Can the beast sue me?

I have heard it seriously said, by a professor of law, that the day may come when a beast or even a *tree* can be represented in court with a civil claim! This would mean that a beast or a tree would be considered a legal *person*. We would have in the law books the case of *Oak tree 10, Lot 3, Concession 4* v. *Harry Smith* with a decision, perhaps, in favor of the tree (Harry has said he will cut it down). Or a criminal case: *The people [the Queen]* v. *Harry Smith*, where Harry was tried for the criminal offence of threatening Moose M with extinction. This would make Moose M one of the people or one of the Queen's subjects. Of course, if the moose or the tree *were* a legal person, *I* could bring a civil suit against *it*, or the state could file criminal charges! I could charge the water-seeking willow tree with destroying my tile bed, and could be awarded damages. How could the tree pay? Or the moose could be charged with the criminal offence of stealing my turnips. I suggest that this (and all the rest of it) is a gross absurdity. But perhaps, you say, beasts (mosquitoes and microbes included?) could have *moral* rights, even if they could not have legal rights; but, once more, while you can certainly kill a beast or hurt a beast, or be cruel to a beast, how could you *wrong* one? If you could, then the beast could require that you make reparation, which is surely absurd. If you say a lawyer could represent the beast in court, we are back into legal rights again.

We might try to make out the following case. In a moment of anger, I kick my dog, although he has been a faithful "friend" and companion and has once even saved my life. I feel sick and miserable and do my best to make amends by being especially kind and loving to my dog in order to make it up to him. This does make sense. I may certainly *feel* that I have wronged the dog, but can I *actually* have wronged him if he is not a person? Rights and justice, which are inseparable, and all the conceptual apparatus that goes with them – reparation, desert, earned merit, punishment, requirement to respect the rights of others – make sense only in connection with persons, and if they seem to make sense for such animals as dogs, cats, and horses that is because of these animals' long association and close relationships with human beings, who may think of them and treat them as if they were persons.

A respected moral philosopher, who shall not be named, once said that if a mother sees a rat about to nibble her baby's toe, she must consider the rights of the rat as well as the rights of the baby. If I don't either allow the rat a bite or find him something else to eat, does that mean I have *wronged* him? Do I *owe* it to him to see that he doesn't go hungry? Can he be righteously indignant and justly seek redress? I refuse to go along with rats' rights. How about you? Of course, we can be *cruel* or *mean* to beasts, and cruelty and meanness, as we know, are base and reprehensible, for this is built into the very meaning of the "thick" moral concepts (vice words) "cruel" and "mean." But is this because the beasts do not *deserve* such treatment? That would only make sense if they *could* sometimes deserve such treatment. Could they? And if so would it then be *just* to be cruel and mean to them? (It is never just to be cruel and mean, even to people.) All of this is surely nonsense. Do we even have *moral obligations* to beasts, leaving aside the question of rights and justice? I can only have moral obligations to a kind of creature that has moral obligations to me, except for human babies, but they may *become* morally obliged to me for the care I have given them as infants. The notion that I might have a moral obligation to a rat, or it to me, or that they might have moral obligations to each other comes strictly from Gary Larson's *The Far Side.*

This is not to say we do not have a moral *responsibility* toward many species of non-human animals: for their care if they are domestic animals, and that includes poultry, cattle, sheep, and pigs (factory farming is an abomination) or for wild animals in captivity. It is also our responsibility to preserve the habitat of animals in the wild and not to wantonly destroy species after species, as we are doing now, by recklessly destroying those natural habitats by the use of insecticides, or in order to create and maintain money-making industries. And there is no justification for torturing lab animals in tests of perfumes and cosmetics. Arguably we may use lab animals for medical testing, perhaps even for psychological research, but there is still a responsibility to take proper care of the animals and not to be needlessly cruel.

4   To call the moral virtues "dispositions of character" may be technically accurate, but it has a very dry ring to it. I would much rather call them "states of the soul" except that this could too easily be misinterpreted.

Chapter 12   The Best Life for All

1   See the following quotations from J. S. Mill, *Utilitarianism*, ed. Oskar Piest (The Liberal Arts Press, New York, 1957). "From the dawn of philosophy, the question concerning the *summum bonum*, or, what is the same thing, concerning the foundation of morality, has been accounted the main problem in speculative thought . . ." (p. 3). "All action is for the sake of some end, and rules of action, it seems natural to suppose, must take their whole character and color from the end to which they are subservient" (p. 4). "The creed which accepts as the

foundation of morals 'utility' or the 'greatest happiness principle' holds that actions are right in proportion as they tend to promote happiness; wrong as they tend to produce the reverse of happiness . . ." (p. 10). "As between his own happiness and that of others, utilitarianism requires him to be as strictly impartial as a disinterested and benevolent spectator" (p. 22). *Utilitarianism* was originally published in three parts in *Fraser's Magazine* (1861). Since then it has reappeared in numerous editions and anthologies. (It is never out of print.)

2 I owe a great deal of what is said in this section to Alasdair MacIntyre (see MacIntyre, *After Virtue*, 2nd edn (Duckworth, London, 1985, pp. 186–97).

3 Ibid., pp. 187–9.

Glossary

The abbreviation (*q.v.*) means that the term used also appears in this glossary.

a priori: knowable independently of observation or experiment
"absolute": (in ethics a term best avoided if possible) non-relative (opposite of "relative")
absolutism: (another term best avoided) the view that there are objective and universal moral truths
adversarial: oppositional (the relation that enemies have to each other)
adversary: an enemy
altruistic: self-denying, self-sacrificing, selfless, not considering oneself but only others
amoral: a term used by someone who does not believe in any morality to describe his or her own attitude
anomie: lack of moral belief (*q.v.*) with its accompanying anxiety
anthropologist: someone engaged in the study of humanity
anthropology: the study of humanity
anti-realism: in ethics, the view that there are and could be no moral truths or facts
applied ethics: the philosophical consideration of particular moral issues such as abortion, war, and capital punishment, or the application of philosophical ethics to particular areas, such as business or medicine
aretaic morality: the aspect or dimension of morality concerned with the good or bad moral character of persons and the virtues and vices that constitute such good or bad character
categorical imperative: (a term originated by Kant) the supreme or governing principle of deontic morality (*q.v.*) determining what acts and omissions

are morally wrong (what omissions and acts are morally obligatory); it forbids doing (or not doing) anything that we could not will that everyone do (or not do) at their pleasure (whenever they feel like it)

claim right: a positive good that I may rightfully demand of another person or persons or collectivity or the state, and which that person or persons or collectivity or the state is morally obliged to give me or do for me (same as "demand right")

cognitivist anti-realism: the view that moral judgments (*q.v.*) are truth claims (*q.v.*) (which non-cognitivists [*q.v.*] deny), but that they are all in error because they are intended to refer to a moral reality (*q.v.*) which could not exist

collectivism: the view that we should never consider only ourselves but always the collectivity of the people (usually identified with the state)

collectivity: any group united by some common interest

commitment to principle: (a phrase used by the prescriptivists [*q.v.*]) moral judgments (*q.v.*) are said not to be statements claiming truth, but indications of the acceptance of imperatives (*q.v.*) demanding actions (or abstentions) of a certain kind

common good: the good of the community as a whole, hence of all its members

communal *eudaimonia*: the thriving or flourishing of the community as a whole

communalism: (the moral theory advocated in this book) moral goodness is an important part of the common good (*q.v.*), which, in turn, is part of the good of each individual; moral goodness, with the institutions that encourage it, is central to the good community; not just any community with its existing institutions will do, although we may have to make do, for the present, with what we have, until changes come about (contrast with communitarianism [*q.v.*])

communitarianism: the view that the common good (*q.v.*) is to be pursued and can be achieved in the context of the existing institutions of a culture, whatever they may be

conformism: "do the done thing"

consensual morality: the norms of conduct (*q.v.*) agreed upon within a given community

consensus: general agreement

consequentialism: the view that we are morally obliged always to act for the maximum good of everyone indifferently

contractarianism: the view that we would be best off if we could dominate everybody but that we should settle for second best by agreeing with everyone else to restrict our conduct in such a way that we do not live in perpetual fear of one another

cultural relativism: the view that morality is entirely a matter of accepted norms of conduct (*q.v.*) within a given culture or tradition

customary morality: the accepted norms of conduct (*q.v.*) within a given culture

definitional: true by definition (as in "No bachelor has a wife")

deliberation: weighing and balancing reasons in order to decide what one ought to do

demand right: same as "claim right" (*q.v.*)

deontic morality: the ethics of moral requirement and permissibility based on the concept of law

disagreement in attitude: (a term used by the emotivists [*q.v.*]) in moral disagreements it is only attitudes, not beliefs, that are opposed

disagreement in belief: disagreement over what is or is not the case

disinclination: a strong aversion to doing something of a certain kind

disposition of character: a settled state of character that disposes one to act in certain ways; the virtues (*q.v.*) and vices (*q.v.*) are said to be dispositions of character

egoistic: concerned only with oneself

emotivism: (a meta-ethical (*q.v.*) doctrine) moral utterances are non-statemental (*q.v.*) expressions of approval or disapproval

empirically verifiable: verifiable (capable of being shown to be true) by observation or experiment

error theory of value: (an expression coined by Mackie) all moral judgments (*q.v.*) are in error since they are meant to refer to a non-natural ("queer") moral reality (*q.v.*) which could not possibly exist

ethical egoism: the view that morality consists in being clever at looking after your own personal interests

ethical universalism: the view that one must see oneself as only one among many, all of whom are on an equal footing

ethics: in philosophy, the philosophical study of morality

ethics of general prescription: an ethics that would provide a complete and general guide to conduct

ethics of limitation: an ethics that places limits on one's freedom to do or not do as one pleases

ethnologist: someone who studies human cultures

ethnology: the study of human cultures

eudaimonia: thriving, flourishing, well-being (happiness in this sense)

evaluative perspective: the moral outlook from within a given culture

expression of attitude: in ethics, affirming or implying or otherwise indicating that one approves or disapproves of some course of action or aspect of character

externalism: the view that reasons for action, hence values, can exist even if they are unrelated to our present desires

fact: anything that is true

fact/value distinction: the view that there is an unbridgeable logical gap between fact and value (facts are one thing; value claims are another)

gerundive: (a term taken over from grammar) implying that something is to be done or not to be done

good (n.): anything of value (that is worth having, getting, or doing)

grounded in reason: capable of being shown to be true by reason; in the case of value judgments (q.v.), including moral judgments (q.v.), capable of being shown to be true by *practical* reason (q.v.)

hedonic value: the value that something has because one likes it or finds it pleasant or agreeable

hedonism: the view that hedonic value (q.v.) is the only value

honesty-related values: values that can be understood in the same way that honesty is, namely as related to moral requirement (q.v.)

human good: anything that is a good for all human beings (e.g. health, achievement, pleasure)

human well-being: eudaimonia (q.v.)

Hume's principle: "No action without desire"

ideal-regarding: motivated by concern for some ideal (e.g. justice)

illicit: not licit; immoral (q.v.)

immoral: violating a valid moral principle or principles without justification or excuse

imperative: a command, order, or instruction

implicit: not stated but implied

imply: convey without stating

individualism: the view that sees people as a collection of individuals rather than members of a community

internalism: the view that reasons for action cannot exist independently of one's existing desires

intersubjective morality: (a term used by Lovibond) the consensual morality (q.v.)

justified on moral grounds: justified by practical reason (q.v.) where the values are moral values

Kantian morality: deontic morality based on the categorical imperative understood individualistically

language of value: the forms of speech we use in making value judgments (q.v.)

liberalism: in this book, the view that advocates the tolerance of the values of other persons and other cultures

licit: morally permissible (*q.v.*)
linguistic practice: our use of language
logical empiricism: logical positivism (*q.v.*)
logical positivism: the doctrine that a meaningful statement must be either empirically verifiable (*q.v.*) or true by definition ("analytic")
***macho* virtues:** the virtues of the aretaic moral view that emphasizes toughness and hardness
meta-ethics: the examination of the meaning, function and use of moral language (*q.v.*)
moral accord: moral agreement
moral authority: a supposed authenticator of morality, e.g. God, the community, one's peers, one's true self
moral beliefs: beliefs that something is morally good or bad, morally right or wrong
moral blame: charging someone with doing something morally wrong
moral code: a set of do's and dont's
moral conservatism: acceptance of the existing consensual morality (*q.v.*)
moral judgment: any judgment imputing moral praise or blame or claiming or implying that something shows good or bad character or is morally wrong, obligatory, or permissible
moral language: the language we use in making moral judgments (*q.v.*)
moral life: a life that is morally good
moral necessity: moral requirement (*q.v.*)
moral nihilism: the view that there is no valid morality
moral philosophy: the philosophical study of morality (same as "ethics")
moral praise: commending somebody for being of good character or doing something supererogatory (*q.v.*)
moral realism: the view that there are objective moral truths and falsehoods and, in that sense, a moral reality (*q.v.*)
moral reality: a realm of moral truths or facts
moral reasons: reasons tied to moral values (*q.v.*)
moral rectitude: always doing what is morally right (= never doing, by act or omission, anything that is morally wrong)
moral requirement: what we must do or not do for (deontic) moral reasons (*q.v.*)
moral right: what we may rightfully demand that others do for us
moral skepticism: doubt that a universal, non-egoistic morality is possible
moral strength: having the strength of will to do what is morally required of one, or of doing what the person who possessed a certain moral virtue would do
moral theory: any account, in general terms, of the nature of morality

moral utterance: a spoken or written moral remark

moral values: values that are connected with the virtues or with moral requirement (*q.v.*)

moral wrongdoing: doing what one morally ought not to do or failing to do what one morally ought to do

morally bad: morally wrong or exhibiting a vicious character

morally binding: morally required (*q.v.*)

morally good: anything that has moral value

morally neutral: morally indifferent (neither morally good nor morally bad)

morally neutral facts: facts having no gerundive (*q.v.*) or attitudinal implications

morally obligatory: morally required (*q.v.*)

morally permissible: what one may or may not do at one's pleasure without violating any moral principle either way

morally required: what a valid moral principle dictates that one must do or not do

morally right: morally permissible to do (except in the phrase "the morally right thing" (*q.v.*)

(the) morally right thing: the only right choice in a difficult moral situation

morally wrong: non-justifiable or inexcusable violation of a valid moral rule or principle

mores: customs and practices of a culture

natural desires: (Kant's term) the desires that come to us in the course of living

naturalistic fallacy: the view that value can be understood in empirical terms

negative moral value: anything that gives us a moral reason *against* doing something

negative right: a permissive right (*q.v.*)

nihilism: the denial of any moral value

non-cognitivism: the meta-ethical (*q.v.*) view that moral thoughts and utterance cannot be statements, but only non-statemental (*q.v.*) expressions of attitudes or commitments to principle

non-natural fact: a (n alleged) fact, supposedly accessible to intuition, that something possesses a non-natural property

non-naturalism: the view that moral judgments express non-natural facts (*q.v.*)

non-objectivist knowledge: (Williams) moral knowledge that exists only from within a particular evaluative perspective (*q.v.*)

non-objectivist truths: (Williams) moral truths that exist only from within a particular evaluative perspective (*q.v.*)

non-reflective: no thought or scrutiny given or necessary

non-statemental: expressed without actually being stated

norms of conduct: conduct that is approved (or not disapproved) within a given culture

objective moral truth: a moral truth that is universal and independent of outlook or perspective

objectively true: true independently of outlook or perspective

open-question argument: (Moore) good cannot be defined because the question "Is that really good?" always remains open

other-regarding: concerned with the good of others

ought judgment: judgment that one has a reason for doing something

permissive right: a right against others (or the state) to leave us alone to live our own lives (often collectively called the right to liberty)

personal moral truth: (subjective relativism) a moral truth alleged to be true for me but not necessarily for anyone else

personal morality: (subjective relativism and prescriptivism) the morality to which I am personally committed, but to which others need not be committed

personal preference: what I personally like or dislike

personal tastes: personal preferences (*q.v.*)

personal values: whatever matters to me

perspectival truths: truths that exist only from within a particular perspective

positive right: claim right (*q.v.*)

practical ethics: applied ethics (*q.v.*)

practical judgment: an ought judgment (*q.v.*)

practical reason: reason based on values to be gained (or not lost)

premise: part of an argument intended to lead to a conclusion

prescribe: issue an instruction to do something

prescriptivism: the meta-ethical (*q.v.*) view that moral judgments (*q.v.*) contain personal commitments to principle

proscribe: forbid

psychological egoism: the view that all human motives are self-regarding

pure subjective relativism: "It's morally right for me if I think it's morally right for me"

radical freedom: (Sartre) there is no reliance on any authority; we make ourselves by our own free choices

rationally justified: in ethics, justified by practical reason (*q.v.*)

reason for choice: value to be gained by a course of action

rectitude: always doing what is morally right (= never doing, by act or omission, anything that is morally wrong) (same as moral rectitude)

right (*a.*): not wrong, licit (*q.v.*)

right (n.): something I may morally demand of others and which they are morally obliged to do

self-interested: concerned with my own purely personal interest

selfish: self-regarding in a morally reprehensible way

selfless: having no concern for oneself

self-regarding: with concern for oneself

sittlich **morality:** (Lovibond) customary (*q.v.*) or consensual morality (*q.v.*)

social evil: something bad for society in general

standards of quality: whatever makes something good of its kind

"suberogation": doing less than is morally required (the ghostly opposite of supererogation [*q.v.*])

subjective: real or valid only from a personal perspective

subjective relativism: the view that I am the creator and authenticator of my own personal morality

subjectivism: the meta-ethical (*q.v.*) doctrine that moral utterances are declarations of approval or disapproval

substantive ethics: contrasted with meta-ethics (*q.v.*), the investigation into what is good or bad, right or wrong

substantive moral theory: a theory which attempts to account for what morality is, what purposes it serves, and what justifies or grounds it

sufficient reason: in ethics, reason or reasons determining that this, all things considered, is what one ought to do

summum bonum: highest good or greatest good

supererogation: doing more than one is morally required to do

suppressed premise: a premise in an argument that is unstated because it is regarded as too obvious to have to be stated

theoretical ethics: (*v.* practical or applied ethics [*q.v.*]) includes both meta-ethics (*q.v.*) and substantive ethics (*q.v.*)

theoretical reason: (*v.* practical reason [*q.v.*]) reason as moving logically from a premise (or premises) to a conclusion

thick concept: (Williams) a "world-related" concept, such as "bully" or "liar," that bears its own moral weight

thin concept: (Williams) a moral concept such as "ought," "right," or "good" implying a "transcendental standpoint" (*q.v.*)

transcendental standpoint: a standpoint outside the perspective of any particular time or place

transcultural: true across cultures

truth claim: any claim to truth (all assertions are truth claims)

truth value: there are two truth values: "true" and "false"; not all utterances have a truth value (e.g. "Whoa!")

ulterior motive: a true but hidden motive

universal: in ethics, applicable to everyone (hence objective and independent of culture or particular persons)

universal morality: a morality applicable to all humankind

universal value: something that is a value for everybody

universalism: any morality rejecting favor to particular persons or groups

universalizability: application of one's moral judgments to everyone in similar circumstances

utilitarianism: the consequentialist (*q.v.*) doctrine that we are always to act for the greatest good of everyone indifferently

valid: in logic, the conclusion follows logically from the premises; otherwise sound, or having to be accepted

value judgment: any judgment affirming or implying that something is good or bad, right or wrong

vice: a disposition (*q.v.*) which contributes to a bad moral character

virtue: a disposition (*q.v.*) which contributes to a good moral character

well-being: *eudaimonia* (*q.v.*)

Index